BEST of the BEST
from
NEW MEXICO
COOKBOOK

Selected Recipes from New Mexico's
Favorite Cookbooks

Sandstone bluffs border the eastern side of El Malpais, whose 114,277 acres of wilderness are filled with volcanic features dating back 115,000 years. Several Indian tribes continue to use the area in their ancestral rituals.

BEST of the BEST
from
NEW MEXICO
COOKBOOK

Selected Recipes from New Mexico's
FAVORITE COOKBOOKS

EDITED BY

Gwen McKee
and
Barbara Moseley

Illustrated by Tupper England

QUAIL RIDGE PRESS
Preserving America's Food Heritage

Recipe Collection©1999 Quail Ridge Press, Inc.

Reprinted with permission and all rights under the name of the cookbooks or organizations or individuals listed below.

The Aficionado's Southwestern Cooking©1985 Ronald Johnson; *The Best from New Mexico Kitchens*©1978 by New Mexico Magazine; *Billy the Kid Cook Book*©1998 Lynn Nusom; *Cafe Pasqual's Cookbook*©1993 Katharine Kagel; *Carob Cookbook*©1990 by Tricia Hamilton; *Christmas in New Mexico Cook Book*©1991 Lynn Nusom; *Christmas Celebration: Santa Fe Traditions*©1996 Clear Light Publishers; *Cocinas de New Mexico*©1994 Public Service Company of New Mexico; *Comida Sabrosa*©1982 Irene Barraza Sanchez and Gloria Sanchez Yund; *Cooking at The Natural Cafe in Santa Fe*©1992 The Crossing Press; *Coyote's Pantry*©1993 Mark Miller and Mark Kiffin; *Families Cooking Together*©1998 Georgia O'Keeffe Friends of the Library; *Fiery Appetizers*©1991 The Crossing Press; *Fiesta Mexicana*©1982 T & E Enterprises; *Fiestas for Four Seasons*©1998-99 Clear Light Publishers; *The Great Chile Book*©1991 Mark Miller; *The Great Salsa Book*©1994 Mark Miller; *Great Salsas by the Boss of Sauce*©The Crossing Press; *Green Chile Bible*©1996-99 Clear Light Publishers; *Happy Camper's Cookbook*©1999 Marilyn Abraham and Sandy MacGregor; *A Little Southwest Cookbook*©1993 Chronicle Books; *Mark Miller's Indian Market Cookbook*©1995 Mark Miller; *Men's Guide to Bread Machine Baking*©1997 by Jeffrey Gerlach, Prima Publishing; *New Mexico Cook Book*©1990 Lynn Nusom; *A Painter's Kitchen*©1997 Margaret Wood; *The Rancho de Chimayó Cookbook*©1991 The Harvard Common Press; *Red Chile Bible*©1998-99 Clear Light Publishers; *Rehoboth Christian School Cookbook*©1981 Tse Yaanichii Promoters; *The Santa Fe School of Cooking Cookbook*©1995 Susan D. Curtis and The Santa Fe School of Cooking, Inc.; *Sassy Southwest Cooking*©1997 Clyde W. Casey; *Savoring the Southwest*©1983 Roswell Symphony Guild Publications; *Savoring the Southwest Again*©1998 Roswell Symphony Guild Publications; *Simply Simpatico*©1981 The Junior League of Albuquerque, Inc.; *Southwest Indian Cookbook*©1978-99 Clear Light Publishers; *The Tequila Cook Book*©1993 Lynn Nusom; *The Very Special Raspberry Cookbook*©1993 The Very Special Raspberry Cookbook Committee.

Library of Congress Cataloging-in-Publication Data

Best of the best from New Mexico : selected recipes from New Mexico's
    favorite cookbooks / edited by Gwen McKee and Barbara Moseley.
       p. cm.
    ISBN 0-937552-93-3
    1. Cookery, American—Southwestern style. 2. Cookery—
    New Mexico.
    I. McKee, Gwen. II. Moseley, Barbara.
    TX715.2.S69B466 1999
    641.59789—dc21   99-38581
                                          CIP

First printing, September 1999 • Second, April 2001 • Third, March 2003 • Fourth, September 2004
Cover photo: Scenic view of the Jemez Mountains in Autumn.
All photographs by Keith Odom, except back cover photo by Greg Campbell.
Design by Cynthia Clark. Printed in Canada

QUAIL RIDGE PRESS
1-800-343-1583 • P. O. Box 123 • Brandon, MS 39043
info@quailridge.com • www.quailridge.com

Contents

Preface 7

Foreword 9

Contributing Cookbooks 13

Beverages & Appetizers 15

Bread & Breakfast....................................39

Soups 67

Salads 83

Vegetables 97

Pasta, Rice, Tacos, etc. 123

Meats 137

Poultry 171

Seafood 193

Cakes 201

Cookies & Candies....................................215

Pies & Desserts 229

A Little Help with Chiles 251

Glossary 253

Catalog of Contributing Cookbooks 257

Index 277

BEST OF THE BEST STATE COOKBOOK SERIES 288

Editors Barbara Moseley and Gwen McKee admiring ristras of chiles.

Preface

If there are beans and corn on the stove, a stack of tortillas nearby, and a ristra of dried chiles against the wall—then you must be in a New Mexico kitchen! Be forewarned: The pungent aroma of roasting chiles and simmering salsas will likely send your senses into a frenzy. And when you taste the resulting dishes, you will quickly understand why the popularity of one of our country's oldest cuisines is rapidly spreading across the country.

Using what the land provides is always the basis from which most local dishes are derived. The Pueblo Indians cultivated such crops as corn, squash, peanuts, beans and potatoes. Influenced first by the Indians, the Spanish, Mexican and Anglo flavors soon intermingled to create flavorful dishes that now stand out as uniquely New Mexican.

But one cannot talk of New Mexican cooking without first mentioning its most important ingredient: chiles! These wonderfully piquant peppers come in different sizes, degrees of hotness, and intensities of flavor, and are used in everything from appetizers to desserts, even wine! (And New Mexicans spell it with an "e"—chile—and leave the "i"—chili—for the meat/bean dish.) As to buying or ordering chiles, it's a good idea to ask the waiter or grocer which ones are hotter, as they can vary. When you are served in a restaurant, you will be asked "red or green?" referring not to your color preference, but to which chiles you want served with your dish. If you can't decide, order your meal "Christmas," and your dish will come with half green and half red chiles. Though today's supermarkets have ready supplies of already prepared products, including fresh, canned, jarred, and powdered chiles, the recipes in this book have easy instructions telling how to peel, bake, broil, dry and crush chiles. You will soon be enjoying the rich, unforgettable fragrance of these wonderfully piquant peppers wafting through your own kitchen, beckoning all who come near.

Tortillas are equally as important to New Mexico cuisine. They are made with either flour or corn, and are filled or topped with meats, chile, beans, cheeses, and/or vegetables, then baked or fried. Burritos, quesadillas, chimichangas and fajitas are made with flour tortillas, while tostadas, chalupas, enchiladas, and taquitos are made with corn tortillas.

A soothing relief from the peppers, the sopapilla is a light pillowy pastry that is sometimes dipped in honey. They are delicious served either as a main course stuffed with meats, beans and cheeses, or as a delicious dessert filled with ice cream and fruit.

Typical New Mexican fare can be as fancy as Mexican Pecan-Toffee Tartlets in Chocolate Chip Cookie Crust, and as simple as Jalapa Hamburgers and Blue Corn Pancakes. The many diversified recipes come from outstanding cookbooks by noted authors as well as junior leagues and churches. They come from cosmopolitan big city restaurants as well as bed and breakfast ranchos. The one thing they have in common is that they are all authentic, delicious, chosen favorite New Mexican recipes. We hope that with these recipes from all across the state, we can help you experience the incomparable taste that the Land of Enchantment has to offer.

We learned so much by testing these recipes, and hope that you will come to appreciate this delightful style of cooking as we have. We have included a helpful listing of chiles on page 251. We have also included a glossary of New Mexican foods that will help you understand and become more familiar with them and the terms used in New Mexican cooking (see page 253).

The fifty-six cookbooks from across the state that have contributed their favorite recipes to this collection are to be commended for their excellence. We have enjoyed working with the authors, cookbook chairman, publishers and chefs who have shared some of their favorite recipes with us. Our thanks to the newspaper food and feature editors who ran our query about New Mexican cookbooks in their papers, and the chambers of commerce who provided us with information that aided us in our search for New Mexico cookbooks.

A special thanks to Keith Odom who lives in Albuquerque and enjoys sightseeing and photographing interesting places. Keith has provided us with the cover photo as well as the chapter opening pictures that are used throughout. We are grateful to friend Mary Ann Wells, who wrote us such a beautiful letter describing New Mexico, that we coerced her into expanding it into a Foreword. And as always our own "best" illustrator, Tupper England, deserves our sincere thanks for adding such flavor with her drawings.

We invite you to become acquainted with the uniqueness of New Mexican cuisine by discovering it firsthand right here in this cookbook. Won't you join us? You're in for a sense-sational treat! Enjoy!

Gwen McKee and Barbara Moseley

Foreword

New Mexico nurtures the soul and the spirit with a landscape so intensely beautiful and varied that everyone within her boundaries is inspired to reach beyond the ordinary. Cooking and food preparations that would be considered mundane endeavors in other places receive a touch of magic here. The spice of imagination is in the air. Special recipes uniting all the elements that feed the body and soul are created regularly by cooks blessed with a knowledge of tradition and a desire for innovation. New Mexican cooks have had the challenge of inventing a cuisine for dining in such places as the shadow of the sacred Taos Mountain. This is a mountain that talks to people, whispering to kindred souls that they can find their true home in her embrace. Uninspired food will not do.

What is a suitable dinner menu when you are surrounded by the animated red-clouded sunsets of White Sands? What is a suitable snack under the night skies of Chaco Canyon where the Milky Way is a thick cloud of stars suspended between heaven and earth that hums with songs of light? New Mexico can convince the most pragmatic people that they are having out-of-this-world experiences, that they have entered a mystic realm. It is scarcely possible to find a corner of the state that is not enchanted, or a place where food is not revered. The dinners that appear on New Mexican tables are as exciting as this collection of recipes implies.

Perhaps special appetites are created from the experience of stepping inside a surreal Georgia O'Keeffe landscape and seeing the world she painted from the inside out. The gold and purple mountains, the hills of splattered colors, the meander of blue rivers across red canyon floors, the prickly green of juniper, cedar and sage are the reality of the countryside around the artist's home in Abiquiu. Does an elegant squash soup, horno-baked bread, green salad and a local wine best combine the sophisticated simplicity of this world? On a near diagonal line from Abiquiu across the center of the state to the southeast, highways run across the plains of Peter Hurd landscapes. His snapshots of this reality transposed to canvas make us yearn for visions of cowboys on horseback. Is this the place for a cowboy supper of beans, biscuits and beefsteak? Somewhere in between these opposing landscapes, and slightly to the north, are the high mountain

pine forests and
Pueblo Indians of the
Taos Society of Artists'
canvases.   Do the col-
ors and shapes call to mind
a supper of grilled trout, blue
corn tortillas, chiles and posole?

For thousands of years American Indians have called this land sacred. The mystic quality of the light speaks the truth of their belief to our hearts. Hispanic and Anglo settlers have adopted the original natives' way of seeing. All of life is sacred, the air we breathe, the ground we walk, the food we eat. Nothing is taken for granted. In the sacred world of New Mexican foods, corn and chile are the kitchen sacraments. A genuine New Mexican dinner must contain both in some form.

Corn is considered a gift from the gods in Native American religions. It is revered as a plant and food. Red, white, blue and yellow varieties are planted and harvested with ceremonies of thanksgiving here each year. Corn pollen and finely ground white cornmeal are sprinkled on the winds to seek blessings for the people and the land. Chile is no less revered. Early Hispanic settlers learned of sacred sites, native places of healing, and built shrines over them. Chimayó is one such place. Pilgrims come to the centuries old, rustic adobe church for a pinch of earth that they believe can produce miracles. Across the plaza, vendors announce that they have "holy chiles" for sale. Grown in the sacred earth of Chimayó how can the chiles be less than holy? Doubtlessly, the farmers of Hatch, and every other chile-producing region of the state, would want you to know that their chiles also have remarkable properties. Hatch is the self-proclaimed "Chile capital of the world" and all roads leading to the processing plants from area farms are strewn with bright red pods that have fallen off the chile wagons. After the green chile harvests in early September, the entire state seems to be wrapped in the aroma of roasting chiles.

But even with an abundance of exotic corn and chile dishes, New Mexican menus are almost never one-dimensional culturally.

Successive waves of Hispanic and Anglo settlers have brought their own ideas of preparing food and cooking which they have married to American Indian traditions to create unique recipes and eating experiences. The chiles, corn, squash, beans, piñons, pumpkins, seeds, tubers, trout, venison, elk and buffalo of the Indians' larder have met all these influences with an exuberance seldom seen elsewhere. Sopas, sopaipillas, cheeses, custards and horno wheat bread from the Hispanic traditions combined with the Anglo love of beef prepared in any fashion, frontier-American cooking and imported gourmet specialties from a myriad of cultures have all embraced the traditional American Indian foods to create unique and exciting recipes. This book offers examples of this marriage of food traditions in recipes that will appeal to everyone. Bien apetito!

Mary Ann Wells
Journalist and author

Mary Ann Wells is the editor of the Taos County Historical Society journal *Ayer y Hoy en Taos*. Her most recently published book is *Searching for Red Eagle: A Personal Journey into the Spirit World of Native America*.

Bandera Crater is located in El Malpais National Monument, a spectacular volcanic area featuring spatter cones, ice caves and lava flows. A breach in the wall caused a 17-mile lava tube system, one of the longest in North America.

Contributing Cookbooks

The Aficionado's Southwestern Cooking

Amistad Community Recipes

The Best from New Mexico Kitchens

Beyond Loaves and Fishes

Billy the Kid Cook Book

Bon Appétit de Las Sandias

Cafe Pasqual's Cookbook

Carob Cookbook

Christmas Celebration: Santa Fe Traditions

Christmas in New Mexico Cook Book

Cocinas de New Mexico

Comida Sabrosa

Cooking at The Natural Cafe in Santa Fe

Cooking with Kiwanis

Coyote's Pantry

The Eagle's Kitchen

Families Cooking Together

Fiery Appetizers

Fiesta Mexicana

Fiestas for Four Seasons

A Fork in the Road

Good Sam Celebrates 15 Years of Love

The Great Chile Book

The Great Salsa Book

Great Salsas by the Boss of Sauce

Green Chile Bible

The Happy Camper's Cookbook

Inn on the Rio's Favorite Recipes

Contributing Cookbooks

The Joy of Sharing

License to Cook New Mexico Style

The Little Southwest Cookbook

Mark Miller's Indian Market Cookbook

Men's Guide to Bread Machine Baking

Mrs. Noah's Survival Guide

New Mexico Cook Book

Our Best Home Cooking

A Painter's Kitchen: Recipes from the Kitchen of Georgia O'Keeffe

Peanut Palate Pleasers from Portales

Rancho de Chimayó Cookbook

Raspberry Enchantment House Tour Cookbook

Recipes for Rain or Shine

Recipes from Hatch

Recipes from the Cotton Patch

Red Chile Bible

Red River's Cookin'

Rehoboth Christian School Cookbook

Saint Joseph's Really Grande Cookbook

The Santa Fe School of Cooking Cookbook

Sassy Southwest Cooking: Vibrant New Mexico Foods

Savoring the Southwest

Savoring the Southwest Again

Simply Simpatico

Southwest Indian Cookbook

The Tequila Cook Book

The Very Special Raspberry Cookbook

What's Cookin' at Casa

The largest array of gypsum dunes in the world stretches for over 230 square miles just outside the famous White Sands Missile Range, where the first atomic bomb was exploded. Located south of Alamogordo.

Perfect Margaritas

Be prepared! These high-octane margaritas just might sweep some of your guests off their feet. They are wonderfully flavored and potent. For the very best margaritas, always squeeze fresh limes (preferably the juicy, thin-skinned, yellowish Mexican variety, which have the traditional pungent flavor.) Whenever I am near the Mexican border or in the Caribbean, I lay aside quantities of the freshly squeezed juice of these limes in half-pint freezer containers or jars and bring them home solidly frozen. In a pinch the dark green, thicker-skinned Persian limes will work, too. Be sure to keep the juice frozen until you use it. Always buy at least 80 proof tequila, made from the blue agave plant.

**8 fresh limes, preferably
  Mexican variety
Coarse salt
½ cup triple sec, or to taste
1½ cups 80- to 92-proof pure
  agave tequila (white preferred)**

**⅓ of a fresh egg white, beaten
  with a fork
Crushed ice**

Squeeze the limes, being certain to get all the flesh plus the juice. Measure and use only ½ cup juice. Reserve the rest. Prepare the glasses. If salt is desired, rub one of the lime rinds around the top rim of each glass. Crunch the glasses into the salt and place in the freezer, allowing at least 30 minutes to frost.

Meanwhile, prepare the margaritas by placing the lime juice, triple sec, tequila, and egg white in the blender. Add enough ice to fill the blender about halfway.

Process. If the texture is not slushy enough, add ice to get the desired texture. Taste and add more triple sec if not sweet enough. Serve in the frosted glasses, either straight up or over ice. Yields 4 large margaritas.

Note: You can freeze leftover margaritas for at least a month.

Fiestas for Four Seasons

My Kinda Cocoa

This is strictly an adult drink for those cold winter nights when coffee won't do—and chocolate will.

1 tablespoon cocoa
3 teaspoons sugar
1 ounce tequila

1 ounce Kahlua
1 cup hot milk
Whipped cream

Spoon the cocoa and sugar into the bottom of a large mug or heavy glass. Stir in tequila and Kahlua, pour in the hot milk and stir well. Top with a dollop of whipped cream and serve. Serves 1.

The Tequila Cook Book

The sun shines most of the time in New Mexico. Farmington recorded 779 days of consecutive sunshine from December 16, 1961 to February 2, 1964.

Indian Nut Mix

A fine crisp nibble for all occasions. It's also a good way to use up left-over tortillas.

Oil for frying
1 corn tortilla, cut in ½-inch
  squares
1 flour tortilla, cut in ½-inch
  squares
Salt
1 tablespoon butter

½ cup piñon nuts
½ cup pumpkin seeds
½ teaspoon red chile
  powder
¼ teaspoon celery salt
¼ teaspoon cumin

Preheat oven to 300°. Heat oil and fry the tortilla squares in batches. When they are crisp and golden, lift out with a slotted spoon onto paper towels. Salt immediately while they are hot. Melt butter in a small frying pan, and sauté piñon nuts and pumpkin seeds for several minutes—or until they start to pop and turn gold. Shake nuts and tortillas together in a paper bag with chile powder, celery salt, and cumin. Line a cookie sheet with paper towels, place the mixture on them, and bake for 10 minutes or until crisp. Serves 4.

The Aficionado's Southwestern Cooking

Mexican Hot Nuts

4 cups walnut, pecan, or
  cashew halves or peanuts
¼ cup butter, melted

2 tablespoons crushed red
  chile
½ teaspoon ground cumin

Combine the nuts and the melted butter, and toss until the nuts are evenly coated. Spread in a baking pan and bake for 15 minutes in a 350° oven. Mix the chile and cumin together in a bowl. Add the nuts and stir well to coat. Return the nuts to the baking pan and bake for another 10 minutes. Drain on paper towels before serving. The nuts will keep for 2-3 weeks, refrigerated. Yields 4 cups.

Note: Heat scale 4. Chopped finely, these nuts can be mixed with stuffing for roasted poultry.

Fiery Appetizers

Valley-of-Fire Pecans

2 cups large pecan halves
¼ cup butter, melted
1½ tablespoons hot red chile
  powder (or to taste)

1½ teaspoons salt

Preheat oven to 375°. Toss pecans with butter, and place in a single layer in a large cast-iron skillet. Place skillet in oven for about 10 minutes or until pecans begin to toast and release a nutty fragrance. Remove from oven, and allow to cool 5 minutes so chile does not burn when added to pecans. Combine chile powder and salt, and sprinkle over warm pecans. Makes 2 cups.

Note: These are best if made with butter. However, peanut oil may be substituted (increase oven temperature to 400°). Do not use margarine, because it will burn.

Savoring the Southwest Again

Mexican Peanuts

1 crushed clove garlic
2 tablespoon peanut oil
1 pound roasted unsalted
  peanuts
1½ teaspoons salt

1 tablespoon chili powder
½ teaspoon cayenne pepper
¼ teaspoon dried cilantro
  (optional)
1 teaspoon lemon juice

Sauté garlic in peanut oil. Stir in the remaining ingredients. Cook for about 2 minutes in the open skillet at medium heat. As soon as they are cool enough to eat they may be served. They keep well in a tin.

Note: Measurements for the chili powder and cayenne pepper may be increased if you like them hot.

Peanut Palate Pleasers from Portales

Party Peanut Ball

1 (8-ounce) package cream
   cheese
1 (8-ounce) jar or roll Old
   English cheese
4 tablespoons Worcestershire
   sauce

8-9 drops hot sauce
½ teaspoon garlic salt
½ cup ground peanuts
Parsley, chopped

Let cheese stand at room temperature. Blend well; add the other ingredients and mix well. Shape into ball or loaf and roll in chopped parsley and chill.

Peanut Palate Pleasers from Portales

Baked Caramel Goodstuff

Set this near your cookie jar and you will find it cuts down on your cookie baking. Great for nibbling!

8 cups puffed wheat cereal
½ cup walnut pieces
½ cup dry roasted peanuts
½ cup pecan pieces
½ cup butter or margarine

1 cup brown sugar, packed
¼ cup corn syrup
¼ teaspoon salt
¼ teaspoon soda
1 teaspoon vanilla

In large bowl combine first 4 ingredients. Melt butter in saucepan, stir in brown sugar, syrup, and salt. Bring to boil, stirring constantly. Boil 5 minutes. Remove from heat and stir in soda and vanilla. Gradually pour over cereal mixture. Stir to coat thoroughly. On greased cookie sheet spread evenly. Bake at 300° for 15 minutes. Stir well and bake 15 minutes more. Cool completely on pan. Break into desired size pieces and store in airtight container.

Savoring the Southwest

Chunky Guacamole

1 large ripe avocado
1 medium tomato
1 small onion
1 small bell pepper

3 long green chiles
Juice of ½ lemon
Salt to taste

Chop all the ingredients fine. Do not mash. Use fresh roasted and peeled chiles, but, if they are not available, use canned or frozen. Mix together with the lemon juice and add salt to taste. Serve as a dip or as a salad with lettuce and corn chips.

The Best from New Mexico Kitchens

Stuffed Jalapeños

Jalapeños
Cream Cheese

Cheddar cheese
Bacon

Slice jalapeños in half lengthwise and remove seeds. Fill with cream cheese and top with Cheddar cheese. Wrap bacon around pepper and fasten with toothpick. Bake at 350° until bacon is done. Preparation is lengthy but worth it!

The Joy of Sharing

Stuffed Jalapeño Chile Peppers

If you can find the red-ripe jalapeño chiles, you are in for a treat. The mature pepper has a rich warm flavor. I fix these stuffed jewels as often as I can.

18 ripe red jalapeño chiles
1 (8-ounce) package cream
   cheese, softened
2 tablespoons lime juice
1 teaspoon ground cumin
1 teaspoon ground red New
   Mexico chile

Dash fresh ground black
   pepper
2 tablespoons vegetable oil
½ cup chopped pecans
½ small white onion
   chopped
Cilantro, finely chopped

Cut jalapeños in half lengthwise. Remove seeds and devein. Set aside. In a medium bowl, combine all ingredients except pecans, onions, and cilantro. Beat with electric mixer until smooth. Stir in pecans and onions. Stuff jalapeños with cream cheese till slightly rounded. Cover and refrigerate at least 8 hours. Serve sprinkled with cilantro.

Sassy Southwest Cooking

Mexican Deviled Eggs

8 hard-boiled eggs
½ cup shredded Cheddar
  cheese
¼ cup mayonnaise
¼ cup salsa

2 tablespoons sliced green
  onions
1 tablespoon sour cream
Salt to taste

Slice the eggs in half lengthwise. Remove yolks and set aside. In a small bowl, mash yolks with cheese, mayonnaise, salsa, onions, sour cream, and salt. Evenly fill the egg whites. Serve immediately or chill until ready to serve. Yields 16 servings.

What's Cookin' at Casa

New Mexico Cherry Bombs

The word bomb is only a slight exaggeration. For a much milder version, use cherry peppers.

24 jalapeño chiles
8 ounces Monterey Jack or
  Cheddar cheese, sliced

Flour for dredging
2 eggs, beaten
Vegetable oil for deep-fat frying

Slit each pepper, remove the seeds with a small spoon or knife, and stuff the peppers with slices of cheese. If necessary, insert a toothpick to hold the peppers together. Dip each chile in the flour, then the egg, then the flour again. Fry in 350° oil until golden brown. Drain and serve. Yields 24. Heat scale 8.

Variations: Stuff the chiles with chorizo, or ground meat with cheese.

Fiery Appetizers

When you bite into a four-alarm chile, don't wait for the fire trucks. The most soothing thing is milk! Swish it around in your mouth—it's the number one fire-putter-outer. There are a few other remedies including buttermilk, yogurt, fruit syrup, peanut butter, and olive oil.

Marinated Mexican Mushrooms

12 ounces (2- to 3-inch)
   white button mushrooms,
   wiped clean and stemmed
⅓ cup virgin olive oil
⅓ cup white wine vinegar
2 garlic cloves, minced
1 teaspoon caribe (crushed
   dried red chile)

½ teaspoon Mexican oregano
¼ teaspoon salt
1 large Spanish onion, thinly
   sliced and separated into rings
Caribe chile for garnish

Put the prepared mushrooms in a heat-proof bowl. Bring the next 6 ingredients to a boil, adding the onions once the mixture begins to boil. Cook and stir frequently until the onions just begin to lose their crispness. Pour the mixture over the mushrooms, and let them marinate at room temperature for at least 2 hours, stirring frequently. Chill about ½ hour—not longer or the oil will thicken. The mushrooms can be made several days before—they keep very well up to a week. They are attractive served in a shallow rectangular or oval bowl, with the mushrooms arranged around the edges and the onions in the center. Add a sprinkle of the caribe for a special touch. Serve with toothpicks. Yields 4 servings.

Fiestas for Four Seasons

Rajas Salsa

An all-purpose salsa; and especially good with steak or fish.

1 large red bell pepper, roasted
   and julienned
1 large yellow bell pepper,
   roasted and julienned
1 large poblano chile, roasted
   and julienned
1 Roma tomato, blackened and
   roughly chopped

4 teaspoons minced fresh
   cilantro
½ teaspoon chopped roasted
   garlic
½ teaspoon salt
1 tablespoon extra-virgin olive
   oil
1 tablespoon fresh lime juice

Thoroughly combine all the ingredients together in a mixing bowl. Yields about 2 cups.

The Great Salsa Book

Green Apple Serrano-Cilantro Salsa

There's a wealth of tart, fresh flavors in this salsa, and W. C. describes it as a "big jumble of flavors in your mouth, mon." He suggests using it as a bed for seafood in place of pasta or rice, serving it with a sparkling wine. This will keep for about a week in the refrigerator.

¼ cup white cider vinegar
1 teaspoon salt
⅓ cup sugar
¼ cup freshly squeezed lime
   juice (Key lime preferred)
½ cup apple juice
12 medium fresh basil leaves,
   chopped
4 Granny Smith medium apples,
   skins left on, cored, seeded,
   and chopped fine
½ medium onion, diced

⅓ cup raspberry vinegar
1 medium red bell pepper,
   seeded and chopped fine
1 medium green bell pepper,
   seeded and chopped fine
1 medium yellow bell pepper,
   seeded and chopped fine
10 fresh serrano chiles, seeds
   and stems removed, minced
½ cup chopped fresh
   cilantro
1 teaspoon salt

In a saucepan, combine the vinegar, salt, sugar, lime juice, apple juice, and basil leaves. Bring to a boil, reduce the heat, and simmer for 5 minutes. Remove from the heat and cool. In a large bowl, combine the apples, onion, raspberry vinegar, bell peppers, serrano chiles, cilantro, and salt and toss well. Add the cooked mixture and toss again. Refrigerate for one hour before servings. Yields 4-5 cups.

Great Salsas by the Boss of Sauce

Mango Salsa

Great on grilled fish or poultry, as a table salsa, or with tortilla chips.

2 mangoes, cut in small dice
1 habanero or 3 or 4 hot chiles
   such as serrano or jalapeño,
   stemmed, seeded, and cut
   in small dice
3 or 4 green onions, sliced thin
   with some green

1 small red bell pepper, cut in
   small dice
¼ cup chopped cilantro
Juice of 1 lime, or to taste
Salt, to taste

Mix all ingredients in a bowl and let stand for an hour to develop the flavor.

Cooking with Kiwanis

Pico de Gallo Salsa

If you have ever eaten at a New Mexico restaurant, you have probably been served this salsa with fresh tortilla chips—a tradition I hope never changes.

2 ripe tomatoes, seeded and
   chopped
1 small red onion, chopped
6 red radishes, chopped
2 serrano chiles, seeded and
   finely chopped
2 jalapeño chiles, seeded and
   finely chopped
½ cucumber, peeled, seeded
   and chopped

½ cup fresh cilantro,
   chopped
1 tablespoon fresh lime juice
1 tablespoon fresh lemon
   juice
1 teaspoon red-wine vinegar
½ teaspoon garlic salt
½ teaspoon lemon pepper

In a glass or plastic bowl, combine tomatoes, onion, radishes, chiles, cucumber, and cilantro. In a small bowl, combine the remaining ingredients. Mix well. Pour over vegetables and toss thoroughly. Serve immediately or cover and refrigerate. (Best served freshly made.) Makes 2½ cups.

Sassy Southwest Cooking

Texas Gunpowder Salsa

Jalapeño powder is available from Southwestern mail-order companies, or you can make your own by dehydrating and grinding jalapeños in a spice mill (be sure to wear a mask). Here's a salsa that's excellent for barbecues, to serve over hamburgers, or with chips. This will keep for about 3 days in the refrigerator.

¾ cup "Texas Gunpowder,"
   or jalapeño powder
1 cup boiling water
1 tablespoon cider vinegar
¼ cup extra virgin olive oil
1 tablespoon dried Mexican
   oregano
3 cloves garlic, minced

1 cup chicken stock
½ cup chopped onion
6 medium Roma tomatoes,
   chopped
2 tablespoons chopped fresh
   cilantro
1 teaspoon salt
1 teaspoon sugar

In a bowl, combine the jalapeño powder and the boiling water, taking care not to inhale the fumes. In a food processor or blender, combine the cider vinegar, olive oil, oregano, garlic, and chicken stock; purée. Add the purée to the jalapeño mix; add the remaining ingredients and mix well. Refrigerate for an hour before serving. Yields 3-4 cups.

Great Salsas by the Boss of Sauce

Jiffy Chile con Queso

1 can condensed cream of
   mushroom soup
1 (6-ounce) roll garlic cheese

1 (4-ounce) can green chiles,
   chopped

Mix the soup and the cheese over heat until the cheese melts. Add the chiles and serve warm with chips, preferably blue corn chips. Serves 15.

Green Chile Bible

Chile Con Queso

1 tablespoon salad oil
¼ cup minced onion
1 (4-ounce) can chopped green
  chilies, drained
½ teaspoon garlic, crushed
⅓ - ½ cup light cream or
  milk

1 (8-ounce) package pasteurized
  process cheese spread, cut in
  cubes
1 cup grated Cheddar cheese
Tortilla chips or fresh
  vegetables for dipping

In a small saucepan, heat oil over moderately high heat. Add onion, chilies, and garlic and cook 5-7 minutes, stirring frequently, until onion is lightly browned. Reduce heat to low and add ⅓ cup of the cream; then add cheeses and stir until mixture is smooth. If necessary, thin sauce with additional cream. Serve in a small chafing dish with tortilla chips or fresh vegetable dippers.

Simply Simpatico

Green Chile Won Tons

1 pound Longhorn Cheddar
  cheese, grated
1 (8-ounce) can green chilies,
  chopped

2 packages won ton skins
Oil

Combine cheese and green chilies. Place one teaspoon of mixture on a won ton skin and fold like an envelope. Fry in 2 inches of hot oil, turning once until golden brown. Drain. Yields 40.

Fiesta Mexicana

Near Carrizozo is the Valley of Fires, one of the best-preserved lava fields in the country, and nearby the ghost town of White Oaks.

Green Chile Pinwheels

8 ounces sharp Cheddar
cheese, grated
8 ounces extra-sharp Cheddar
cheese, grated
2 cups flour

¼ pound butter, softened
3 tablespoons water
Chopped green chilies to taste
(about 2 small cans)

Combine cheeses and flour, mixing thoroughly so cheese is coated with flour. Add butter and water and work mixture with hands until well blended. Divide cheese mixture into 4 parts and form each into a ball. Roll between two sheets of waxed paper, like pie crust. Remove top sheet of waxed paper and cover entire cheese surface with chile. Lift edge and roll as you would a jelly roll. Twist ends of waxed paper and refrigerate for at least 30 minutes before slicing. At this point they may be frozen for later baking, or stored in refrigerator for up to a week.

When ready to bake, preheat oven to 350°. Slice rolls about ¼-inch thick. Place on ungreased cookie sheets and bake 12-15 minutes or until golden. These freeze well.

Good Sam Celebrates 15 Years of Love

Chile Cheese Roll

1 pound longhorn cheese
3 small packages cream cheese
1½ teaspoons red chile
pepper, powdered

1 teaspoon minced garlic
1 cup finely chopped pecans
Paprika

Grate cheese, add cream cheese, red pepper, garlic, and nuts. Mix well with hands. Roll out on paprika sprinkled wax paper.

Recipes from Hatch

Shrimp Cheese Ball

2 (4½-ounce) cans tiny
   shrimp, drained
1 (8-ounce) package cream
   cheese, room temperature
8 ounces Cheddar cheese,
   grated, room temperature

1 teaspoon dillweed, chopped
1 teaspoon parsley, chopped
½ teaspoon garlic salt
¼ teaspoon cayenne pepper
½ cup almonds, sliced

Mix all the ingredients together, except almonds. Roll into a ball
and chill in the refrigerator until firm. Then roll in the almonds
and serve with your favorite crackers.

Christmas in New Mexico Cook Book

Armadillo Eggs

1 dozen fresh whole large
   jalapeños
½ pound marbled (Jack and
   Cheddar) cheese

2 pounds sausage (pork
   breakfast roll)
1 box original flavor
   Shake-n-Bake coating mix

Wash jalapeños; leave stems intact. Slit one side of each pepper with paring knife. Gently squeeze peppers by ends to open,
remove all seeds. Set aside. Cut cheese into ¼-inch square
strips. Stuff cheese strips into peppers. Set aside. Make one
dozen sausage patties, ¼-inch thick, diameter large enough to
cover entire pepper. Place each pepper slit-side down in middle
of patty; wrap patty around pepper. Roll all peppers in coating
mix and place on cookie sheet. Bake 25-30 minutes at 350°,
until sausage is done.

What's Cookin' at Casa

Indienne Cashew Spread

½ cup chopped cashews
5 tablespoons Major Gray's
  Chutney, chopped
½ teaspoon lemon juice

1 (8-ounce) package cream
  cheese
¼ teaspoon curry powder
Apple rings

Mix together the cashews, chutney, lemon juice, cream cheese, and curry powder. Spread on cool, unpeeled apple rings or Triscuit crackers. Covers 15 apple rings.

Recipes from the Cotton Patch

Cilantro Mousse

1 cup mayonnaise
1 bunch cilantro, stems
  removed
3 tablespoons sweet cream
½ medium-size onion,
  chopped
1 small serrano chile pepper,
  seeded and chopped

1 teaspoon chicken consommé
  granules
2 envelopes unflavored gelatin,
  dissolved in ½ cup boiling
  water
Saltine crackers

Process first 6 ingredients in a food processor until blended. Add gelatin, and blend well. Place in a well-greased mold, and chill until set. Unmold onto a serving platter, and serve with saltines.

Savoring the Southwest Again

Heavy-Duty Nacho Sauce

For nachos, you can always heat a jar of Cheez-Whiz in the microwave and pour it over corn chips. OR you could make this beer-cheese sauce. It is so good that you can dip tortilla chips or even steamed flour tortillas in it—and call it a meal.

1 cup chopped onion
2 medium-sized cloves garlic, crushed
¼ cup olive oil
½ teaspoon ground cumin
½ teaspoon ground coriander
½ teaspoon mild red chile powder, or more to taste
1 teaspoon salt

¼ teaspoon freshly ground black pepper
1 bell pepper, chopped
2 tomatoes, chopped
¼ cup flour
1 (12-ounce) can beer at room temperature
2 cup grated brick or Monterey Jack cheese

Sauté onion and garlic in olive oil with spices and salt. When onion is translucent, add peppers and tomatoes; sauté 10 minutes more. Stir in the flour and cook 5-10 minutes. Add the beer and cook over medium heat another 15 minutes, stirring often. Cover and heat very low and let simmer an hour or two, stirring every 15 minutes. Uncover and remove from heat and let cool, about 45 minutes. To serve, reheat slowly, sprinkle in the cheese as it melts. Serve hot.

License to Cook New Mexico Style

Albuquerque Delight

1 can refried beans (with onion and green chile, if available)
1 package taco seasoning mix
3 avocados, mashed (or 1 package frozen avocado mix)
2 teaspoons lemon juice
2 tablespoons minced onion
Dash of garlic salt
4 ounces sour cream
1 cup chopped green chilies
½ pound Monterey Jack cheese, grated
½ pound Longhorn Cheddar cheese, grated
2 ripe tomatoes, chopped
1 small can pitted black olives, sliced for garnish

Blend refried beans with taco mix. Spread into large pie dish. To mashed avocados, add lemon juice, onion, and garlic salt (omit if using frozen avocado mix). Spread avocado mixture over bean layer. Add layers of sour cream, green chilies, and cheeses. Garnish with tomatoes and olives and serve with tortilla chips. Serves 12.

Fiesta Mexicana

Many Layered Nacho Dip

Watch it disappear!

1 (16-ounce) can refried beans
1 package taco seasoning mix
1 (8-ounce) carton sour cream
1 (6-ounce) carton frozen avocado dip, thawed
1 (4½-ounce) jar stuffed green olives, or black olives, chopped (save a few for garnish)
2 large tomatoes, diced
1 small onion or green onions, chopped
1 (4-ounce) can diced green chili (or fresh)
1½ cups grated Monterey Jack or Cheddar cheese
Paprika

Combine beans and taco seasoning, stirring well. Spread in a greased 12x8x2-inch dish. Layer remaining ingredients as listed, ending with cheese. Sprinkle with paprika and place a few olives on top. Refrigerate until serving time. Good served with blue corn tortilla chips.

Saint Joseph's Really Grande Cookbook

Broccoli-Hamburger Dip

2 pounds hamburger
1 onion, chopped
2 (10-ounce) packages
 chopped broccoli
1 stick butter

4 garlic cheese rolls
2 cans cream of mushroom soup
4 small cans chopped green
 chilies

Brown hamburger; drain off fat. In a separate pan, brown chopped onion and broccoli in stick of butter. Melt cheese and combine with soup and green chilies. Serve hot. Leftovers can be frozen and heated later.

Our Best Home Cooking

Harlequin Dip

2 (4-ounce) cans chopped
 green chilies
2 (4½-ounce) cans chopped
 black olives
3 tomatoes, chopped

4 green onions, chopped
2 tablespoons wine vinegar
1 tablespoon oil
Salt and pepper to taste

Combine all ingredients and mix well. Use as a dip with crisp tortilla chips. Makes 8-10 servings.

Simply Simpatico

Mushroom Turnovers

PASTRY:

½ pound butter, room
   temperature
1 (8-ounce) package cream
   cheese, room temperature

1½ cups flour
½ teaspoon salt

Blend butter thoroughly with cream cheese. Add flour and salt. Work together until smooth. Chill in refrigerator for several hours. When ready to make the turnovers, start the filling.

FILLING:

3 tablespoons butter
½ pound fresh mushrooms,
   finely chopped
1 medium onion, finely
   chopped
½ teaspoon salt

¼ teaspoon thyme
Dash cayenne pepper
Dash ground nutmeg
2 tablespoons flour
3 tablespoons sour cream
3 tablespoons dry sherry

Melt butter over medium heat. Add mushrooms and onion. Sauté a few minutes until slightly soft. Add the salt, thyme, cayenne pepper, and nutmeg. Sprinkle the 2 tablespoons flour over the mixture and blend well. Cook for 3-4 minutes. Remove from heat and stir in the sour cream and dry sherry. Chill the mushroom filling in refrigerator for a few minutes. Proceed to roll the pastry out on a floured board to ⅛-inch thickness. Cut into circles with a 3-inch round cookie cutter. Place a scant teaspoon full of filling on each circle. Fold the circles in half and press the edges together with a fork. Prick the top of each turnover a few times with a fork. Place the turnovers on an ungreased cookie sheet. Bake for 15 minutes in a 425° oven or until pastry is lightly browned. Serve hot. Makes about 30 turnovers.

Note: The unbaked prepared turnovers freeze well and stay indefinitely. They can be taken directly from the freezer and baked without defrosting. Just bake them a few minutes longer.

Recipes from the Cotton Patch

Carnitas Caliente

Carnitas are Mexican "little pieces of meat" often served at breakfast but perfect as alarming appetizers.

3 teaspoons red chile powder
¼ teaspoon freshly ground
  black pepper
1 teaspoon ground cumin
3 cloves garlic, minced

2 teaspoons finely chopped
  fresh cilantro
¾ teaspoon salt
1 pound boneless pork, trimmed
  and cut into 1-inch cubes

Combine all the spices and rub the pork cubes with the mixture. Let sit at room temperature for an hour. Bake the cubes on a rack over a baking sheet for 1½ hours at 300°, or until the meat is quite crisp. Pour off the fat as it accumulates. Serves 6.

Note: Carnitas can be prepared in advance and reheated. They can also be frozen. To reheat, thaw overnight in the refrigerator and bake in a 350° oven for 5-8 minutes, or until heated. Heat scale 3.

Fiery Appetizers

Cocktail Meatballs

Every time we serve these, they're the first thing on the cocktail table or buffet to disappear.

1 egg	1 teaspoon red chile powder
½ cup tequila	1 teaspoon ground black
1 teaspoon Worcestershire	pepper
sauce	1 pound ground beef
1 tablespoon fresh parsley,	1 cup bread crumbs
chopped or 1 teaspoon dried	½ cup Parmesan cheese
½ teaspoon celery seed	3-4 tablespoons canola oil

Whisk the egg with the tequila, Worcestershire, parsley, celery seed, chile, and pepper. Combine the mixture with the ground beef, bread crumbs, and Parmesan cheese. Form the mixture into balls the size of a walnut. Heat the oil in a large frying pan and sauté the balls, turning gently to brown on all sides. When cooked through, place on paper towels to drain and then serve with the Chinese Style Dipping Sauce or your favorite barbecue sauce. Serves 6-8.

CHINESE STYLE DIPPING SAUCE:

¼ cup light soy sauce	¼ teaspoon ground ginger
2 tablespoons sesame oil	3 green onions, chopped,
¼ cup tequila	(include green)

Mix all the ingredients together and serve to dip egg rolls, wonton, sushi, or pot stickers, or use over chop suey or chow mein instead of plain soy sauce.

The Tequila Cook Book

The Continental Divide runs through much of the state of New Mexico.

Tangy Chicken Tidbits

For a terrific tangy variation, skewer these tidbits, alternating the chicken with cherry tomatoes, and baste with the cayenne sauce while grilling.

3 tablespoons butter
1 tablespoon sesame oil
1 teaspoon cayenne powder
½ cup Dijon-style mustard
⅓ cup cider vinegar
2 tablespoons brown sugar,
   firmly packed

3 tablespoons honey
1 tablespoon soy sauce
2 pounds boneless chicken
   breast, skinned and cut into
   1-inch cubes

Melt the butter and oil in a pan, add the remaining ingredients, except the chicken, and simmer for 5 minutes. Add the chicken and sauté until the chicken is browned on all sides, about 10-15 minutes. Serve the chicken, along with the sauce, in a chafing dish with toothpicks. Garnish with parsley. Yields 50-60. Heat scale 4.

Fiery Appetizers

The magnificent Cathedral of Saint Francis of Assisi is a significant departure from Santa Fe's pueblo architecture. Referred to as "The Mother Church," it is one of the first Roman Catholic churches built in the southwest.

Blue Corn Muffins

These excellent muffins are light and moist and actually more gray in color than true blue. The blue corn, from which the meal is ground, has religious significance for the Southwestern Indians who have grown it for centuries.

1½ cups white flour	1 teaspoon sugar
1 cup blue cornmeal	1½ cups milk
3 teaspoons baking powder	2 large eggs, well beaten
1 teaspoon baking soda	⅓ cup vegetable oil

In a large bowl, combine the dry ingredients. In another bowl, combine the milk, eggs, and oil and add them to the dry ingredients. Mix just enough to combine. Fill well-greased muffin pans two thirds full and bake at 400° for about 20 minutes. Makes 12 regular-size muffins.

A Little Southwest Cookbook

Blue Corn: The ground meal made from blue corn is nuttier in flavor, higher in protein, and lower in starch than the meal made from either white or yellow corn, and it produces a more fragile tortilla. The color of the kernel and the meal is gray-blue. If the kernel is popped, the popped corn is white.

Green Chile Muffins

These are moist and do not crumble. They go well with all New Mexican meals. Try the different cornmeals for variety.

¾ cup milk
1 (8-ounce) can cream-style corn
⅓ cup melted butter, or vegetable oil
2 eggs, beaten
1½ cups white, yellow or blue cornmeal
1 teaspoon baking powder
½ teaspoon baking soda
1 teaspoon salt
1 teaspoon sugar
1½ cups mixed shredded Cheddar cheese and Monterey Jack cheese
1 (4-ounce) can chopped New Mexico chiles, drained

Preheat oven to 400°. Line 18 muffin cups with paper liners, or grease and flour each cup. In a medium-size bowl, stir together milk, corn, butter, and eggs. In a large bowl, whisk together cornmeal, baking powder, baking soda, salt, and sugar. Add mixture from medium-size bowl to dry ingredients and mix just until combined. Do not overmix.

Spoon a large spoonful of batter into each prepared muffin cup and top with a little cheese mixture and green chile, dividing evenly and reserving a little for sprinkling on top. Top with remaining batter and reserved cheese and green chile. Each cup should be two-thirds full. Bake 25-30 minutes, or until muffins are golden and a wooden pick inserted into the center comes out clean. Makes 18 muffins.

Sassy Southwest Cooking

Broccoli Cheese Cornbread

1 box cornbread mix
1 medium onion, finely chopped
2 cups grated cheese
Pinch salt
4 eggs
1 box frozen chopped broccoli, thawed and well drained

Mix all ingredients together and place in greased 9x12-inch pan. Bake at 350° for 25 minutes or until golden brown.

The Joy of Sharing

Skillet Corn Bread

This spicy skillet bread, sparked with both green and red chiles, is best served hot from the oven.

1 cup yellow cornmeal
½ cup all-purpose flour
2 tablespoons sugar
½ teaspoon salt
½ teaspoon baking soda
½ teaspoon baking powder
1 tablespoon Chimayó chile powder
1 cup buttermilk
2 large eggs, beaten
2 fresh green New Mexico or other green chiles, roasted, peeled, seeded, and diced

1 fresh red jalapeño chile, seeded, and minced
1 red bell pepper, roasted, peeled, seeded, and diced
1 cup mild Cheddar cheese, shredded
½ pound cooked ham, finely diced
4 tablespoons unsalted butter

Preheat the oven to 400°. In a large mixing bowl, whisk together the cornmeal, flour, sugar, salt, baking soda, baking powder, and chile powder. Pour the buttermilk and eggs into the dry mixture and stir to combine. Add the chiles, red pepper, and cheese to the batter and mix thoroughly.

In a medium cast-iron skillet, cook the ham in butter until it is nicely browned. Pour the ham and butter from the skillet into the batter and stir, then pour the batter back into the hot skillet and set on the center rack of the preheated oven. Bake the corn bread until it is firm and crusty, 30-40 minutes. Remove from the oven and turn out on a rack to cool, or cut into wedges straight from the skillet. Serves 8-12.

Red Chile Bible

New Mexico is the fifth largest state in area behind Alaska, Texas, California, and Montana, and was the 47th state admitted to the Union. With few sizeable natural lakes, New Mexico has important artificial bodies of water including Elephant Butte Reservoir, as well as Conchas Lake, Caballo and Navajo Reservoirs, and Lake Sumner.

Door Knobs
(Hush Puppies)

1 cup cornmeal
½ cup flour
1 teaspoon salt

½ teaspoon soda
2 tablespoons sugar
1 cup buttermilk

Mix and dip by teaspoonful into deep hot fat, about 4 inches deep. Cook until browned. Turn floating knobs over. Drain on paper towels and eat while hot.

Red River's Cookin'

Blue Corn Meal Pancakes

Blue cornmeal is used in the northern part of New Mexico more than in the southern part. Like olives, martinis, and rhubarb, it is an acquired taste—but one well worth going to the effort of getting to know.

1 cup blue cornmeal
1 cup all-purpose flour
2 teaspoons baking powder
½ teaspoon salt
1½ cups milk

2 eggs, well beaten
½ cup vegetable oil
½ cup sour cream
¼ cup green chile, chopped

Mix together blue cornmeal, flour, baking powder, and salt in a mixing bowl. Stir in milk, then the eggs, and beat. Slowly beat in the oil. Drop by tablespoonful onto a hot griddle. Mix sour cream and green chile together. Using a small ice cream scoop, put a scoopful on top of each stack of pancakes. This makes a great side dish for your "authentic" Christmas table. Yields approximately 12 pancakes.

Christmas in New Mexico Cook Book

Beer Biscuits

This is a quick and easy biscuit recipe that uses a prepared biscuit mix. The beer gives the biscuits a unique, delightfully light flavor.

4 cups Bisquick
1 tablespoon cooking oil
2 tablespoons sugar

1 (12-ounce) can beer, room
   temperature

Preheat oven to 400°. Mix all the ingredients together and pour into greased muffin tins. Fill only ½ full. Let sit about 20 minutes. Bake for 15 minutes or until the biscuits are nicely browned. Yields 24 biscuits.

Billy the Kid Cook Book

Ranch Biscuits

1 package yeast
1 teaspoon sugar
½ cup warm water
5 cups flour
3 teaspoons baking powder

1 teaspoon soda
½ teaspoon salt
2½ tablespoons sugar
2 cups buttermilk
½ cup oil

Mix yeast, sugar, and water. Let stand. Mix flour, baking powder, soda, salt, and sugar. Add buttermilk, oil, and yeast mixture to flour mix. Mix well. If too thin, add flour. Put in the refrigerator. Let rise 10-15 minutes after they are cut. Bake at 450° for 10-15 minutes.

Amistad Community Recipes

Ácoma Pueblo, also called Sky City, sits atop a 357-foot mesa, located 12-miles south of Interstate 40 between Laguna and Grants.

Sour Cream Bread

This picture-perfect loaf is not only tall and light, but wonderfully tasty. You'll make this one more than once.

1-POUND LOAF:

¼ cup water
⅔ cup sour cream
2 cups bread flour
1½ teaspoons sugar

¾ teaspoon salt
2 tablespoons dry milk
  powder
1½ teaspoons yeast

1½-POUND LOAF:

½ cup + 1 tablespoon water
¾ cup sour cream
3 cups bread flour
2 teaspoons sugar

1 teaspoon salt
3 tablespoons dry milk
  powder
2 teaspoons yeast

Follow bread machine directions for making white bread.

The Men's Guide to Bread Machine Baking

The Ultimate Sandwich Bread

I haven't found anyone who doesn't like this bread, hence its name. The loaf is tall and light, which pleases even finicky eaters or children. The addition of both whole wheat and rye flours give the bread a rich, full flavor that satisfies those with more sophisticated taste, yet the flavor is not so over-powering that it dominates sandwich fillings. One of my best loaves—a personal favorite.

1-POUND LOAF:

⅔ cup water
1½ tablespoons canola oil
1 cup bread flour
¾ cup whole wheat flour
¼ cup rye flour

1½ tablespoons vital gluten
1½ tablespoons sugar
¾ teaspoon salt
1½ teaspoons yeast

1½-POUND LOAF:

1 cup water
2 tablespoons canola oil
1¾ cups bread flour
1 cup whole wheat flour
⅓ cup rye flour

2 tablespoons vital gluten
2 tablespoons sugar
1 teaspoon salt
2 teaspoons yeast

Follow bread machine directions.

The Men's Guide to Bread Machine Baking

Garlic Focaccia

DOUGH ADDITIONS:
3 tablespoons olive oil
6 garlic cloves, peeled and
coarsely chopped

DOUGH:
1 cup water
3 cups bread flour
1 teaspoon sugar
½ teaspoon salt
1 teaspoon freshly ground black
pepper
2 teaspoons yeast

TOPPING:
6 tablespoons olive oil
2 tablespoons coarse (kosher)
salt
2 tablespoons freshly grated
black pepper

Sauté the garlic in the oil over medium heat until the garlic is lightly browned, and allow it to cool completely. Load the garlic and the remaining dough ingredients into the bread pan, select the dough setting, and press start. When the cycle ends, pull the dough out, punch it down, and knead it briefly on a floured surface to release gas. Allow to rest for 15 minutes.

Roll or press out the dough into a rectangle to fit a 15½ x 10½-inch jelly roll pan or large baking sheet. Generously grease the pan with olive oil and place the dough in the pan. Drip 3 tablespoons of the topping oil over the top, prick the dough with a fork 25-30 times, cover with plastic wrap, and set aside to rise for 30-45 minutes, or until doubled.

Bake in a preheated 375° oven for 20 minutes, or until golden brown. Before serving, drizzle the remaining 3 tablespoons of oil over the bread, season with salt and pepper, cut into squares, and serve warm.

The Men's Guide to Bread Machine Baking

Irish Soda Bread

4 cups Wondra Flour
1½ teaspoons baking soda
1 teaspoon salt
2 tablespoons caraway seeds
¾ cup sugar

1 cup raisins
2 eggs slightly beaten
2 tablespoons butter
1½ cups buttermilk

Mix dry ingredients and raisins. Mix eggs, butter, and buttermilk. Add to dry ingredients. (It will be the consistency of thick wallpaper paste—don't get upset). Put in iron frypan or porcelain clad cast iron pot which is slightly greased. Cut cross on top. Bake in 350° oven for 1¼ hours. Cool in pan for 20 minutes, then turn out on cooling rack. (Check bread after one hour. If it is chestnut brown, it is done—can burn easily if not watched).

Saint Joseph's Really Grande Cookbook

Empanadas de Fruta

1½ cups flour
1 teaspoon baking powder
1 teaspoon salt

8 tablespoons shortening
4-6 tablespoons water
Butter or oleo, optional

Sift flour, baking powder, and salt together. Cut in shortening and mix well. Add enough water to make dough easy to handle. Roll out dough to ⅛ inch thickness. Cut in rounds 3-4 inches in diameter. Fill each round with fruit. Press edges of dough together. Brush with butter and bake until brown.

FRUIT FILLING:
2 cups canned fruit, drained
1 cup sugar

1 teaspoon cinnamon
½ teaspoon cloves

Blend all thoroughly. Fill pastry rounds.

Recipes from Hatch

Navajo Fry Bread with Cilantro Butter and Raspberry Honey

3 cups flour
1½ teaspoons baking
   powder
½ teaspoon salt
1⅓ cups warm water
Shortening

Use either all white or half whole wheat flour. Mix flour, baking powder and salt. Add warm water and mix. Dough should be soft but not sticky. Knead until smooth. Tear off a chunk about the size of a peach. Pat and stretch until it is thin. Poke a hole through the middle, and drop into sizzling hot deep fat (lard is the traditional shortening, but you might prefer to use vegetable oil). Brown on both sides. Drain and serve hot.

Top with cilantro butter (whipped butter to which cilantro has been added) or raspberry honey (a mixture of ½ honey and ½ raspberry jam). Makes 6-8 pieces.

Contributed by McGrath's, Albuquerque.

Raspberry Enchantment House Tour Cookbook

Sopaipillas

Light, airy pillows of fried bread are the pride of Rancho de Chimayó. The golden puffs of dough accompany all meals. They can be stuffed with savory or sweet fillings. A cooking thermometer that registers up to at least 410° is required for this recipe.

2 cups flour
1 teaspoon salt
1 teaspoon baking powder
1½ teaspoons sugar
(optional)
1½ teaspoons oil, preferably
canola or corn

½ cup lukewarm water
¼ cup evaporated milk, at
room temperature
Oil, preferably canola or corn,
for deep-frying, to a depth of
2 inches
Honey, as an accompaniment

Sift together the flour, salt, baking powder, and, if desired, sugar into a large mixing bowl. Into the dry ingredients, pour the oil and mix with fingertips to combine. Add the water and the milk, working the liquids into the dough until a sticky ball forms.

Lightly dust a counter or pastry board with flour, and knead the dough vigorously for one minute. The mixture should be "earlobe" soft and no longer sticky. Let the dough rest, covered with a damp cloth, for 15 minutes. Divide the dough into 3 balls, cover the balls with the damp cloth, and let them rest for another 15-30 minutes. If not for use immediately, the dough can be refrigerated up to 4 hours.

Dust a counter or pastry board lightly with flour, and roll out each ball of dough into a circle or oval approximately ¼-inch thick. Trim off any ragged edges and discard them. To avoid toughening the dough, it should only be rolled out once. With a sharp knife, cut each circle of the dough into 4 wedges. Cover the wedges with the damp cloth. Don't stack the wedges, because they are likely to stick together.

Layer several thicknesses of paper towels near the stove. In a wok or a high-sided, heavy skillet, heat the oil to 400°. Give the oil your full attention, so that while it is heating, the temperature does not exceed 400°. If the oil smokes before reaching the proper temperature, it cannot be used for this recipe, because there is a danger of it catching fire. Make sure you are

(continued)

(continued)
using fresh, high-quality oil.

Exercising care to avoid a possible burn, gently drop a wedge of dough into the hot oil. After sinking in the oil briefly, it should begin to balloon and rise back to the surface. Cautiously spoon some of the oil over the sopaipilla after it begins to float. When the top surface has fully puffed—a matter of seconds—turn the sopaipilla over with tongs, again being extremely cautious. Cook it until it is just light golden, remove it with tongs, and drain it on paper towels. If a sopaipilla darkens before it is fully puffed, decrease the temperature by a few degrees before frying the remaining dough. Make 2-3 sopaipillas at a time, adjusting the heat as necessary to keep the oil's temperature consistent. Drain the fried breads on the paper towels. Arrange them in a napkin-lined basket and serve immediately with honey. Makes 12 sopaipillas.

The Rancho de Chimayó Cookbook

Ginger Bread

½ cup sugar	¾ teaspoon baking soda
½ cup oil	1 teaspoon powdered ginger
½ cup molasses	1 teaspoon cinnamon
1 egg	1½ cups flour
½ teaspoon salt	½ cup boiling water

Heat oven to 350°. Mix sugar, oil, molasses and egg together. Add salt, baking soda, ginger, cinnamon, and flour and mix well. Add boiling water and stir. Pour into a greased 8x8-inch pan. Bake 35 minutes at 350°.

Cooking with Kiwanis

Peanut-Carrot-Pineapple Holiday Bread

3 cups sifted flour
1 teaspoon soda
1 teaspoon salt
1 teaspoon cinnamon
3 eggs, beaten
3 cups sugar
1 cup cooking oil
2 cups finely grated carrots
1 (9-ounce) can crushed
  pineapple, drained
2 teaspoons vanilla
1 cup chopped peanuts

Sift flour, soda, salt, and cinnamon together. Place eggs and sugar in mixer bowl. Beat at medium speed until mixed. Beat in oil, a small amount at a time. Stir in flour mixture, carrots, pineapple, vanilla, and peanuts. Pour batter in two greased loaf pans. Makes 2 small loaves. Bake at 350° for 60 minutes.

Peanut Palate Pleasers from Portales

Cranberry-Orange Bread

2 cups sifted flour
½ teaspoon salt
1½ teaspoons baking powder
½ teaspoon soda
1 cup granulated sugar
1 egg, beaten slightly
2 tablespoons melted butter
½ cup orange juice
2 tablespoons hot water
½ cup chopped nuts
1 cup coarsely cut cranberries
1 tablespoon grated orange rind

Preheat oven to 350°. Sift dry ingredients together; add egg, melted butter, orange juice, and water. Mix only until dry ingredients are moistened. Fold in nuts, cranberries, and orange rind. Pour into a greased 9x5-inch loaf pan. Let stand 20 minutes, then bake for 50 minutes, or until bread tests done. When cool, wrap in waxed paper. The bread improves in flavor and slices more easily if allowed to stand for 24 hours before cutting. Makes 1 loaf.

Simply Simpatico

Banana Walnut Buttermilk Bread

This rich bread freezes beautifully.

1½ cups sugar
½ cup unsalted butter,
  softened
2 large eggs
4 very ripe bananas, mashed

1 teaspoon vanilla
1 teaspoon baking soda
⅓ cup buttermilk
1½ cups unbleached flour
1 cup finely chopped nuts

In a large bowl cream together the sugar and butter; add eggs one at a time, beating well after each addition. Beat in mashed bananas and vanilla, and continue beating until mixture is smooth. In a measuring cup stir baking soda into the buttermilk and add it to the banana mixture along with the flour and chopped nuts. Stir the batter until it is just combined. Pour batter into a greased and floured 9x5-inch loaf pan and bake in a 350° oven for one hour or until a cake tester inserted in the center comes out clean. Transfer the bread to a rack and let it cool in the pan for 10 minutes. Turn the bread out onto a rack and let it cool completely. Makes 1 loaf.

Simply Simpatico

Mom's Streusel-Filled Coffee Cake

This recipe has been in my family for generations. I can't remember celebrating a holiday and not having "Mom's Coffee Cake" warm from the oven. My guests at the Inn love this recipe.

CAKE:

3½ cups flour	½ cup shortening
1 tablespoon baking powder	2 eggs
1 teaspoon salt	1 cup milk
1½ cups sugar	1 tablespoon vanilla

STREUSEL:

1 cup brown sugar	¼ cup melted butter
2 tablespoons cinnamon	1 cup chopped nuts
¼ cup flour	

Mix cake ingredients well and place half of the batter in the bottom of a greased springform pan. Mix the streusel ingredients together with a fork. Add half the streusel over cake batter, then add the rest of the batter and top with remaining streusel. Bake in a preheated oven at 350° for about 45 minutes.

Inn on the Rio's Favorite Recipes

Breakfast Pear Loaf

A wonderful alternative to banana bread.

½ cup butter, softened
1 cup sugar
2 eggs
¼ cup milk
1 teaspoon vanilla extract
2 cups flour

1 teaspoon baking powder
½ teaspoon baking soda
¼ teaspoon nutmeg
1 cup coarsely chopped pears
½ cup chopped walnuts or
    pecans

Preheat oven to 350°. Grease a 9x5-inch glass loaf pan. Beat together the butter and sugar until creamy. Add the eggs, milk, vanilla, and mix well. In a separate bowl, sift together the dry ingredients. Combine with the butter mixture and stir thoroughly. Fold in the chopped pears and nuts. Stir until just blended. Spoon batter into greased pan. Bake for one hour, or until a toothpick inserted in the middle comes out clean. Do not over bake. Makes one loaf.

Inn on the Rio's Favorite Recipes

Mom's Apple Bread

3 eggs
1 cup oil
2 cups sugar
2 cups flour
1 teaspoon vanilla

1 teaspoon cinnamon
1 teaspoon baking soda
Dash of salt
2 cups chopped apples
1 cup nuts

Mix eggs, oil, and sugar in large bowl. Add flour, vanilla, cinnamon, baking soda, salt, apples, and nuts. Pour into greased loaf pans. Bake one hour at 350°. Makes 3 loaves.

What's Cookin' at Casa

Cocas
(Little Spanish Pizzas)

Best made with a pizza stone.

DOUGH:

3 teaspoons active dry yeast

12 tablespoons (¾ cup) warm water (110°)

2 tablespoons fine cornmeal

12 tablespoons (¾ cup) whole milk

4 tablespoons extra virgin olive oil

1 teaspoon salt

2 tablespoons rye flour

3½ cups unbleached white flour

FILLING:

1 cup roasted red bell peppers, chopped

1 cup New Mexico or Anaheim chiles, chopped

1 cup red onion, chopped

1 cup black olives, chopped

1 cup corn, grilled and removed from cob, or substitute frozen corn nibblets

1 cup cooked (preferably grilled) and shredded chicken breast

¼ cup goat cheese

½ cup Monterey Jack cheese, shredded

½ cup chopped cilantro

Dry red pepper flakes in shaker

¼ cup olive oil to brush over pizza dough when shaped, and on edges after it comes out of the oven

Place the yeast in a small bowl. Dissolve it in the warm water and set it in a warm place for 4 minutes. Combine the cornmeal, milk, and oil in a large mixing bowl. Add the yeast mixture, salt, and rye flour and mix well. Then gradually add the white flour until the dough is soft and workable.

Turn out onto a lightly floured surface and knead for 5 minutes. Sprinkle with a little flour as needed to keep the dough from sticking to the surface. Place the dough in a heavy oiled bowl and turn the dough once so it is coated with oil. Let the dough rise in a warm place until it has doubled in size, about 40-45 minutes.

Preheat the oven to 500° at least 30 minutes with a pizza stone on the lower third of the oven. To form the Cocas, divide

(continued)

(continued)

the dough into 4 equal balls. Roll out on a lightly floured surface, turning to keep the shape round. Roll the dough to about ⅛-inch thickness, slightly thicker at the edges.

Lay the dough on an oiled pizza pan or cornmeal-dusted wooden peel. Brush with olive oil. Use any desired combination of fillings listed above. Sprinkle cheese over the Cocas, place them in the oven on the pizza stone, and bake for 10 minutes or until golden brown. Brush the edges with oil and sprinkle with chopped cilantro and/or dry red pepper flakes. Serves 4-6.

Note: A very hot oven is needed to cook pizzas or Cocas. To ensure the proper temperature, use a pizza stone.

Christmas Celebration: Santa Fe Traditions

Easy Applesauce Loaf

Mix this quick bread up in a matter of minutes. Slices of Easy Applesauce Loaf make excellent sandwiches for tea when put together with whipped cream cheese. This recipe can easily be doubled.

⅔ cup sugar
⅓ cup canola oil
2 large eggs
2 tablespoons milk
1 teaspoon vanilla extract
1 cup applesauce
2 cups flour

1 teaspoon baking powder
½ teaspoon baking soda
½ teaspoon salt
½ teaspoon cinnamon
¼ teaspoon nutmeg
½ cup chopped walnuts

Preheat oven to 350°. Grease a 9x5-inch glass loaf pan. With an electric mixer, beat together the sugar and oil until creamy. Add eggs, milk, vanilla, and applesauce. Mix well. In a separate bowl, sift together the dry ingredients. Combine the two mixtures and fold in the chopped nuts. Pour batter into pan. Bake for one hour or until a toothpick inserted in the center comes out clean. Makes one loaf.

Inn on the Rio's Favorite Recipes

Grits and Cheese Casserole

1½ cups grits
6 cups water
1½ sticks oleo
1 pound American cheese
3 eggs, beaten

2 teaspoons salt
1 teaspoon savory salt
Tabasco and Worcestershire, to taste

Cook grits in boiling water as directed. Add oleo and grated cheese. Fold in eggs and seasonings. Pour into greased casserole. Bake one hour at 325°.

The Joy of Sharing

Company Eggs and Cheese

14-15 slices white sandwich bread
1 cup grated sharp Cheddar cheese
1 cup grated Monterey Jack cheese
1 (4-ounce) can chopped green chilies

7 eggs
½ tablespoon dry mustard
1 teaspoon salt
3 cups milk
1 cup crushed cornflakes, or enough to cover
¼ cup melted butter

Preheat oven to 350°. Remove crusts from bread and cut slices in half. Place half the bread in a buttered 9x13-inch pan. Layer with Cheddar cheese, Monterey Jack cheese, and green chilies. Cover with remaining bread. Beat eggs with dry mustard, salt, and milk. Pour over casserole and let stand in refrigerator 12 hours or overnight. Before baking, cover with cornflakes and drizzle with butter. Bake for 30-40 minutes at 350°. Makes 8-12 servings.

Cooking with Kiwanis

Huevos Rancheros

Although usually associated with breakfast, Huevos Rancheros is a hearty regional favorite at any time of the day, almost always accompanied by "refried" beans.

Oil, preferably corn or canola,
  to a depth of ½ inch
6 (5-inch) corn tortillas
12 eggs

2-3 cups green chile sauce,
  warmed
Shredded lettuce and chopped
  tomato, for garnish

Arrange several layers of paper towels near the stove.

Heat the oil in a large skillet until it ripples. With tongs, dip a tortilla into the hot oil and cook it until it is softened and pliable, a matter of seconds. Remove the tortilla immediately and drain it on the paper towels. If you don't act quickly enough, the tortilla will become crisp. Repeat with the rest of the tortillas. Carefully pour out of the skillet all but enough oil to generously coat its surface. Reserve the extra oil.

Arrange each tortilla on a plate and set aside. Place the skillet back on the stove and heat the oil over low heat. Fry the eggs, 2-3 at a time, turning once after the whites have set and the yolk has thickened. (For health reasons, each should be fried until the yolk sets.) Top each tortilla with two eggs, arranged side-by-side. Continue until all the eggs are fried, adding a bit of the reserved oil when the skillet becomes dry. Pour ⅓ - ½ cup of green chile sauce over each serving. Garnish the plates with lettuce and tomato. Serve with scoops of "refried" beans and Spanish rice, if desired.

The Rancho de Chimayó Cookbook

Butch Cassidy and his "Wild Bunch" were cowhands at the WS Ranch near Glenwood in the 1890s.

Huevos Rancheros

Our huevos rancheros are thick with chile sauce and cheese, unlike most versions I've had elsewhere. Huevos rancheros are the preferred breakfast on the working cattle ranches in Mexico, so have a big day planned for this hearty beginning!

4 cups black beans or pinto beans

4 cups red chile sauce or green chile sauce (or 2 cups each)

4 blue corn or whole-wheat or white-flour tortillas, plus 4 whole-wheat tortillas for serving

2 tablespoons vegetable oil, if using corn tortillas

2 tablespoons clarified butter

8 eggs

3 cups grated Monterey Jack cheese

½ cup finely sliced scallions for garnish

Preheat a broiler. Place the beans and chile sauce(s) in separate saucepans over medium-low heat and heat to serving temperature, stirring frequently to prevent scorching.

If using blue corn tortillas, brush each tortilla on both sides with vegetable oil. Place a dry skillet over high heat. When the pan is hot, add the tortillas, one at a time, and heat, turning once, until soft, about 5 seconds on each side. (If using flour tortillas, this step is unnecessary.)

In a sauté pan melt the butter and cook the eggs as desired: fried, over easy, sunny-side-up, or scrambled.

Place a corn or wheat tortilla on each of 4 flame-proof serving plates. Spoon one cup of the beans over each tortilla and top with the eggs, placed in the center. Ladle one cup of the chile sauce over each serving. Sprinkle the cheese over all. Slip under the broiler until the cheese melts and bubbles, just a few minutes. Garnish with the scallions and serve piping hot. Accompany with a warmed whole-wheat tortilla for each person. Serves 4.

Cafe Pasqual's Cookbook

Mexican Omelet

¼ cup diced yellow onion
3 large fresh mushrooms
1 teaspoon butter
3 eggs
¼ teaspoon pepper
Dash salt
¼ teaspoon milk

Hot pepper sauce
¼ cup jalapeño-flavored
    processed American cheese,
    cubed
1 teaspoon red salsa (very hot)
2 strips crisp bacon, crumbled

Sauté onion and mushrooms together in the butter. Take out of the pan and reserve. Beat eggs, add pepper, salt, milk, and hot pepper sauce. Put into the same pan over medium heat. Sprinkle the cheese over egg mixture. Add onions and mushrooms and spread salsa over the top. Sprinkle the bacon on top and cook until moist and set but not hard. Serve as is or with tomato salsa and a warm flour tortilla. Serves 1.

New Mexico Cook Book

Switchback trails lead down into Carlsbad Caverns.

Green Chilaquiles Omelet

These beauties can be made in relays and kept warm in the oven, or you can make a double recipe in an 8-inch omelet pan and cut the omelet in quarters to serve. They look very pretty garnished with tomato quarters and a sprig of fresh coriander.

1 corn tortilla	½ cup green chile sauce, heated
Oil for frying	½ cup Monterey Jack cheese,
Salt	grated (or Cheddar)
Ground cumin	1 tablespoon butter
2 eggs	

Cut the tortilla's round edges off so you have a square. Cut the square in half, stack the halves, and cut into matchstick strips. Fry in hot oil until crisp, drain on paper towels, and sprinkle with salt and a little cumin immediately. Beat eggs in a bowl with a little salt, and have sauce and cheese ready.

Melt butter in a 6-inch omelet pan over medium heat. When it sizzles, pour the eggs in. When they start to set, lift the edges with a fork to let unset egg run under, then spread with sauce. Keep lifting the edges to let any runny egg under, but don't let the omelet overcook—the edges should be set, but the top should still be a little undercooked. Remove from the heat, sprinkle with tortilla strips, and then cheese. Run under a broiler for a minute or so to melt the cheese, then slip face up onto a plate. Serves 1.

The Aficionado's Southwestern Cooking

Carlsbad Caverns has been described as the 8th Wonder of the World. It contains 83 separate caves, including the nation's deepest limestone cave—1,597 feet—and third longest. The temperature is a constant 56 degrees. Besides the beauty of the glistening formations in the cave chambers, there are spirals of bats that exit the cave nightly from May through October.

Breakfast Burritos

Breakfast Burritos are popular at the Albuquerque Balloon Fiesta in October, where everyone gets up before dawn to watch 500 to 600 hot-air balloons ascend.

2 strips bacon, fried
Scrambled egg
Shredded Monterey Jack
   cheese

Flour tortilla
Red or green salsa to taste

Roll bacon, egg, and cheese in flour tortilla. Serve with salsa.

Variations: Cooked crumbled or sliced chorizo may be substituted for bacon for a spicier burrito. Fried, grated or cubed potatoes can be added.

License to Cook New Mexico Style

Chile Egg Puff

10 eggs
½ cup flour
1 teaspoon baking powder
½ teaspoon salt
1 pint cottage cheese
1 pound Cheddar cheese,
   shredded

½ cup butter
2 (4-ounce) cans diced green
   chilies
1 teaspoon MSG (optional)

In the bowl of an electric mixer, beat eggs until light and lemon colored. Add flour, baking powder, salt, cottage cheese, Cheddar cheese, butter, and green chilies. Blend smoothly. Pour mixture into buttered 9x13-inch pan. Bake at 350° for 35 minutes or until brown. Serves 6.

Recipes from Hatch

Farmer's Breakfast Casserole

3 cups frozen, shredded
hash browns
¾ cup shredded Monterey
Jack cheese
1 cup diced, fully cooked ham
¼ cup chopped green chilies
or onions

4 eggs
1 (12-ounce) can evaporated
milk
¼ teaspoon pepper
⅛ teaspoon salt

Place potatoes in an 8-inch square baking dish. Sprinkle with cheese, ham and chilies or onions. Beat eggs, milk, pepper and salt. Pour over all. Cover and refrigerate for several hours or overnight. Remove from the refrigerator 30 minutes before baking. Bake, uncovered, at 350° for 55-60 minutes until a knife inserted near the center comes out clean. Yields 6 servings.

Our Best Home Cooking

Early Morning Casserole

1 pound sausage
4 tablespoons oleo
12 eggs

1 can mushroom soup
1 can chopped green chilies
Grated cheese

Scramble and cook sausage until brown. Drain on paper towels and put in ovenproof pan. Melt butter in skillet; scramble eggs until soft. Pour over sausage and add mushroom soup (undiluted). Add chopped chilies and cover with grated cheese. Bake at 350° for 10 minutes or until heated through.

Amistad Community Recipes

Almost three quarters of New Mexico's population lives in urban areas. Thirty-three percent of the land in New Mexico is owned by the federal government.

Spicy Southwest Bake

As a busy innkeeper, I love this flavorful dish's make-ahead preparation. Guests love this Southwest-style dish with sour cream and fresh salsa.

½ pound pork or turkey sausage	4 slices bread
1 large onion, diced	6 large eggs
1-3 teaspoons hot pepper flakes	1 cup milk
	1 cup salsa
	1 cup shredded Cheddar cheese

Brown sausage and onions together. Add the hot pepper flakes. One teaspoon for mild, 3 for hot and spicy. Lightly spray an 7x11-inch baking dish with non-stick cooking spray. Line the baking dish with the bread slices. Sprinkle the sausage/onion mixture over the bread. Mix the eggs, milk, and salsa together. Pour over the bread slices. Top with the cheese. Cover with foil and refrigerate overnight.

At brunch or breakfast time, put casserole in a preheated 350° oven for 45 minutes. Take off the foil and heat for 10 more minutes. Remove from oven and let cool 10 minutes before serving. Serve with extra salsa, hot or mild, and sour cream. Enjoy!

Inn on the Rio's Favorite Recipes

Salsa Rancherita

This succulent sauce compliments egg or burrito dishes.

2 tablespoons minced onion	2 cloves garlic, chopped
3 tablespoons butter	1 tablespoon oregano
4 fresh tomatoes, chopped	1 teaspoon salt
1 cup chopped green chile	¼ teaspoon pepper

Sauté onions in butter until they are transparent. Add tomatoes, chile, garlic, and spices. Simmer over medium heat 10 minutes or until mixture comes to a boil. Serve hot over egg or burrito dishes. Makes 2 cups.

Comida Sabrosa

Soda Dam is a volcanic deposit within the Jemez Caldera. The geothermal and hot springs systems are caused by groundwater that flows near the top of igneous rock that still may be partially molten.

A Santa Fe Soup

1 avocado
8 ounces plain yogurt
1 (14½-ounce) can chicken
   broth, or homemade broth
1 clove garlic, pressed
12 sprigs cilantro, chopped or
   Chinese parsley, or regular
   parsley

Juice of ½ lemon
1 small green chile or jalapeño,
   chopped
Paprika

Put all ingredients in blender, excluding paprika. Blend well. Chill several hours. Serve with paprika sprinkled on top. Good served with cucumber sandwiches. This will keep for several days. Do not freeze. Serves 1-4.

Savoring the Southwest

Gazpacho

Serve this cooling summer classic with fresh hot tortillas, quesadillas, or crisp corn chips and guacamole.

1 medium white or yellow onion, diced

3 cloves garlic, pressed or minced

½ teaspoon salt

1 tablespoon extra virgin olive oil

5 cups vegetable stock, divided

9 ripe tomatoes, cored

2 cucumber, trimmed and peeled

5 ripe tomatoes, finely diced

1 small hot green chile (jalapeño), seeded and minced

2 mild green chiles (Anaheim), or 1 green bell pepper, seeded and finely diced

1 red bell pepper, finely diced

2 tablespoons minced parsley

2 tablespoons minced cilantro

¼ cup lemon juice

2 tablespoons lime juice

Salt and black pepper, to taste

Sauté the onion and garlic with the salt in the olive oil until the onion is very sweet and golden brown. Transfer this mixture to blender container, add 3 cups vegetable stock, and blend until fairly smooth. Pour into a large bowl. Place the 9 cored tomatoes, one cucumber, and 2 cups vegetable stock in the blender container and blend until almost smooth. (This may need to be done in 2 batches.) Add this mixture to the stock and onion liquid. Add the remaining diced and minced vegetables, herbs, and juices to the soup. Season to taste with salt and black pepper. Chill and serve. The Gazpacho should be cold, tangy, and spicy. It will keep, covered, in the refrigerator for up to 2 days. Serves 6-8.

Cooking at the Natural Cafe in Santa Fe

Bloody Mary Soup

2 tablespoons butter
1 medium onion, diced
3 stalks celery, diced
2 tablespoons tomato purée
1 tablespoon sugar
5 cups V-8 vegetable juice

1 tablespoon salt (optional)
2 teaspoons Worcestershire
  sauce
¼ teaspoon pepper
1 tablespoon fresh lemon juice
4 ounces vodka

Melt butter in large saucepan. Sauté onion and celery in butter over medium heat. Add tomato purée and sugar. Cook for one minute. Add V-8 juice and simmer for 8 minutes. Stir in remaining ingredients. Strain and serve hot or well chilled. If using a food processor or blender, there is no need to strain.

Bon Appétit de Las Sandias

Route 66 Diner—Fabulous '50s food and eye-popping period decor make this diner a must-eat for visitors to Albuquerque. On Central Avenue (old Route 66).

Tortilla Soup

1 bunch green onions, sliced
thinly on the diagonal
¼ cup white wine (or broth)
8 cloves garlic, roasted
8 small Roma tomatoes, peeled,
seeded and chopped
1 cup green chile, roasted,
peeled and chopped (or
use frozen)

3 (14-ounce) cans low-sodium
chicken broth
4 tablespoons cilantro leaves
½ cup Soubise Sauce (optional)
8 corn tortillas, cut in thin strips
and baked at 300° until crisp
Garnishes: non-fat sour cream,
lime wedges, chopped
jalapeños

Place green onions in a soup pot with tightly-fitting lid. Add a little broth or white wine to steam. Prepare garlic by simmering whole, unpeeled cloves in water for 5 minutes. Drain and peel. Set on a baking sheet in a 300° oven for 20 minutes. While garlic is roasting, prepare tomatoes, measure chile and open broth. Mash roasted garlic while adding to onions; add tomatoes, chile and broth. Cook 30 minutes. Add cilantro and cook an additional 15 minutes, thickening with Soubise Sauce, if desired. Ladle into bowls and float corn tortilla strips on top. Pass the garnishes.

SOUBISE SAUCE:
1 cup diced onion
3 cloves garlic, minced
½ cup long-grain rice
½ cup non-fat dry milk
powder

1 quart chicken stock
(homemade, canned or
reconstituted with bouillon
granules; low-sodium
preferred)

Place onion and garlic in a heavy saucepan; cook over low heat, stirring constantly, for about 5 minutes. Add rice, milk powder, and stock. Cook for about 45 minutes, until rice is tender. Transfer to food processor or blender; process until smooth. The mixture will keep in the refrigerator several days to be used as a non-fat thickening agent. Makes 8 servings.

The Very Special Raspberry Cookbook

Taco Soup

2 pounds ground meat
1 onion, chopped
1 can chopped green chile
1 can hominy or corn or both
2 cans pinto beans

3 cans tomatoes
1 package dry taco mix
1 package dry Hidden Valley
 Salad Dressing Mix
2½ cups water

Brown the ground meat and onion together. Add the remaining ingredients. Mix all together and simmer 30 minutes. Serves 12-15.

Our Best Home Cooking

Autumn Soup

1 pound ground beef
1 cup diced onions
1 cup sliced carrots
1 cup diced potatoes
1 cup diced celery
4 cups water
2 teaspoons salt

4 tablespoons bottled Kitchen
 Bouquet
½ teaspoon pepper
2 bay leaves
1 teaspoon basil
1 (28-ounce) can peeled
 tomatoes, with liquid

Brown meat, drain off fat. Stir in remaining ingredients. Bring to a boil, then cover and simmer for 20 minutes.

Variation: After simmering for 10 minutes, add any pasta such as large shell pasta, then cover and simmer 10 minutes or until pasta is tender.

The Eagle's Kitchen

Prairie Soup

2 (1-pound, 14-ounce) cans
  tomatoes, chopped
¼ teaspoon garlic salt
¼ teaspoon vinegar
¼ teaspoon sugar or sugar
  substitute
1 pound ground round
2 bouillon cubes
4 cups hot water
1 cup finely chopped carrots
  (2 medium carrots)

1 cup finely chopped celery
  (4-5 stalks celery)
1 cup finely chopped green
  pepper
1 cup finely chopped potatoes
1 medium onion, finely
  chopped
1 tablespoon dry parsley
Salt and pepper

Simmer tomatoes, garlic salt, vinegar, and sugar. Sauté ground round slowly until brown, drain off any fat and add to tomatoes. Dissolve bouillon in hot water. Add bouillon and all vegetables to tomatoes. Add parsley and salt and pepper to taste. Simmer about one hour. Makes about 2 quarts.

Variation: Two tablespoons tiny pasta or 2 tablespoons barley can be added in place of the potatoes.

Savoring the Southwest

Old Town Soup

6 tablespoons butter
⅓ cup flour
½ cup milk
½ cup light cream
3 cups chicken broth

1 cup chopped cooked chicken
  or turkey
Hatch green chile to taste
Tortilla chips
Cheese, grated

Melt butter in saucepan. Blend in flour. Add milk, cream and broth. Cook and stir constantly until mixture thickens and comes to a boil. Add chicken and chile. Heat. To serve, break up tortilla chips and put in a bowl. Pour soup over chips and sprinkle you favorite cheese on top. Freezes well. Serves 3-4.

Families Cooking Together

Corn Soup

This soup, with its south-of-the-border flavors, is popular throughout the Southwest. Served with tostadas and a green salad, it makes a complete meal.

3½ cups corn kernels,
   preferably fresh
1 cup chicken stock
2 tablespoons butter
2 cups milk
1 clove garlic, minced
1 teaspoon oregano

Salt and pepper
2 tablespoons canned green
   chilies, diced, drained
1 cup peeled, seeded, chopped
   tomatoes
1 cup cubed Monterey Jack
   cheese

Purée corn and stock in a blender or food processor. Place purée in a saucepan with butter. Stir and simmer 5 minutes. Add milk, garlic, oregano, salt and pepper and bring to a boil. Reduce heat, add chilies, simmer 5 minutes. Divide tomatoes among 4 soup bowls. Remove soup from heat and add cheese. Stir until just melted. Ladle over tomatoes in bowls.

A Little Southwest Cookbook

Caldo de Queso con Calabacitas

4 cups water
4-6 potatoes, cut up
4 carrots, cut up
6 tablespoons oil or butter
1 onion, diced
2 ribs celery, diced
½ sweet red pepper
6 tablespoons flour
4 cloves garlic, minced
4 cups chicken broth

4 zucchini, sliced
2 cups milk
8 ounces Velveeta, cut in chunks
1 cup half-and-half
3-4 Anaheim green chilies,
    roasted, seeded and chopped
    (cut down amount if too hot)
Salt and white pepper to taste
Bottled hot sauce may be added
    to taste

In a large 4-quart pot, add water, potatoes, and carrots. Let it come to a boil and then turn down heat a little and cover with a lid. In a sauté pan, melt butter or oil over medium heat. Add diced onion, celery, and red pepper. Sauté until wilted and add flour and cook until flour barely turns color (if too thick, add a little more oil). Take off heat and stir in garlic. Add some warmed chicken broth to the roux mixture a little at a time, stirring constantly. When vegetables are barely done, add roux mixture to pot along with rest of broth and sliced zucchini and continue to simmer.

In another small pan, place 2 cups of milk with the cheese, barely heating the milk, but enough to melt cheese. Add chilies to this. Add the milk, cheese and chile mixture to large pot of soup. Stir. Lastly add one cup half-and-half. Taste and adjust seasonings. Heat, but do not let boil. Serve with hot corn tortillas.

Bon Appétit de Las Sandias

The state bird is the roadrunner. A member of the cuckoo family, they are brown, long-legged, long-billed birds that blend into their desert environment. The roadrunner's popularity soared with the release of an animated cartoon featuring the wily roadrunner and an inventive coyote who never gave up trying to catch him. "Beep Beep!"

Secret Soup

2 cans pinto beans
2 cans jalapeño pinto beans
1 can kidney beans
1 can corn
1 small can chopped green
   chilies
2 cans chicken broth
1 can stewed tomatoes
Cilantro to taste

4-5 cloves garlic, minced
1 onion, chopped fine
1 tablespoon olive oil
1 package taco seasoning
   mix
1 package dry ranch dressing
   mix
4 cups chopped chicken
   (optional)

Rinse all beans. Put first 8 ingredients in soup pot and stir to mix. Sauté garlic and onion in olive oil; add to pot. Add dry mixes and stir well. Add chicken, if desired. Simmer for one hour. Better made the day before.

The Joy of Sharing

Make-a-Meal Soup

1 onion, chopped
1 tablespoon pure vegetable
   oil
1 pound smoked sausage,
   thinly sliced
3 cups water
2 chicken bouillon cubes
1 teaspoon salt
¼ teaspoon pepper
1 bay leaf

½ teaspoon thyme
3 carrots, chopped
3 celery stalks, chopped
¼ head cabbage, cut in 1-inch
   chunks
2 tablespoons uncooked rice
1 (8-ounce) can tomato sauce
1 (15-ounce) can kidney beans
1 (28-ounce) can whole
   tomatoes

In a large saucepan, brown onion in oil until tender. Add remaining ingredients. Cover and simmer for 30 minutes. Makes 8 servings.

Our Best Home Cooking

Minestrone Soup

This is the perfect soup to highlight the flavors of the garden in early August, when all the vegetables are available.

½ cup minced onion
⅓ cup diced celery
2 tablespoons safflower oil, or olive oil
4 cups chicken or vegetable broth
1 of 2 garlic cloves
1 cup diced carrots
1 cup shredded cabbage
1 cup string beans, cut into ½-inch pieces
1 cup diced zucchini

2 medium tomatoes, peeled, seeded, and chopped roughly
1 cup chopped spinach
Herb salt, to taste
Freshly ground pepper, to taste
Cooked beans: navy, kidney, fava, or garbanzo (optional)
Precooked pasta (optional)
Parmesan or Romano cheese, as garnish
Parsley, as garnish

In a large soup pot, sauté the onion and celery in the oil. When they become tender and transparent, add the chicken broth and bring the mixture to a low simmer. Squeeze the garlic through a press and stir it into the liquid. Add all remaining vegetables, except the spinach, and simmer for 2 hours. Stir in the spinach during the last 2 minutes of cooking. Add the herb salt and freshly ground pepper to taste. Serves 4-6.

Cooked navy beans, kidney beans, fava beans, or garbanzo beans are also good in the soup. A small amount of precooked pasta is another addition. Finely chopped parsley and freshly grated Parmesan or Romano cheese can be added before serving.

A Painter's Kitchen

Hearty Black Bean Soup

2 cups dried black beans,
    soaked overnight in 8 cups
    of water
1 bay leaf
3 tablespoons butter or oil
2 onions, chopped
2 stalks celery, sliced

2 carrots, diced
2 cloves garlic, minced
1 tablespoon lemon juice
½ teaspoon cumin seed
½ teaspoon oregano
4 cups tomato juice

Bring the beans, water, and bay leaf to a boil in a large kettle. Lower the heat and simmer until the beans are soft—a full hour. Meanwhile, heat the butter or oil in a large skillet, and add the onions, celery, carrots, and garlic. Stew over low heat for 10 minutes or until tender. When the beans are soft, add the vegetables to the kettle, along with the lemon juice, cumin, oregano, and tomato juice. Bring to a boil. Discard the bay leaf and serve. Serves 8-10.

Savoring the Southwest

Sinister Stew

2 medium-size yellow or white
    onions
2 tablespoons vegetable oil
2 pounds lamb stew meat cut
    into chunks
4 cloves garlic
2 bay leaves
¼ teaspoon ground thyme

1 cup red wine
½ teaspoon dried parsley
½ teaspoon ground black
    pepper
¾ cup chopped green chile
    (fresh or canned)
1 or 2 tablespoons chopped
    jalapeños (to taste)

Peel and chop the onions. Heat oil in a large pan and sauté the onions for 5 minutes. Add rest of ingredients to the onions and cook, covered, over very low heat for 4-5 hours, or until the lamb is nice and tender. Remove bay leaves and garlic cloves and serve. Served with rice and bread, this makes an excellent (albeit hot) dish. Serves 6-8.

New Mexico Cook Book

Hopi Corn Stew
with Blue Corn Meal Dumplings

2 pounds stewing beef, cut
   into 1-inch cubes
2 tablespoons lard or oil
1 medium-sized onion,
   chopped
1 small sweet green pepper,
   chopped

1 tablespoon ground red chili
4 cups frozen corn kernels
1 medium-sized pumpkin, peeled
   and cubed
2 tablespoons whole wheat flour
Salt to taste

In a large heavy saucepan, sauté meat in lard or oil until light-ly browned. Transfer meat to a plate. Sauté onion and green pepper in same pan until onion is slightly wilted. Return meat to pan with chili powder, add enough water to cover meat, and simmer for 1½ hours. Add corn, pumpkin, and salt to taste and simmer until tender. Add flour mixed with 2 tablespoons of water to stew. Add dumplings and simmer, covered, for 15 min-utes.

BLUE CORN MEAL DUMPLINGS:
2 cups ground blue corn meal
2 teaspoons baking powder
1 teaspoon salt

¼ cup lard or other shortening
¾ cup milk

Combine corn meal, baking powder, and salt. Cut in lard or other shortening until mixture looks like meal. Add milk to form a soft but still stiff dough. Drop mixture by spoonfuls into stew. Yields 6 servings.

Southwest Indian Cookbook

The Hopi are descended directly from the Anasazi and are thought to have lived in the region since about 1150 AD. Hopi ways and traditions are distinctly dif-ferent from those of the Navajo or New Mexico Pueblo peoples, and some of their cer-emonies, such as the famous Snake Dance, are strictly closed to the public. A well-known Hopi craft is the carved wood kachina doll; unique to the Hopi, they originated as religious symbols.

Holiday Tortilla Stew

3 cups chicken breast,
  shredded
2 Anaheim chiles
1 red bell pepper
2 ears yellow corn or
  1 package frozen corn
4 large tomatoes
1 pound chorizo, sautéed
  and drained
2 strips lean bacon, chopped
2 medium onions, chopped
2 teaspoons fresh oregano
  or 1 teaspoon dried

1½ teaspoons ground cumin
4 cloves garlic, crushed
6 cups fresh chicken stock
Salt and pepper to taste
4 cups zucchini, diced
12 corn tortillas
1 cup vegetable oil
Fresh cilantro
Juice of 2 limes
1 cup sour cream (optional)

Grill or broil the chicken, chiles, bell pepper, and corn until blistered on all sides. Remove the skins and seeds from the chiles (use rubber gloves) and bell pepper. Coarsely chop. Cut the kernels of corn off the cobs. Parboil the tomatoes to remove the skins, chop coarsely, and set them aside.

Sauté the chorizo and drain off and discard all the fat. In a Dutch oven or large pot, fry the bacon until crisp; then remove and chop it, saving the drippings. Add the chopped onions to the bacon drippings and sauté them until they are clear, 3-5 minutes.

Add the tomatoes, chicken, chorizo, oregano, cumin, garlic, and chicken stock. Bring to a boil. Reduce the heat to a simmer. Salt and pepper to taste. Cover and cook 20-30 minutes. Stir in the chopped chiles, bell pepper, corn, and zucchini and cook another 10-15 minutes.

Before serving, cut the corn tortillas into 1-inch strips and fry them until crisp in the vegetable oil. Drain on paper towels. Ladle the stew into bowls and garnish the bowls with tortilla chips, fresh cilantro, and lime juice. If desired, dollop sour cream on top. Or ladle the stew into bowls and let guests add their own garnishes. Serves 12.

Christmas Celebration: Santa Fe Traditions

Green Chile Stew

Great on a cold winter night.

2 tablespoons olive oil
3 pounds turkey thighs, skinned, boned, and cut into bite-size pieces
1 large onion, chopped
2 cloves garlic, minced
2 cups chicken or turkey stock
1 cup dry white wine
1 tablespoon tomato paste
1 (28-ounce) can diced or crushed tomatoes
3 cups water

3-4 large green chiles, roasted, peeled, and chopped
4 medium potatoes, peeled and diced
2 cups frozen corn kernels
½ teaspoon ground oregano
½ teaspoon ground cumin
1 tablespoon chopped fresh parsley
1 teaspoon freshly ground black pepper
1 teaspoon salt

Heat the olive oil in a large soup pot and sauté the turkey and onion together until the turkey is lightly browned. Add garlic, chicken or turkey stock, wine, tomato paste, tomatoes, and water. (Add water slowly until desired consistency.) Cook over medium-high heat for 20 minutes. Add the rest of the ingredients; cover and simmer over low heat for another 45 minutes or until the turkey and potatoes are tender. If you want a soupier consistency, use 1 - 2 additional cups of water, or a mixture of stock and water. Serves 4-6.

A Fork in the Road

Green Chile Stew

Traditional in many homes.

2 pounds boneless pork, cut
   into 1-inch cubes
3 tablespoons all-purpose
   flour
2 tablespoons butter
1 cup chopped white onion
2 garlic cloves, minced
3 cups peeled, chopped ripe
   tomatoes

1 teaspoon salt
½ teaspoon dried-leaf oregano
¼ teaspoon ground cumin
20 fresh New Mexico chiles,
   roasted, peeled, seeded,
   deveined, and chopped

Toss pork with flour, to coat. In a 4-quart Dutch oven or heavy pot, heat butter and add pork cubes a few at a time. Stir to brown. Push to side of pot and add onion, garlic and cook until onion is soft. Stir in browned pork. Add tomatoes, salt, oregano, and cumin. Cover and simmer one hour; add water as necessary and stir occasionally. Add chiles, simmer 30 minutes and add water as necessary. Makes 4 servings.

Sassy Southwest Cooking

New Mexicans swear a bowl of green chile stew not only clears the sinuses with one good bite, but packs enough Vitamin C to help stave off a cold.

Camel Rock, a curious natural rock formation north of Santa Fe, can be found roadside on the Tesugue Indian Reservation.

Fresh Fruit Salad
with Spicy Avocado Dressing

SALAD:

1 large mango, peeled and sliced

3 apricots, peeled and quartered

3 plums, peeled and quartered

2 cups strawberries, halved

1 small bunch green grapes, washed and stemmed

1 pound mixed lettuces

AVOCADO DRESSING:

½ medium avocado, peeled and mashed

½ cup plain yogurt

1 tablespoon honey, or to taste

2 scallions, minced (white part only)

½ teaspoon lemon zest

¼ teaspoon orange zest

⅛ teaspoon salt

¼ teaspoon ground cumin

⅛ teaspoon freshly ground black pepper

½ teaspoon minced Fresno or red jalapeño chile

2 tablespoons light cream or to taste

Whisk the dressing ingredients together in a medium bowl, or mix in a blender, if you prefer. Adjust seasoning to taste, and drizzle over mixed fresh fruits and greens. Serves 6-8.

Note: The Avocado Dressing also goes well with cold chicken or turkey; and, if you omit the honey and add half a minced garlic clove, it partners beautifully with cold shrimp or scallops, or with a bowl of summer vegetables.

Red Chile Bible

Orange-Almond Salad

¼ cup salad oil
2 tablespoons sugar
2 tablespoons malt vinegar
¼ teaspoon salt
⅛ teaspoon almond extract
6 cups torn mixed greens

3 medium oranges, peeled,
   sliced crosswise and halved
1 cup thinly sliced celery
3 tablespoons sliced green onion
⅓ cup toasted slivered almonds

In a screw-top jar combine oil, sugar, vinegar, salt, and almond extract. Cover and shake well to dissolve sugar and salt. Chill. In a large salad bowl, combine greens, oranges, celery, and onion. Sprinkle with almonds. Pour dressing over and toss gently to coat. Serve at once. Makes 6-8 servings.

Simply Simpatico

Avocado Salad

1 clove garlic, minced
2 tablespoons grated onion
2 tablespoons finely chopped
   capers
1 tablespoon chopped parsley
1 teaspoon chopped chives
½ teaspoon sugar
½ cup olive oil
2 tablespoons tarragon vinegar

1 teaspoon salt
½ teaspoon pepper
1 avocado, chopped
2 heads romaine lettuce,
   washed and chilled
1 head endive, washed and
   chilled

Combine all the ingredients (except the lettuce) in a salad bowl and mix well. Tear the lettuce leaves into thirds and add to the dressing. Toss lightly and chill. Toss again before serving.

Red River's Cookin'

Strawberry Spinach Salad

2 bunches spinach
2 pints strawberries, washed and quartered

Arrange spinach and strawberries in layers in a glass bowl. Add dressing at last minute and toss. Enjoy!

DRESSING:

½ cup sugar
1½ teaspoons minced onion
2 tablespoons sesame seeds
1 tablespoon poppy seeds
¼ teaspoon Worcestershire
   sauce

¼ teaspoon paprika
½ cup vegetable oil
¼ cup cider vinegar

Put sugar, onion, sesame and poppy seeds, Worcestershire sauce, paprika, oil and vinegar in blender. Blend on low until mixed.

Families Cooking Together

24-Hour Vegetable Salad

10-15 fresh mushrooms,
   sliced
¼ cup chopped green onions
2 cucumbers, peeled and sliced
¼ cup chopped fresh parsley
1 large green pepper, sliced
3 large tomatoes, cut into
   wedges

6 ounces Swiss cheese, cut into
   thin strips
1 (6-ounce) can whole pitted
   black olives
½ teaspoon garlic salt
½ teaspoon salt
¾ cup Italian salad dressing

In a large deep glass bowl, layer first 8 ingredients in order given; top with drained olives. Add garlic salt and salt to the salad dressing, stir and pour over top of salad. Cover and refrigerate for at least 12 hours, better if it stays 24 hours. Toss and serve. Serves 6.

Savoring the Southwest

Wilted Lettuce Salad

SALAD:

1 bunch leaf lettuce, torn   6-8 radishes, thinly sliced
4-6 green onions, thinly sliced

Toss lettuce, onion, and radishes in a large salad bowl; set aside.

DRESSING:

4-5 bacon strips   1 teaspoon sugar
1 tablespoon lemon juice   ½ teaspoon pepper
2 tablespoons red wine vinegar

In a skillet, cook bacon until crisp. Remove to paper towels to drain. To the hot drippings, add lemon juice, vinegar, sugar, and pepper; stir well. Immediately pour dressing over salad; toss gently. Crumble the bacon and sprinkle on top. Yields 6-8 servings.

Mrs. Noah's Survival Guide

Mexican Salad

1 large head lettuce, shredded   1 cup water
1 onion, chopped   1 (10½-ounce) bag fritos
1 or 2 tomatoes, chopped   Catalina dressing
1 pound hamburger meat   Colby or Cheddar cheese
1 package taco seasoning   (optional)

Combine lettuce, onion, and tomatoes in large salad bowl; set aside. Brown hamburger meat, drain; add taco seasoning mix and water. Let simmer and cook down. When done, add to salad mixture; add Fritos. Toss with Catalina dressing. Add grated cheese, if desired.

Recipes for Rain or Shine

New Mexico Burning Salad

SALAD:

3 cups shredded lettuce
1 (15-ounce) can dark red
  kidney beans
2 medium tomatoes, chopped

1 chopped avocado
1 small zucchini, chopped
½ cup green chile

DRESSING:

⅓ cup olive oil
½ cup lime juice

½ teaspoon cumin
½ teaspoon salt

Toss salad ingredients in bowl. Mix dressing ingredients and pour over salad. Serve in bowls garnished with olives, cubed provolone cheese, and corn chips.

Cooking with Kiwanis

Bean Salad

2 cups cooked pinto beans
2 cups cooked green beans
1 large onion, peeled and
  thinly sliced
2 cloves garlic, peeled and
  mashed
1 large sweet pepper, seeded
  and thinly sliced

½ cup sugar
1 teaspoon ground red chili
2 teaspoons salt
⅓ cup vinegar
½ cup oil

Combine pinto and green beans, onion, garlic, and pepper in a large bowl. Combine sugar, chili, salt, and vinegar in another bowl. Slowly pour in oil, beating constantly. Pour over beans and toss thoroughly. Allow beans to marinate, covered, for at least 2 hours in the refrigerator before serving. Yields 6-8 servings.

Southwest Indian Cookbook

Raspberry Green Salad

1 head romaine or green leaf
    lettuce
2 (10½-ounce) cans
    mandarin oranges, drained
15 cherry tomatoes,
    quartered
1 small jicama root, peeled
    and julienned

Fresh raspberries for garnish
    (optional)
1 avocado, sliced
⅔ cup toasted almonds
⅓ cup chopped fresh basil
1 mango, cut in small pieces

Layer all ingredients in glass or Lucite bowl for best color display. Toss just before serving with Raspberry Vinaigrette.

RASPBERRY VINAIGRETTE:

1 (12-ounce) can cran-raspberry
    frozen juice concentrate
1 (16-ounce) jar seedless
    raspberry jam
1 teaspoon white pepper

2 cups red wine vinegar
2 teaspoons minced fresh garlic
½ teaspoon salt
2-4 cups safflower oil

Process all ingredients except oil until smooth in processor or blender. Divide in 4 parts. Freeze 3 parts in sealed freezer bags. (They will keep in freezer indefinitely.) Slowly add one cup safflower oil to remaining part in processor. (Leftover mixed salad dressing will keep in a covered jar in the refrigerator for at least a week.) To use frozen portion, defrost. Put in blender and drizzle in ½ - 1 cup safflower oil. Makes 8-10 servings.

Note: You may vary the amount of lettuce. Do not substitute the safflower oil. It has a distinctive taste that glorifies the fruit.

The Very Special Raspberry Cookbook

Randy's Raspberry Vinaigrette

1 pint fresh raspberries
½ pint sun-dried cranberries
1 cup cranberry juice cocktail
1 teaspoon Dijon mustard

½ cup raspberry vinegar
1 cup olive oil
Juice of 1 lime
Pinch of salt, to taste

In a saucepan, heat raspberries and cranberries with cranberry juice cocktail. Transfer to food processor and add Dijon mustard and vinegar. Turn to high speed and incorporate oil slowly until emulsified. Add lime juice and salt.
Contributed by Stephen's, Albuquerque.

Raspberry Enchantment House Tour Cookbook

Mexican Cole Slaw

6 cups red and green cabbage, shredded
3 tablespoons cilantro or parsley, chopped
1 red bell pepper, thinly sliced
1 red onion, thinly sliced
1 (4-ounce) can green chilies, chopped and drained

Juice of 2 limes
2 cloves garlic, minced
¼ cup white wine vinegar
1 tablespoon sugar
½ teaspoon salt
¼ teaspoon Tabasco sauce
¼ cup water
⅓ cup olive oil

Place cabbage, cilantro, red pepper, onion, and chilies in a glass bowl. In a jar with a tight-fitting lid, combine the lime juice, garlic, vinegar, sugar, salt, Tabasco, water, and oil. Shake well. Pour dressing over the slaw and toss to coat well. Marinate refrigerated, tightly covered, with plastic wrap, for at least 12 hours, tossing frequently. Drain and serve well chilled. The salad can be made up to 3 days in advance, but drain it after 2 days and keep it tightly covered.

Bon Appétit de Las Sandias

Cabbage Salad
with Apple and Walnuts

½ small green or red cabbage
1 small apple with a sweet
and tart flavor

½ cup walnuts, broken
Herb Salad Dressing

Cut the cabbage half into 2 pieces and core them. Then slice the cabbage into fine shreds no wider than ⅛-inch and into pieces 2 inches long. Core and quarter the apple, then cut into small chunks about ¼-inch thick and ½-inch square. (You may want to peel a commercially produced, nonorganic apple.) Chop or break the walnuts so that they are about the same size as the apple chunks. Mix the cabbage, apple, and walnuts together in a salad bowl. Add the Herb Salad Dressing and stir again. Serves 4-6.

HERB SALAD DRESSING:

2 teaspoons each: lovage,
tarragon, dill, basil, parsley
2 tablespoons olive oil
2 tablespoons safflower oil,
or other high-quality
vegetable oil
1 teaspoon lemon juice, or
more to taste

¼ teaspoon whole seed mustard
2 garlic cloves
Herb salt, to taste
Freshly ground pepper, to taste
Pinch of sugar (optional)
Chives, as garnish

Wash the herbs and pat them dry. Then chop all herbs medium-fine, except the chives. Blend the olive and safflower oils with a fork, add the lemon juice and mustard. Squeeze one medium garlic clove through a garlic press and add it to the liquid. Then add the chopped herbs to the dressing. Add herb salt and freshly ground pepper to taste. Add a pinch of sugar ,if the mixture is too sour. Allow this dressing to stand for an hour, if possible, so that the herb and garlic flavors can permeate the dressing. This quantity will dress a salad for 4-6 people.

A Painter's Kitchen

Christmas Eve Salad

3 oranges, peeled and
    sectioned
3 bananas, peeled and sliced
1 grapefruit, peeled and
    sectioned

½ cup pine nuts
½ cup grenadine
1½ cups shredded coconut

Mix all the ingredients together and refrigerate until ready to serve. Serves 4-6.

Christmas in New Mexico Cook Book

Jicama Salad with Watercress, Radishes, and Chiles

2 medium jicama, about
    1½ -2 pounds, peeled, sliced
    ¼-inch thick, and cut into
    ¼-inch-thick sticks
1 cup slivered red onion
1⅓ cups julienned radishes
3-5 jalapeños, stemmed,
    seeded,ribbed, and thinly
    sliced lengthwise

2 bunches watercress, large
    stems removed
⅓ cup coarsely chopped fresh
    cilantro
½ cup freshly squeezed lime
    juice
1 tablespoon cider vinegar
2 tablespoons sugar
1 teaspoon salt or to taste

In a large bowl gently toss the jicama, red onion, radishes, chiles, watercress, and cilantro. Refrigerate until ready to use. In a small bowl whisk together the lime juice, vinegar, sugar, and salt until the sugar is dissolved. Pour dressing over salad and toss to coat thoroughly. Adjust seasonings and serve immediately. Yields 6 servings.

The Santa Fe School of Cooking Cookbook

Jicama is a crisply textured, slightly sweet, edible tuber resembling a brown-skinned turnip; sometimes called Mexican potato. Sticks of peeled jicama, dipped in a little salt and hot chile powder and squirted with lime, make a terrific, low calorie snack.

Pat's Pasta Salad

1 package tricolored pasta
4 tablespoons extra virgin
   olive oil
½ bunch green onions
1 medium jar green olives with
   pimentos

½ to ¾ cup chopped fresh
   parsley
½ cup pecan halves
4 ounces hard salami

Prepare pasta until al dente. Drain pasta, rinse with cold water and drain well. Pour pasta into large salad bowl. Pour juice from olives and reserve liquid. Add olives to pasta. Chop green onions into thin pieces and add to pasta. Add parsley and pecan halves. Slice salami into bite-sized pieces and add to pasta. Mix olive oil and olive juice together. Pour onto pasta and toss gently. Chill. Toss again before serving.

The Eagle's Kitchen

Tuna Macaroni Salad

1½ cups cooked macaroni
1 small can water packed tuna, drained

¼ cup chopped celery
3 hard-boiled eggs, chopped
1 small onion, chopped

DRESSING:
½ cup Miracle Whip
¼ cup French dressing
¼ teaspoon mustard

1 teaspoon sugar
½ teaspoon vinegar

Mix salad ingredients together. Mix Dressing ingredients together and pour over macaroni salad. Chill for 2 hours.

The Joy of Sharing

Red Hot Salad

¼ cup red hot candies
1 cup boiling water

1 small package cherry Jell-O
2 cups applesauce

Dissolve red hots in water. Add to Jell-O. Add applesauce. Stir and set in refrigerator. Serves 8.

Recipes for Rain or Shine

Tiny Green Beans and Baby Red Potatoes in Salsa Vinaigrette

What was once the bounty of early spring in the Southwest can now be enjoyed all year. Prepared this way, a pair of favorite vegetables have a Tex-Mex tang and can accompany a wide variety of Southwestern menus. You can vary the type of salsa here to suit your palate and the other dishes in your meal.

15 tiny red potatoes, well scrubbed and with a ½-inch belt of skin removed
1½ pounds fresh small green beans, rinsed with stems removed, leaving tips
1 cup water
¼ cup white vinegar
¼ cup extra virgin olive oil, preferably Spanish
½ cup fresh salsa, or to taste
8 fluffy red lettuce leaves, rinsed
16 thin strips of red bell pepper

In a saucepan bring water about one inch deep to a boil. Add the potatoes and green beans and cover. Simmer about 5 minutes, or until the potatoes are just tender, not mushy. (Peek once or twice to be sure the water has not evaporated.) Combine the vinegar, oil, and salsa. When the vegetables are just done (do not overcook!) drain excess liquid, cover, and allow to dry out on the surface over a low flame—about 5 minutes.

Toss with the vinaigrette; keep tossing every 15 minutes or so until the vegetables have absorbed most of the liquid. After about an hour, place the lettuce leaves on individual plates, then arrange the green beans and potatoes in an attractive pattern. Garnish with a crisscross of bell pepper strips and chill. Yields 8 servings.

Fiestas for Four Seasons

Peanut Salad

2 cups shelled, roasted and
  salted peanuts
⅓ cup oleo
1 large package Cool Whip,
  divided
1 (8-ounce) package cream
  cheese
1 cup sugar

1 large box frozen strawberries,
  thawed, drained, reserve
  liquid
1 large can crushed pineapple,
  drained, reserve liquid
1 box strawberry-banana Jell-O

Prepare peanuts in the food processor until they are finely crushed; set aside 2 tablespoons to sprinkle on the top of finished salad. Mix with oleo and spread in the bottom of a 9x13-inch flat dish and bake at 350° for 10 minutes. Set aside to cool. Mix ½ cup Cool Whip with cream cheese and sugar. Spread over cool peanuts. Add enough water to liquids from strawberries and pineapple to make 2 cups. Add Jell-O to liquid and boil for 2 minutes. Let this mixture nearly set. Add the fruit. Spread over the creamed mixture and top with rest of Cool Whip and sprinkle peanuts on top.

Peanut Palate Pleasers from Portales

The International UFO Museum and Research Center in Roswell is fast becoming the clearing house for information related to UFOs and their phenomenon. The founders were participants in the Roswell Incident of 1947.

Zuñi Succotash

3 cups canned pinto beans,
  drained
1½ cups fresh or frozen corn
  kernels
1½ cups fresh string beans,
  chopped
1 teaspoon sugar

1 teaspoon salt
Pepper to taste
1½ cups water
4 tablespoons butter or
  shortening
2 tablespoons shelled sunflower
  seeds, crushed

In a large heavy saucepan, place all the ingredients, except for the sunflower seeds, in water with 2 tablespoons butter. Simmer for 15 minutes or until vegetables are tender. Add sunflower seeds and remaining butter and continue to simmer until mixture thickens. Yields 6 servings.

Southwest Indian Cookbook

Spicy and Saucy Stir-Fry

Well worth the effort of chopping.

2 cups rice
¼ cup peanut, corn, or
  safflower oil
1 teaspoon mustard seeds
½ cup finely chopped onion
3 minced garlic cloves
1 green or red bell pepper,
  chopped
1 cup potato cubes
½ cup water
1 cup cubed cauliflower
1 cup cubed broccoli
1 cup cubed eggplant

1 cup thin sliced celery
1 teaspoon ground turmeric
1 teaspoon ground cumin
1 teaspoon ground coriander
½ cup water
1 cup cut snow peas or string
  beans
1 cup chopped cabbage
1 large chopped tomato
1 teaspoon salt
¼ teaspoon cayenne
Juice of 1 lemon or lime

Put rice to steam (15 minutes by pressure cooker yields most nutrients). Heat oil over moderate heat and add mustard seeds. Allow to pop in hot oil. Add onions; cook for several minutes. Add garlic and bell pepper; cook for 2 minutes. Add potato and ½ cup water and cover to steam for 10 minutes. Add cauliflower, broccoli, eggplant, and celery. Mix well and add turmeric, cumin, and coriander. Add ½ cup water; stir well and cover for 5-10 minutes (until taters are tender). Add peas (beans), cabbage, and tomato and stir well. Add salt and cayenne; cook and stir for 5 minutes. Add steamed rice to the veggies; put lemon juice on top and serve. Serves 6.

Variations: Garnish with coriander leaves. Serve with apricot jam or chutney on the side. Serve with Indian bread or pita bread. Sauté tofu or tempeh cubes in toasted sesame oil and add with rice.

A Fork in the Road

Vegetable Enchilada

A Sunday brunch pleaser.

6 cups assorted vegetables,
  cut into small pieces
  (zucchini, broccoli, carrots,
  cauliflower, onion, etc.)
2 tablespoons vegetable oil
⅛ teaspoon chili powder or
  to taste

¼ teaspoon cumin
Salt and pepper to taste
1 cup Cheddar cheese, grated
1 cup Jack cheese, grated
12 flour tortillas
1 jar chile salsa

Cook veggies in oil until crispy-tender. Add spices and ½ of each cheese. When cheese melts, fill tortillas with mixture and roll closed. Place filled tortillas in baking dish and spoon salsa and remainder of cheese over the enchiladas. Bake at 350° until hot. Serves 6.

A Fork in the Road

Hominy Cheese Casserole

2 cans yellow or white hominy
1 can mushroom soup
1 can Ro-Tel tomatoes

1 cup Cheddar cheese
Crushed corn chips

Mix all ingredients except corn chips. Put in 2-quart casserole dish and cover with corn chips. Bake for 35 minutes at 350°.

Mrs. Noah's Survival Guide

Calico Corn

½ cup sliced fresh mushrooms
⅓ cup chopped green pepper
⅓ cup chopped onions
2 tablespoons butter
1 (16-ounce) can whole kernel
corn, drained

1 (2-ounce) jar pimientos,
drained and diced
2 tablespoons celery flakes
Dash cayenne or hot pepper
sauce

Place mushrooms, green pepper, onion, and butter in 1½-quart glass or ceramic dish. Microwave uncovered 1-2 minutes or until tender. Add remaining ingredients. Microwave covered 1-3 minutes or until heated through, stirring once during cooking.

License to Cook New Mexico Style

Green Chile Corn Casserole

1 box Jiffy Corn Muffin Mix
2 eggs
½ stick butter or margarine,
softened
⅔ cup milk
1 (4-ounce) can chopped
green chilies, undrained

4 ounces Cheddar or Jack
cheese, grated (optional)
¼ teaspoon ground cumin
1 (16-ounce) can whole kernel
corn, drained
1 (16-ounce) can creamed corn

Mix all ingredients together with an electric mixer to incorporate margarine, adding corn last. Bake at 350° in your favorite 2-quart baking dish for one hour or until set.

Families Cooking Together

There are four ingredients that make up most Southwestern dishes: the tortilla, pinto bean, cheese and chile. New Mexico dishes, though mistakenly referred to as "Tex-Mex" or "Mexican," actually reflect a blend of Hispanic and Indian cultures.

Corn Cakes with Calabacitas and Queso Blanco Salsa

This dish is beloved by our vegetarian and nonvegetarian patrons alike. I was inspired to create it in order to offer the centuries-old calabacitas, the Southwest's classic corn and squash sauté. The white cheese salsa is essentially the chile con queso of Old Mexico, but made with ingredients available north of the border. These corn cakes may be served as an appetizer or as a lunch or brunch main course.

QUESO BLANCO SALSA:

¼ cup unsalted butter
1 white onion, chopped
5 Italian plum tomatoes, peeled and chopped
4 fresh mild green chiles such as New Mexico or Anaheim, roasted, seeded, peeled, and chopped
1 red bell pepper, seeded, deveined, and diced

1 yellow bell pepper, seeded, deveined, and diced
¼ teaspoon salt
¼ teaspoon freshly ground black pepper
½ cup half-and-half
½ pound cream cheese, cut into small pieces
½ teaspoon cayenne pepper

Melt the butter in a large sauté pan over medium heat. When the butter sizzles, add the onion and sauté until translucent, about 7 minutes. Add the tomatoes, chiles, red and yellow bell peppers, salt, and black pepper. Cook for 10 minutes, stirring frequently.

Reduce the heat and add the half-and-half, stirring well. When heated through, add the cream cheese. Cook, stirring frequently, until the cheese melts and the mixture is thick, about 12 minutes. Stir in the cayenne pepper and remove from the heat. Let cool, cover, and refrigerate until 30 minutes before serving. (You may prepare the salsa up to 3 days in advance.) Just before serving, reheat the salsa by placing it in the top pan of a double boiler over gently simmering water; stir frequently to prevent scorching. Adjust to taste with cayenne pepper.

(continued)

(continued)

CORN CAKES:

⅓ cup finely diced red bell pepper

1 cup fresh or thawed, frozen corn kernels

3 eggs

¾ cup milk

½ cup all-purpose flour

⅓ cup stone-ground yellow cornmeal

2 tablespoons unsalted butter, melted and cooled

1 teaspoon salt

2 dashes of Tabasco sauce

½-1 teaspoon cayenne pepper

¼ cup finely minced scallions, including the green tops

¼ cup stemmed fresh cilantro (coriander) leaves, chopped

3 tablespoons freshly grated Parmesan cheese

Melted butter for cooking

Combine the bell pepper, corn, eggs, milk, flour, cornmeal, butter, and salt in a blender or in a food processor fitted with the metal blade. Process for about 30 seconds. Transfer the mixture to a large bowl, and stir in the Tabasco sauce, cayenne pepper, scallions, cilantro, and Parmesan cheese. Cover and let stand for 30 minutes at room temperature.

Preheat oven to 250°. Warm a 7-inch nonstick sauté pan over medium heat until hot. Brush the pan with melted butter. When the butter sizzles, ladle 3 or 4 tablespoons of batter into the center of the pan, then tilt and swirl the pan to spread the batter thinly over the pan's surface. Cook until lightly browned on the bottom, about 2 minutes. Flip the cake and cook until the second side browns slightly, another minute. Slide the cake out onto a plate and cover with waxed paper. Make 6 cakes in all in this manner, brushing the pan with butter as needed. As the cakes are cooked, stack them, slipping a sheet of waxed paper between them to prevent sticking, and place in the oven to keep warm until serving. They may be cooked up to one hour ahead of serving.

(continued)

(continued)

CALABACITAS:

2 tablespoons butter, melted

2 cups fresh or thawed, frozen corn kernels

1 cup finely diced red bell pepper

1 cup finely diced zucchini

2 fresh poblano chiles, stemmed, seeded, and finely chopped

Fresh cilantro (coriander) sprigs for garnish

Warm a 7-inch nonstick sauté pan over medium heat until hot. Brush the pan with the melted butter. When it sizzles, add all the remaining ingredients. Cook, shaking the pan to rearrange the ingredients frequently, until the vegetables are just heated through and slightly softened, 3-4 minutes.

To assemble, place the corn cakes on individual plates and divide the calabacitas evenly among them, spooning it on one-half of each corn cake. Fold the other half over to form a half-moon. Ladle the warm salsa over all. Garnish with cilantro sprigs. Serves 6.

Note: Canned green chiles may be used in place of the fresh; be sure to rinse them with water before adding to the salsa.

Cafe Pasqual's Cookbook

Calabacitas

The Spanish settlers of Chimayó, following the example of the Pueblos, grew a good deal of squash, one of the few vegetables that flourished in the area. During the harvest season they feasted on this mélange of zucchini and yellow crookneck squash mixed with green chile and corn, drying the remainder of the summer squash crop for use during the winter months.

4 tablespoons oil, preferably corn or canola

4-6 medium zucchini, or a mix of zucchini and other summer squash, to yield approximately 5 cups when sliced into bite-size chunks

1 medium white onion, chopped

2 cups corn, fresh or frozen

½ cup chopped, roasted green chile, preferably New Mexico green or Anaheim, fresh or frozen

3 tablespoons water, or more as needed

½ teaspoon salt

Grated mild Cheddar cheese (optional) for garnish

In a large skillet, heat the oil, and add the squash and the onion. Sauté the vegetables over medium heat until they begin to wilt. Add the corn, green chile, water, and salt. Cook, covered, over low heat until tender, about 15-20 minutes. Another tablespoon or two of water can be added if the vegetables become dry. Remove from the heat and mix in the cheese, if desired. Serve immediately. Makes 6-8 side-dish or 4 main-dish servings.

The Rancho de Chimayó Cookbook

In 1950 Hot Springs, New Mexico took the challenge by television host, Ralph Edwards, to rename their town Truth or Consequences after his show. However, you can still get hot mineral baths there.

Torta de Calabacitas

5 tablespoons butter, divided
1 large onion, chopped
2 teaspoons ground cumin
3 large zucchini, trimmed and
　shredded
3 garlic cloves, minced

Salt to taste
3 tablespoons minced, seeded
　jalapeño
3 (11-inch) flour tortillas
4 cups shredded Monterey Jack
　cheese

Melt 3 tablespoons butter in a heavy skillet over medium heat; add onion and cumin, and sauté until tender, about 9 minutes. Add zucchini and garlic to onion mixture; sauté until mixture is dry and zucchini is tender, about 14 minutes. Season mixture with salt, and add jalapeño; cook 2 minutes. Transfer mixture to a bowl to cool.

　　Place one tortilla on an oiled, flat plate; sprinkle one-fourth of cheese over tortilla. Spread half of zucchini mixture over cheese; sprinkle one-fourth of cheese over top. Top cheese with second tortilla, and repeat layers, ending with third tortilla. Press stack firmly to compact. Heat one tablespoon butter in a heavy 12-inch skillet over medium heat; slide torta into skillet. Cover and cook until bottom is golden brown, about 4 minutes. Using spatula, slide torta onto plate. Add remaining one table-spoon butter to skillet. Invert torta into skillet, and cook until bottom is golden brown, about 4 minutes. Transfer to a serving platter. Let stand 5 minutes, and cut into wedges. Makes 6 servings.

Savoring the Southwest Again

Zucchini Casserole

½ stick butter
3-4 cups diced zucchini
Garlic, salt, pepper, to taste
1 can Cheddar cheese soup
2 cups canned green beans,
  drained

1-1½ cups tomato sauce
¼ cup Parmesan cheese
Cheese slices

Melt butter in pan; soften zucchini. Add spices, soup, beans, tomato sauce. Sprinkle with Parmesan cheese and cook until zucchini is done. Garnish with several slices of cheese and heat until cheese melts.

Rehoboth Christian School Cookbook

Zucchini Casserole for the Diabetic

1 large zucchini
½ onion
2 small pink unpeeled potatoes
4 ounces fresh mushrooms
1 (16-ounce) can Italian
  tomatoes

1 stalk celery
1 teaspoon basil leaves
1 teaspoon olive oil
1 tablespoon vegetable broth
  seasoning

Cut zucchini into ½-inch slices. Dice onion and potatoes, slice mushrooms, chop celery, dice tomatoes, and crush basil leaves. Combine the fresh vegetables in a covered casserole. Add the oil and broth seasoning. Cover the casserole and cook in the oven at 350° for one hour. Serves 4.

What's Cookin' at Casa

El Camino Real de Tierra Adentro, the Royal Road, is the trail where brave travelers had to cross the fast moving currents of the Rio Grande in a time before bridges. In the 1500s it was a trail of discovering America's Southwest. It wanders North from Mexico's historic Chihuahua City to the oldest capital city in the United States, Santa Fe.

Zucchini Boats

3 plump zucchini
1 clove garlic
½ cup onion, chopped
6 tablespoons butter, divided
2 tomatoes, chopped
1 (4-ounce) can green chilies,
   chopped

¾ cup bread crumbs
¼ cup Parmesan cheese
Salt and pepper to taste
1 tablespoon parsley

Wash zucchini and cut in half lengthwise. Scoop out shells and reserve pulp. Sauté garlic and onion in 3 tablespoons butter until onion is transparent. Remove garlic clove. Add zucchini pulp, tomatoes, and chilies to sautéed onions and mix well. Fill shells with mixture. Melt remaining butter and mix with bread crumbs, cheese, salt, pepper, and parsley. Heap each zucchini boat with bread crumb mixture. Cover and bake in buttered baking dish at 350° for 30 minutes.

Fiesta Mexicana

Holiday Squash

1 butternut squash
   (approximately 2½ to 3
   pounds)
¼ cup butter or margarine
1 cup raisins

2 apples, finely chopped
¼ cup brown sugar
½ teaspoon grated nutmeg
½ teaspoon salt
½ cup Piñon nuts

Cut squash in half. Scoop out seeds and add a small amount of water. Wrap with plastic wrap and cook in microwave until soft enough to scoop the squash out of the shell. Mash and mix the squash with the other ingredients. Spread out evenly in a lightly greased Pyrex square baking dish. Bake in a 325° oven for about 20 minutes. Serves 4-6.

Christmas in New Mexico Cook Book

Eggplant Mexicano

5 slices bacon, chopped
1 onion, chopped
2 fresh tomatoes, chopped
2 jalapeños, seeded and
  chopped
½ cup chicken broth
½ cup dry white wine

1 teaspoon salt
½ teaspoon freshly ground
  black pepper
2 medium eggplants, peeled and
  cut into cubes
1 cup colby cheese, shredded

Preheat oven to 325°. Fry the bacon, remove from pan and reserve. Sauté onion in the bacon drippings. Add the tomatoes, jalapeños, chicken broth, wine, salt and pepper. Line the bottom of a glass casserole dish with half of the eggplant, spoon half of the tomato mixture over eggplant, then sprinkle with half of the cheese and bacon. Repeat process ending with the cheese. Bake for 45 minutes, or until the eggplant is done and the cheese is melted and lightly browned. Serves 4-6.

Billy the Kid Cook Book

Grilled Polenta with Red Chile Sauce and Black Beans

Polenta is warming and satisfying. To get the maximum flavor, toast the cornmeal first and then cook it thoroughly. This brings out the sweetness and makes it easy to digest. The polenta needs to cool completely before it is sliced, so plan to make it in the morning to serve it at night, or cook it the day before serving.

1 teaspoon extra virgin olive oil
2½ cups stone-ground yellow
   cornmeal
5¾ cups cold water, divided
¾ teaspoon salt
¼ cup grated Parmesan cheese

2 tablespoons unsalted butter,
   melted
½ teaspoon extra virgin olive oil
2-4 tablespoons extra virgin
   olive oil, or unsalted butter,
   for grilling

Oil a 5x8-inch loaf pan with the one teaspoon olive oil. Set aside. Toast the cornmeal over medium heat in a heavy skillet until it is fragrant but not browned. Immediately pour the corn-meal into a bowl and let cool.

In a medium heavy-bottomed saucepan, bring 3 cups water and the salt to a boil. Whisk together the cooled cornmeal and the remaining 2¾ cups water. Pour this mixture into the boiling water, stirring constantly. When the polenta begins to boil, cover the pot and reduce the heat to low. Cook the polenta until it is very thick and soft, 45-55 minutes.

Stir in Parmesan cheese and melted butter, then spoon the polenta into the oiled pan, pressing the polenta firmly into the pan using either your hand or a spoon that has been dipped in cold water. Sprinkle on the ½ teaspoon olive oil and rub it over the surface of the polenta. Let the polenta cool, then cover it with waxed paper or plastic wrap and store in the refrigerator until you are ready to grill it. It will keep this way for 2 days.

To grill the polenta, invert the pan onto a cutting board and tap firmly. The polenta may come out the first time, but if not, simply run a knife around the edge of the pan and try again. Slice the polenta into twelve ½-inch pieces. Rinse or wipe the knife with cold water between each cut. In a heavy skillet over medium-high heat, grill the polenta slices in the 2-4 table-spoons olive oil until they are golden and crisp on both sides.

(continued)

(continued)

Serve immediately with Red Chile Sauce. Serves 6.

RED CHILE SAUCE:

5 cloves garlic, pressed
2 tablespoons extra virgin
 olive oil
2 tablespoons yellow cornmeal
½ cup ground New Mexico
 red chile

2½ cups vegetable stock or
 water
¼ teaspoon black pepper
⅛ teaspoon dried oregano
2 tablespoons unsalted butter
¾ teaspoon salt

In a medium saucepan over medium heat, sauté the garlic in the olive oil until golden. Add the cornmeal and cook one minute, stirring constantly. Add the red chile and continue cooking only until fragrant. Do not let the chile brown or the sauce will taste bitter.

Remove the pan from the heat and slowly whisk in the stock, then bring the sauce to a boil over medium heat. Reduce the heat and simmer 10-15 minutes. Add the black pepper, oregano, butter, and salt and simmer until the flavors mingle, 5-10 minutes more. This sauce will keep, covered, in the refrigerator, for up to 4 days. Makes 3 cups.

BLACK BEANS:

2 cups black turtle or black
 mitla beans, sorted and
 washed
5-7 cups water
1 clove garlic, pressed
⅛ teaspoon peeled and grated
 fresh ginger

⅛ teaspoon ground New
 Mexico red chile
1 teaspoon ground cumin
Pinch nutmeg
1 teaspoon salt

Soak the beans in the water overnight before cooking, or bring the beans and water to a boil, cook for 5 minutes, then let stand for one hour before proceeding. Cook the beans in a large saucepan until they are quite tender but still whole, 1-2 hours. Or you may cook the beans with 5 cups water in a pressure cooker until done, approximately 45 minutes. Make sure that the beans are done before seasoning them, because the salt will inhibit further softening.

Add the remaining ingredients to the cooked beans and stir well. Serve hot. Serves 6.

Cooking at the Natural Cafe in Santa Fe

Black Beans with Garlic and Chipotle Chiles

These beans make a great side dish, or they can be used as a filling for burritos.

1 pound black turtle beans (2 cups), picked over for stones
2 tablespoons vegetable oil or olive oil
1 cup chopped onion
2 teaspoons minced garlic
4 bay leaves
2 teaspoons Mexican oregano
2 teaspoons dried epazote*
3 dried chipotle chiles
4-5 quarts water
4 tablespoons vinegar, to taste
1-2 teaspoons salt, to taste
2 tablespoons Amontillado sherry

Soak the beans in water to cover overnight. Heat the oil in a 4-quart pot and sauté the onion for 3 minutes. Add the garlic and continue cooking for 2 minutes. Add the bay leaves, oregano, epazote, and chiles and sauté for one minute. Add 3 quarts of the water and bring to a boil. Reduce the heat and simmer, uncovered, for 2-3 hours, or until the beans are soft. Add the remaining water as needed during cooking. Add the vinegar and salt and continue to cook slowly for 30 minutes more. Taste and adjust seasonings. Stir in the sherry before serving. Serve or reserve for later use.

*Epazote is a pungent herb native to Mexico and commonly used in long-simmered dishes, such as black beans.

The Santa Fe School of Cooking Cookbook

Petroglyphs—Prehistoric Indian paintings of animals, warriors, and abstract images on granite boulders in Southwest Albuquerque.

Indian-Style Pinto Beans

Ah, beans! A New Mexican loves pinto beans! He may eat the kidney, navy and stringed varieties, but when it comes to a showdown in the kitchen, the pinto bean will always win. Slow-simmering with just the right spices, a little bacon fat, and stirred lovingly by "Mamacita," the pinto bean has long been the foundation upon which many a New Mexican meal is built.

1 pound dried pinto beans	1 teaspoon garlic salt
3 quarts water	1 teaspoon salt
½ pound bacon, cut into pieces	1 teaspoon ground black pepper
1 medium-size yellow onion, finely chopped	2 teaspoons dried red chile powder

Wash the beans thoroughly, removing any stones or bad beans. Soak overnight in cold water, changing the water at least once. Cook the bacon for a few minutes; add onion and cook until transparent. Put the beans into a large pot with the bacon and onion; cover with water and simmer, covered, for four hours or until beans start to soften. Add garlic salt, salt, pepper, and chile powder, and cook for 30 minutes. Serve hot. Serves 6-8.

New Mexico Cook Book

Bart's Barbecue Green Beans

A real crowd pleaser.

6 slices bacon, diced
1 onion, chopped
4 (1-pound) cans cut green
  beans, drained

1 cup firmly packed brown
  sugar
1 cup catsup

Cook bacon and onion together in medium-sized skillet over medium heat until bacon is crisp. Remove with slotted spoon and place in ungreased 2-quart baking dish. Add green beans. Mix brown sugar and catsup in medium-sized bowl. Fold into green beans. Bake covered at 250° for 3 hours. Serves 6-8.

Recipes from the Cotton Patch

Southwestern Spinach

2 (10-ounce) packages frozen, chopped spinach
2 tablespoons chopped onion
4 tablespoons butter or margarine
2 tablespoons flour
½ cup evaporated milk
½ cup spinach cooking water
½ teaspoon black pepper
¾ teaspoon celery salt
¾ teaspoon garlic salt
1 cup sharp cheese, grated
1 teaspoon Worcestershire sauce
1 (4-ounce) can chopped green chiles
Buttered bread crumbs

Preheat oven to 350°. Cook the spinach according to the package directions. Drain, reserving ½ cup liquid. Sauté the onion in butter until soft. Blend in the flour. Add the milk and spinach water slowly, stirring constantly to avoid lumps. Cook until smooth and thickened. Add the remaining ingredients except the bread crumbs. Pour into a 9-inch square baking dish and top with the bread crumbs. Bake 25 minutes. Serves 6-8.

Green Chile Bible

Spinach Bake

5 large eggs
1½ cups ricotta cheese
1 tablespoon minced onion
2 teaspoons flour
½ teaspoon dry mustard
1 (10-ounce) package frozen chopped spinach, cooked and well drained
Parsley (optional)

Mix all ingredients except spinach and parsley. Stir in spinach. Pour into 1½-quart casserole. Sprinkle parsley, if desired. Bake at 350° for approximately 35 minutes, until knife inserted near the center comes out clean.

Good Sam Celebrates 15 Years of Love

Sautéed Kale with Garlic and Vinegar

This is a basic method for cooking greens that works equally well with nearly all the leafy greens. It also makes a simple pasta dish; put on some pasta to cook while you sauté, and when the noodles are done, toss them together with the greens, moistened with a little more olive oil and a ladle of the pasta cooking water.

2 bunches kale (about 2 pounds)
3 tablespoons olive oil
Salt

2 cloves garlic
1-2 tablespoons red wine vinegar

Strip the kale leaves off their stems and cut away the tough mid-ribs of any large leaves. Chop coarsely and wash in plenty of water. Drain well, but do not spin dry. Heat a large sauté pan and add the olive oil and enough kale to cover the bottom of the pan. Allow these greens to wilt down before adding more. When all the kale has been added, season with salt; stir in the garlic and cover the pan. The greens will take anywhere from just a few minutes to 15 minutes to cook, depending on their maturity. When they are tender, remove the lid and allow any excess water to cook away. Turn off the heat and stir in the vinegar.

Note: Kale can be served with roast chicken or other meats, or as part of an antipasto platter, in which case, allow the kale to cool, squeeze it dry with your hands, arrange on the platter, and drizzle with very good olive oil.

A Fork in the Road

Roswell is the site of the International UFO Museum and Research Center. The 1947 Roswell Incident (alleged flying saucer crash) is chronicled in 11,000 square feet of exhibits devoted to the alien enigma.

Stuffed Sweet Peppers

4 large sweet red peppers
1 pound ground lamb
1 tablespoon butter or lard
1 small onion, chopped
1 cup raw mushrooms, coarsely
 chopped
½ teaspoon salt

½ teaspoon coriander
½ teaspoon cumin
¼ teaspoon freshly ground
 pepper
3 large tomatoes, peeled, and
 coarsely chopped
1 cup soft bread crumbs

Remove tops and seeds from peppers and rinse peppers. Sauté lamb in butter in a large heavy skillet. Add onion and mushrooms and cook until slightly wilted. Add remaining ingredients and simmer, stirring occasionally, for 25 minutes. Remove from heat and allow to cool. Fill peppers with meat mixture. Place peppers in a baking pan and bake in a preheated 350° oven for one hour or until the peppers are tender. Yields 4 servings.

Southwest Indian Cookbook

Hungarian Stuffed Bell Peppers

6 medium bell peppers
2 tablespoons oil or shortening
3 cloves garlic
1 medium onion, finely chopped
½ cup fresh parsley, chopped
½ cup long-grain rice, uncooked

1½ cups chicken stock or broth
1 pound ground pork or chicken
1½ teaspoons paprika
1 egg
Salt and pepper, to taste

Core peppers and use tops for filling; set aside. Heat large covered frying pan and add oil. Sauté garlic, onion, and chopped pepper tops until tender. Add parsley and rice and sauté a few minutes. Add ½ cup chicken stock and cover. Simmer for 10 minutes; allow to cool.

In a large bowl, combine the ground meat, paprika, egg, salt and pepper with rice mixture. Mix well. Fill peppers just to top; do not pack firmly, as rice will expand during cooking. Place filled peppers in a Dutch oven and add remaining cup chicken stock to bottom of pot. Cover and simmer very gently for 45 minutes, keeping temperature very low or peppers will break. Move the peppers around in the pot to prevent sticking. After 45 minutes, pour the Paprika Gravy over the peppers, cover and simmer for 20 minutes more.

PAPRIKA GRAVY:
4 ounces butter
4 ounces flour
2 quarts water
4 chicken bouillon cubes

2-3 tablespoons paprika
1½ teaspoons thyme
1 bay leaf
1 teaspoon white pepper

Make a roux with the flour and butter and brown. Add water and bouillon cubes or use quarts chicken stock. Add spices which can be adjusted to taste. Simmer all ingredients for 30-45 minutes over low heat for flavor to develop.

Beyond Loaves and Fishes

Roasted Scarlet Potatoes

1½ pounds (2 large) baking
  potatoes, scrubbed
2 tablespoons canola oil
½ teaspoon sweet paprika
1 teaspoon Chimayó chile
  powder

⅛ teaspoon ground cumin
¼ teaspoon dried Mexican
  oregano
Salt and freshly ground pepper,
  to taste

Preheat the oven to 375°. Cut the potatoes in half crosswise, then cut each half into 4 wedges. In a heavy, cast-iron skillet, heat the oil to moderately hot and stir in the ground spices. After 30 seconds, add the potato wedges, sprinkle with oregano and salt and pepper to taste, and toss the potatoes in the oil and spices to coat. Transfer the skillet to the hot oven and roast the potatoes about 40 minutes, turning occasionally, until tender and browned. Serves 4.

Red Chile Bible

Cattle King Potatoes

3 pounds potatoes
1 clove garlic
Salt
½ pound mushrooms
⅓ cup butter, divided

2 egg yolks
½ cup cream
¼ cup minced parsley
Pepper

Peel potatoes, cut in uniform size, boil with garlic and salt until tender. Meanwhile, slice and sauté the mushrooms in one tablespoon of the butter. Mash potatoes with remaining butter. Beat egg yolks with cream and mix into the potatoes along with the mushrooms and parsley. Add more salt if necessary and pepper to taste. Pile in a buttered baking dish and bake at 375° until brown. Serves 8-10.

The Best from New Mexico Kitchens

Garlic Potatoes

8-10 medium-sized potatoes
1 stick oleo
½ cup sour cream
1 (8-ounce) package cream
   cheese

½ teaspoon garlic salt
Salt and pepper to taste

Boil potatoes, drain and mash. Add oleo, sour cream, cream cheese, and seasonings. Whip with electric mixer. Bake in buttered casserole at 350° for ½ hour. May be made the day before and refrigerated.

Recipes for Rain or Shine

Twice Baked Chile Potatoes

3 large white baking potatoes
1 tablespoon olive oil
6 tablespoons butter, divided
¼ cup yellow onion, minced
2 cloves garlic, minced
3 green chiles, roasted, peeled,
   seeded and chopped

Salt to taste
1 teaspoon freshly ground black
   pepper
¼ cup milk
Parmesan cheese
Paprika

Preheat oven to 400°. Wash, scrub and dry the potatoes; coat lightly with oil. Bake for one hour or until the potatoes are done. Heat 2 tablespoons of the butter in a frying pan; sauté onions and garlic until onions are soft. Add green chiles, salt and pepper to the pan and cook over low heat, until the chiles are warmed through.

Cut potatoes in half lengthwise and scoop out the pulp, being careful not to cut through the skin of the potato. Mix potato pulp with the chile and onion mixture. Stir in the 4 remaining tablespoons of butter and the milk, and spoon the pulp back into the potato shells. Sprinkle with Parmesan cheese and paprika, return to the oven, and heat at 300° for 15-20 minutes or until the potatoes are warmed through. Serves 6.

Billy the Kid Cook Book

Sweet Potato and Apple Casserole

3 medium sweet potatoes,
  sliced
2 large apples, sliced
2 cups small (miniature)
  marshmallows
¾ cup sugar

1 teaspoon salt
1 teaspoon cinnamon
2 tablespoons cornstarch
½ cup water
4 tablespoons butter

Spread half of the potatoes in a 3-quart casserole. Add apples and marshmallows; repeat layers. Mix sugar, salt and cinnamon. Sprinkle over mixture. Dissolve cornstarch in water. Pour over mixture. Dot with butter. Cover and bake at 350° for one hour.

Our Best Home Cooking

Ginger Yams

1 (29-ounce) can yams
  (reserve liquid)
12 ginger snaps, crushed
½ cup orange juice
2 tablespoons honey
2 tablespoons brown sugar
¼ teaspoon cinnamon

⅛ teaspoon nutmeg
2 tablespoons margarine or
  butter
½ cup chopped nuts
1 orange, washed well
Marshmallows

Mash the yams with liquid. Add ginger snaps, orange juice, honey, brown sugar, spices, margarine, and nuts. Mix with each addition. Slice the orange as thin as possible and place over the yams. Bake at 350° for 30 minutes. Put marshmallows loosely on top and return to oven until marshmallows are melted and browned. Serves 4-6.

Good Sam Celebrates 15 Years of Love

Zucchini Relish

12 cups coarsely shredded
   zucchini
4 onions, chopped
4 bell peppers, chopped
2 large jars pimientos
2 jalapeño peppers, chopped
½ cup pickling salt

6 cups sugar
2 tablespoons mustard seed
1 tablespoon celery seed
1½ teaspoons turmeric
4 cups cider vinegar
2 cups water

Combine all the vegetables. Sprinkle with pickling salt and let set overnight. Rinse and drain. Combine the sugar, mustard seed, celery seed, turmeric, vinegar, and water. Pour over the vegetables. Bring to boil; boil gently 5 minutes.

Fill hot jars to within ½ inch of the tops; adjust lids. Process in boiling water bath for 5 minutes. (Start timing when water returns to boil.) Makes 9 pints.

Beyond Loaves and Fishes

The legend of the Loretto Chapel is a favorite. A mysterious carpenter appeared in answer to the Sisters of Loretto's novena to build a much needed staircase to the choir loft. After completing this incredible feat (the staircase, built without nails, only wooden pegs, has two 360-degree turns and no visible means of support), he vanished without pay. After searching (even running an ad in the local newspaper) and finding no trace of the man, some concluded that he was St. Joseph himself.

Loretto Chapel, Santa Fe, is known for its miraculous circular staircase that makes two 360-degree turns and stands without any visible means of support. The stairway's mysterious carpenter remains unknown.

Fettucine with Zucchini-Basil Sauce

1 zucchini, cut into ¼-inch slices
2 tablespoons olive oil
1 small onion, peeled and finely diced
2 medium cloves garlic, peeled and minced
¾ cup whipping cream
¾ cup slivered fresh basil (or ½ cup pesto)
2 tablespoons minced parsley
½ teaspoon salt
¼ teaspoon freshly ground pepper
8 ounces fettucine noodles, cooked according to package directions
½ cup freshly grated Parmesan cheese

Stack the zucchini slices, a few at a time, and cut into ¼-inch sticks. Set aside. Heat the olive oil in a heavy frying pan over medium-low heat; add the onion and garlic and sauté slowly for 5 minutes. Add the zucchini sticks; turn the heat up to medium and continue to sauté for 5 minutes. Add the whipping cream, basil, parsley, salt, and pepper; turn the heat up to medium-high and slowly boil for 1-2 minutes. The sauce will have thickened at this point. Remove from the heat. Drain the fettucine through a colander and put back into the hot pan. Pour the sauce over the fettucine; add the Parmesan cheese and stir to coat the noodles. Serve the fettucine immediately on warm plates. Serves 4.

A Fork in the Road

Dutch Lasagna

LAYER 1:

1½ pounds ground beef
1 teaspoon garlic powder
2 tablespoons chopped parsley
1 tablespoon basil
1½ teaspoons salt
1 (28-ounce) can tomatoes
2 (6-ounce) cans tomato paste

Brown ground beef; drain off excess fat. Add garlic, parsley, basil, salt, tomatoes, and tomato paste; simmer for ½ hour, stirring occasionally.

LAYER 2:

6-7 slices lasagna noodles, cooked,
    drained and rinsed in cold water

LAYER 3:

1 (16-ounce) creamed cottage
    cheese
⅓ cup Parmesan cheese
2 eggs, beaten
1 teaspoon salt
½ teaspoon pepper

LAYER 4:

1 pound Mozzarella cheese, sliced

Combine cottage cheese and Parmesan cheese; add eggs, salt and pepper. To assemble: Pour a thin layer of No. 1 in bottom of greased 9x13x2-inch baking dish. Cover with ½ layer of No. 2. Spread on ½ of layer No. 3. Cover with ½ of layer No. 4. Cover with ½ of remaining layer No. 1. Repeat all layers ending with No. 1. Cover with foil and bake at 350° for 20 minutes. Uncover and bake 20 minutes longer. Let set 15 minutes before serving.

Rehoboth Christian School Cookbook

Rockhound State Park, near Deming, New Mexico, offers would-be prospectors a chance to discover their own rocks and gems.

Chile Pie

Not really a "pie," this is more like a quiche without a crust. Delectable as a main dish for lunch, it could also make a light supper. And how about doubling the recipe, making it in a rectangular baking dish, and cutting in small squares to serve at a party?

4-6 whole green chiles
1 cup grated Jack or longhorn
   cheese
4 eggs

1 cup scalded half-and-half or
1 cup evaporated milk
1/2 teaspoon garlic salt

Line a buttered 8 or 9-inch pie pan with chiles (fresh, canned or frozen). Sprinkle with the cheese. Beat eggs and combine with half-and-half and garlic salt. Pour over cheese. Bake at 325° for about 40 minutes or until the custard has set. Cut in wedges and serve. Serves 4.

The Best from New Mexico Kitchens

Southwestern Quiche

1 unbaked (9-inch) pie shell
4 eggs
1 teaspoon salt
1 teaspoon onion salt or
   1/2 cup minced onion
1 teaspoon red chile powder

1 teaspoon black pepper
1 cup chopped mushrooms
1 cup chopped green chiles
2 cups heavy cream or 1 cup
   evaporated milk
1 cup grated Swiss cheese

Prepare pie crust and set aside. Separate eggs; beat egg yolks; then whip egg whites until foamy. Fold egg whites into yolks along with salt, onion, red chile powder, black pepper, chopped mushrooms, and green chiles. Add cream or evaporated milk to mixture and blend well. Layer cheese over bottom of pie crust; pour egg mixture into pie crust. Bake at 425° for 25-30 minutes or until quiche is browned and solid. Serve hot. Makes 6-8 wedges.

Variation: Crumble 1/2 pound cooked pork sausage or 1 cup crumbled bacon (cooked) over top of egg mixture before baking.

Comida Sabrosa

Anne's Quiche

Ann Davenport's quiches have become legendary in the Santa Fe area and have been widely copied. Little wonder! Anne takes a basic quiche recipe made with cream—like the one below—and orchestrates her own delectable variations.

1 (9 to 10-inch) deep pastry shell
1 egg white
1 cup finely minced ham
1½ cups grated Swiss cheese
2 eggs
2 egg yolks
1½ cups scalded cream
½ teaspoon salt
Pepper to taste
1 cup fresh sweet corn kernels, about 3 ears (optional)
1 (4-ounce) can chopped green chile or ½ cup chopped fresh green chile
½ cup minced green onions

Brush the pastry shell with beaten egg white. Bake at 425° until the crust is set, but not brown. Spread the minced cooked ham over the bottom. Sprinkle with the cheese. Beat the eggs and egg yolks with the scalded cream. Add salt and pepper to taste. Slice the corn kernels from the cob with a sharp knife and remove any bits of corn silk. Add with the chopped green chile and minced green onions. Pour this mixture over the cheese and bake at 350° until the custard has set. This could also be baked in 2 (7-or 8-inch) crusts. Or it could be baked in a 9-inch square baking dish and cut in squares to serve at a cocktail party.

The Best from New Mexico Kitchens

Chicken and Sausage Jambalaya

2 tablespoons vegetable oil
1 cup smoked ham, diced
½ cup sausage, diced
2 cups uncooked chicken, diced
1 onion, chopped
4 celery ribs, chopped
1 green pepper, chopped
4 cloves garlic, minced
1 teaspoon oregano
1 teaspoon salt
1 teaspoon pepper
1 teaspoon cayenne
½ teaspoon thyme
2 cups long grain converted rice
1 cup tomatoes, chopped
3 cups chicken stock
3 cups shrimp, peeled and deveined

Heat oil in a large, heavy pot. Add ham and sausage; brown lightly. Remove from pan and set aside. Add chicken and brown. Remove from pan and set aside. Add half of onion, celery, and pepper to the pot, cooking until soft and well browned. Toss in remaining vegetables and garlic. Cook over moderate heat until softened. Return meats to pot with all the seasonings. Cook for 5 minutes. Add rice and stir for a few minutes before adding tomatoes and stock. Bring mixture to a boil, lower heat, cover pot and simmer over low heat for 20-25 minutes until liquid is absorbed and rice is tender. Add shrimp during the last 5 minutes. When rice is done, toss mixture, cover and let rest for 5 minutes. Serve hot.

Families Cooking Together

The Palace of the Governors, built by the Spanish in 1610 in Santa Fe, is the oldest public building in the U.S., and the Mission of San Miguel of Santa Fe is one of the oldest churches in the country.

Chile Rice Navidad

½ cup chopped onions
½ stick butter
1½ cups uncooked, washed
   white rice

3-4 cups hot chicken stock or
   broth
Pinch of saffron

Sauté the onions in the butter. Add the rice and stir well. Pour in the hot chicken stock and saffron and bring the mixture to a boil. Cover and simmer for 15 minutes. While the rice is cooking, assemble the follow ingredients:

1 pint sour cream
1 roasted red bell pepper,
   chopped
1 (6-ounce) can chopped
   green chiles

3-4 drops Tabasco sauce
1 cup Monterey Jack or sharp
   Cheddar cheese, diced
¼ cup fresh green onions,
   chopped

Mix the sour cream with the chopped bell pepper, green chiles, Tabasco sauce, and diced cheese. Remove the rice from the stove and pour in ½ the sour cream mixture. Pour into a buttered 8x10-inch baking dish. Top with the remaining sour cream mixture. Bake in a 350° oven for about 15 minutes, until golden brown. Sprinkle with chopped green onions. Serves 6-8.

Christmas Celebration: Santa Fe Traditions

Sherried Orange Rice

Better than potatoes any day.

1 cup raw rice
1 teaspoon salt
½ teaspoon thyme
½ cup minced onion
½ cup seedless raisins
1 medium unpeeled orange,
   sliced and quartered

1 (10½-ounce) can chicken
   broth
6 tablespoons orange juice
⅓ cup dry sherry

In a greased 2-quart casserole, combine rice, seasonings, onion, raisins, and orange slices. Bring chicken broth, orange juice, and sherry to a boil. Pour over rice mixture; stir once. Cover and bake in a preheated 350° oven about 45 minutes. Serve with pork or chicken. Serves 6.

A Fork in the Road

Rice and Chile Bake

1 cup rice
2 cups sour cream
1 cup green chile, chopped

1 cup Monterey Jack cheese,
   cubed
1 teaspoon salt

Cook rice according to package directions, undercooking slightly. Combine all ingredients and place in a greased casserole. Bake at 350° for 15 minutes or until cheese melts and mixture is thoroughly heated. Serves 6-8.

Fiesta Mexicana

Santa Fe is the capital of New Mexico. Having been established in the early 1600s while it was still under Spanish rule, Santa Fe holds the distinction of being the seat of government longer than any other capital in the U.S. Santa Fe is the oldest and highest-elevation capital in the United States.

Tacos, Shed Style

To many a visitor to New Mexico, The Shed in Santa Fe epitomizes all the mouth-watering attributes of New Mexico cooking at its finest. And there are those who say if you haven't had lunch at The Shed, you haven't been to Santa Fe.

1 pound lean ground beef
1 cup homemade chile sauce or
   canned enchilada sauce
12 blue corn tortillas
Cooking oil

1 pound longhorn cheese,
   grated
Chopped lettuce
Chopped onions
Chopped tomatoes

Brown the ground beef in a heavy skillet and drain off all grease. Mix in the chile sauce. Fry tortilla quickly in hot oil until they are limp. Drain. Allowing 2 to a plate (use oven-safe plates), place 2 tablespoons of the meat mixture on each tortilla. Add a spoonful of the cheese, lettuce, onions, and tomatoes to each. Fold tortilla over and sprinkle with more grated cheese. Place in 425° oven until the cheese melts. Serves 6.

The Best from New Mexico Kitchens

Chimichangas
(chim-ee-CHON-gahs)

1 pound ground beef
1 (10-ounce) can tomatoes
  and green chiles
1 (1¼-ounce) package taco
  seasoning mix

12 (8-inch) flour tortillas
3 cups shredded lettuce
3 cups grated Cheddar cheese
½ cup sliced green onion
1½ cups cooked red chile sauce

In a skillet, brown ground beef. Drain. Add tomatoes-and-green-chiles and seasoning. Simmer 5 minutes. Spoon 3 table-spoons of meat near one edge of a tortilla. Fold nearest edge over meat; fold both ends in like an envelope. Roll tortilla and secure with toothpicks. Fry in 1-inch hot oil until golden on each side. Drain on paper towels and keep warm. To serve, top each chimichanga with lettuce, cheese, onion, and chile sauce. Makes 12.

Variation: Chimichangas can also be made with roast pork or cooked chicken.

License to Cook New Mexico Style

Green Chile Cream Chicken Enchiladas

CREAM CHEESE FILLING:

1-2 large onions, sliced thin or chopped
2 tablespoons butter
2 cups diced cooked chicken
½ cup roasted sweet pepper or red bell pepper or pimiento
2 (3-ounce) packages cream cheese, diced
12 corn tortillas (blue preferred)

Sauté onion in large skillet in butter until limp and beginning to brown. Remove from heat and add chicken, red pepper, and cream cheese; mix well. Fry tortillas in small amount of oil in frying pan or microwave. Spoon ⅓ cup filling in center of tortilla and roll up. Place, seam-side down, in a shortening-sprayed 9x13-inch baking dish. Fill all tortillas in this way.

GREEN CHILE SAUCE:

2 cloves garlic, minced
½ cup onion, minced
¼ cup oil
1 tablespoon flour
1 cup chicken broth or water
1 cup green chilies, diced
Salt and pepper to taste
½ cup chopped tomato (optional)
2 cups Jack Cheese, shredded

Sauté garlic and onion in oil. Blend in flour and add broth and green chilies. Add chopped tomato, if desired. Bring to a boil and simmer 15-20 minutes. Pour Green Chile Sauce over filled tortillas. Sprinkle with 2 cups shredded Jack cheese. Bake covered for 10 minutes at 375°. Uncover and bake another 10 minutes.

Bon Appétit de Las Sandias

Governor King's
Chicken Enchilada Casserole

2 tablespoons onion, chopped
1 small can chopped green
   chilies
2 tablespoons butter
1 large can enchilada sauce
1 can cream of chicken soup

1 small can evaporated milk
2 cups chicken broth
1½ dozen corn tortillas
1 stewing chicken, cooked,
   boned and chopped
2 cups grated longhorn cheese

Sauté onions and chilies in butter. Combine all liquids and add to onion and chile mixture. Simmer to blend flavors. Break tortillas into pieces. Place in casserole in layers with chicken and cheese, ending with cheese. Pour sauce mixture over all. Refrigerate for several hours or overnight. Remove and bake in 350° for one hour. Makes 6-8 servings.
Contributed by governor of New Mexico, Bruce King.

The Very Special Raspberry Cookbook

Green Enchilada Casserole

1 can cream of mushroom soup
1 can cream of chicken soup
1½ cups milk
1 (8-ounce) carton sour cream
1 (4-ounce) can diced green
   chiles

Diced onions
Salt and pepper
Garlic salt
1 dozen corn tortillas
Longhorn Cheddar cheese,
   grated

Combine mushroom soup, chicken soup, milk, sour cream, chiles, onions, salt, pepper and garlic salt. Cook over medium heat until thick. Fry corn tortillas lightly in oil; drain on paper towels. Layer tortillas in casserole dish or dip tortillas in above sauce and then layer. Pour sauce over tortillas and then grated cheese over sauce. Repeat layers of sauce and cheese. Bake at 375° for approximately 20 minutes.

Note: You can add chicken or other meat as a layer also.

Recipes from the Cotton Patch

Chile Relleno Casserole

1 (7-ounce) can whole green
    chiles
2 cups grated Monterey Jack
    cheese

2 eggs
1 cup milk
Salt and pepper to taste

Carefully split chiles lengthwise and open flat. Remove seeds. Divide 1½ cups cheese among chiles. Place on center of chiles and roll them up starting at pointed end. Place seam-side down in greased 9x5x3-inch loaf pan. Beat eggs, milk, salt and pepper. Pour over chiles and sprinkle with remaining cheese. Bake at 375° for 40 minutes or until puffed and brown.

Rehoboth Christian School Cookbook

Sausage and Bean Burritos

¾ pound chorizo, casing
    removed, and crumbled
    (Mexican sausage)
1 medium-sized onion
1 cup picante sauce
1 teaspoon ground cumin
1 (16-ounce) can pinto or red
    kidney beans, rinsed and
    drained

10 flour tortillas, heated
1½ cups grated Monterey
    Jack or Cheddar cheese
Chopped tomato and avocado
Shredded lettuce
Ripe olive slices

Cook chorizo sausage with onion; drain. Stir in picante sauce and cumin; simmer 5 minutes or until most of the liquid has evaporated. Stir in beans. For each burrito, spoon generous ⅓ cup sausage mixture in the center of each tortilla. Top with 2 tablespoons cheese. Add tomato, avocado, lettuce, and olives as desired. Fold tortilla over one end of filling and roll. Serve with additional picante sauce. Makes 5 servings.

License to Cook New Mexico Style

Fiesta Casserole

1 (9¼-ounce) can tuna
1 can condensed cream of
 mushroom soup
1 soup can water or milk
1 medium onion, chopped
3 stalks celery, chopped
1 (8-ounce) can corn
1 teaspoon garlic powder
1 teaspoon salt
1 teaspoon coarsely ground
 black pepper

1 (12-ounce) package egg
 noodles
¼ pound mushrooms
1 tablespoon butter or
 margarine
8 whole green chiles, peeled
1 (8-ounce) package Cheddar
 cheese, sliced

Preheat oven to 375°. Combine the tuna, mushroom soup, water or milk, onion, celery, corn, garlic powder, salt, and pepper in a saucepan. Heat the mixture to a boil; then remove from heat. Cook the noodles according to the package directions. Sauté the mushrooms in butter until lightly browned.

In a casserole, layer the egg noodles, then tuna mixture, then green chiles, then 4 slices of cheese. Repeat. With the mushrooms, form a circle on top and place the remaining cheese in circle. Bake 30-40 minutes. Excellent cold as well as hot. Serves 6-8.

Green Chile Bible

Shiprock, located near Four Corners, USA, is a towering rock formation rising an impressive 1,700 feet from the surrounding plain. The monument figures prominently in Navajo legend.

Chiles Rellenos Dulces
(Sweet Chile Meat Balls)

1 egg
¼ cup milk
2 pounds beef or pork, boiled
   and ground
1½ cups brown sugar
1 cup chopped raisins

1½ teaspoons allspice
1 teaspoon salt
1 cup chopped green chile
1 cup flour
Shortening

Beat egg and milk in a small mixing bowl. Set aside. Combine meat, sugar, raisins, allspice, salt, and chile with 2 tablespoons of egg mixture. Form mixture into ½-inch balls. Dip balls into remaining egg mixture and roll in flour. Heat 2 inches of shortening in a heavy pan on medium-high heat. Fry sweet chile meat balls in hot shortening until golden. Drain on absorbent towels. Freezes well. Yields approximately 3-4 dozen.

Cocinas de New Mexico

Six Layer Dinner

3 peeled, sliced raw potatoes
½ cup chopped green pepper
½ cup chopped onion
¾ cup uncooked rice
3 cups sliced raw carrots

1 pound hamburger, cooked
   and crumbled
1 (8-ounce) can tomato sauce
1 (8-ounce) can water

Layer in order given in a buttered rectangular baking dish. Cover and bake 1½ hours at 350°. Serves 4-6.

Rehoboth Christian School Cookbook

The city of Ruidoso got its name from the river that flows nearby, which is "noisy" in Spanish. On Labor Day, the Ruidoso Downs hosts the quarter horse race with the world's richest purse.

Meatballs Diablo

2 tablespoons bacon drippings
   or olive oil
1 medium onion, finely
   chopped
1 pound lean ground beef
½ pound ground pork
3 eggs
2 dashes of Tabasco, or to taste

½ cup dried bread crumbs
½ teaspoon ground cumin
1 clove garlic, minced
½ teaspoon ground nutmeg
1 tablespoon chopped fresh
   parsley
Cooking oil

Heat the bacon drippings or oil in a frying pan, and cook the onion until soft. Mix together the ground beef and ground pork in a mixing bowl and stir in the onions. Lightly beat the eggs and add to the meat mixture. Stir in the Tabasco, bread crumbs, cumin, garlic, nutmeg, and parsley, and form into balls approximately the size of walnuts. Fry the meatballs in the cooking oil over medium heat until well browned and done through. Place meatballs in Red Chile Sauce and serve with rice. Yields 2 dozen meatballs.

RED CHILE SAUCE:
2 tablespoons butter
2 tablespoons all-purpose flour
1½ cups beef stock or broth
¼ cup red wine
1 clove garlic, finely minced

1 teaspoon ground New Mexico
   red chile
½ teaspoon salt
½ teaspoon freshly ground
   black pepper

Melt the butter, stir in the flour and stir constantly, letting the flour brown slightly. Slowly stir in the beef stock and wine. Stir until the sauce starts to thicken, then turn down the heat to simmer. Stir in the garlic, chile, salt and pepper. Let cook over low heat until just heated through.

Billy the Kid Cook Book

Chile Rellenos Bake

1 pound ground beef
½ cup chopped onion
½ teaspoon salt
¼ teaspoon pepper
2 (4-ounce) cans diced green chilies

6 ounces (1½ cups) Cheddar cheese, shredded
1½ cups milk
¼ cup flour
4 eggs, beaten

Brown beef and onion; drain off fat. Sprinkle meat with salt and pepper. Place half of the chilies in a 10x6x1½-inch baking dish. Sprinkle with cheese; top with meat mixture. Arrange remaining chilies over meat. Combine remaining ingredients; beat until smooth. Pour over meat and chilies mixture. Bake at 350° for 45-50 minutes or until inserted knife comes out clean. Cool 5 minutes. Serves 6.

Red River's Cookin'

Easiest-Yet Tortilla Casserole

1 can cream of chicken soup
1 soup can milk
1 small onion, finely chopped
1 small can diced green chilies

1 package corn tortillas
1 pound hamburger
2 cup grated Cheddar cheese

Combine soup, milk, onion, and chilies in pan and bring to a slow boil. Tear tortillas into small pieces and add to soup mixture. Brown hamburger and drain. Add to soup mixture. Alternate layers of soup mixture and grated cheese in casserole dish, ending with cheese. Bake at 350° for 30 minutes. Serves 5-7.

Rehoboth Christian School Cookbook

Beef Tortilla Pizza

1 pound ground beef
1 medium onion, chopped
1 teaspoon oregano
1 teaspoon ground cumin
1 teaspoon salt
4 large flour tortillas

4 teaspoons olive oil
1 medium tomato, chopped
Mexican toppings: cilantro,
   sliced olives, 1 cup Jack
   cheese, etc.

Sauté beef with chopped onion. Pour off drippings. Sprinkle with oregano, cumin, and salt. Place tortillas on two large baking sheets. Lightly brush tortillas with olive oil. Bake in preheated 400° oven for 3 minutes. Remove from oven and top tortillas with beef mixture, then divide tomato and desired Mexican toppings over beef-covered tortillas. Bake at 400° for 12-14 minutes more. (If doing all 4 tortillas at once, rearrange baking sheets halfway through baking time.)

Bon Appétit de Las Sandias

Southwestern Tamale Pie

1 pound ground beef
1 small onion, diced
1 (10¾-ounce) can cream of
   chicken soup
1 (10¾-ounce) can golden
   mushroom soup
1 cup evaporated milk

1 (4-ounce) can taco sauce
1½ cups chopped green
   chile
1 dozen corn tortillas
1½ cups grated Cheddar or
   Monterey Jack cheese

Brown meat with onion in large skillet; drain excess fat. Add soups, milk, taco sauce, and green chile. Simmer all ingredients together about 10 minutes. Cut corn tortillas into strips. (Tortillas do not need to be fried.) Layer on bottom of 2-quart casserole dish with meat mixture and cheese; continue alternating layers; top layer should end with cheese. Cover casserole and bake at 350° for one hour. Makes 5-6 servings.

Option: Use one cooked, boned, diced chicken in place of ground beef.

Comida Sabrosa

Jalapa Hamburgers

Jalapeños are named after Jalapa, the capital of Veracruz, Mexico. The jalapeños coupled with the tequila give these hamburgers a great lift.

2 pounds ground beef
1 teaspoon Worcestershire
sauce
¼ cup tortilla chips, finely
crushed

1 teaspoon Dijon mustard
1 jalapeño, chopped
½ teaspoon ground black pepper
¼ cup tequila

Mix all ingredients together and form into equal-sized patties. Grill over charcoal, fry or broil until done to taste. Serve on Mexican rolls or in pita bread. Serves 4-6.

The Tequila Cook Book

Tyrone Steak

Although the area around Silver City and Tyrone was known for its mining, ranching was also important to the region. On the ranch, steak was often just cooked in a little lard in a cast iron skillet. Here is a different, easy and very tasty way to prepare a cut of meat that might not be tender enough just grilled or broiled.

4 tablespoons all-purpose flour
2 teaspoons ground red chile, divided
1 teaspoon ground black pepper
1 boneless round steak (2 to 2½ pounds and about 1 inch thick)

3 tablespoons cooking oil
1 large onion, peeled and chopped
1 clove garlic, finely chopped
1 cup crushed tomatoes
1 tablespoon vinegar
Water to cover

Mix flour with one teaspoon of the ground chile and the black pepper. Dredge steak in the flour mixture. Heat the oil in a heavy skillet or Dutch oven (cast iron works best) and sauté the chopped onion and garlic until onions are soft. Add steak to the pan and sear on both sides. Add tomatoes, vinegar, the remaining ground chile and enough water to cover the meat. Cover the pan, reduce heat and cook over low heat for 1½ hours or until the meat is tender. Serves 4-6.

Billy the Kid Cook Book

By AD 1300 thousands of Pueblo people, descendants of the Anasazi, lived in 18 towns along the Rio Grande from Taos south to Isleta (below present-day Albuquerque). The Pueblos were advanced in domestic arts and crafts—pottery, weaving, and home decoration. Some of their adobe dwellings were five stories high. They domesticated turkeys, and in the fields near their towns, they raised corn, beans, and squash for food, and cotton for weaving into blankets. In the 15th century the serenity of their lives was shattered by the arrival of the nomadic Navajo and Apache tribes. The newcomers raided the prosperous Pueblo settlements for food, clothing, tools, and Pueblo children, whom they enslaved, initiating four centuries of warfare. (Source: Encarta)

Southwestern Stuffed Flank Steak

1 (2-pound) flank steak, well trimmed

Cut steak on 3 sides to make a pocket, and fold open to lie flat. Pound until flat and tenderized.

MARINADE:

1 cup dry red wine	1 tablespoon red chili powder
2 tablespoons olive oil	¼ cup onion, minced
2 cloves garlic, minced	½ teaspoon red pepper
1 teaspoon cumin	flakes

Combine marinade ingredients, and cover steak, then place in a glass dish or a Ziploc bag with marinade. Leave in refrigerator for a minimum of two hours.

STUFFING:

2 tablespoons olive oil	3 cloves garlic, minced
½ cup red pepper, chopped	1½ cup cornbread stuffing mix
½ cup green pepper, chopped	½ teaspoon cayenne pepper
½ onion, chopped	½ cup water

Heat oil in skillet over medium heat. Add peppers, onion, and garlic. Sauté, stirring constantly for 5 minutes, or until tender-crisp. Add stuffing mix, cayenne pepper, and water. Blend.

Remove steak from marinade and pat dry. Discard marinade. Cover steak with stuffing mixture and roll up, jelly-roll style. Secure the flap with toothpicks, skewers, or tie with kitchen twine. Bake in a preheated 400° oven for 50 minutes. Transfer to a carving board, tent with foil and let stand 10 minutes. Carve into 1 or 1½-inch slices. Serves 6.

Bon Appétit de Las Sandias

Capitan is the birthplace and burial site of the world's most well-known bear. In May of 1950, man-caused fires destroyed 17,000 acres of forest and grasslands. A fire crew rescued a badly singed bear cub clinging tenaciously to the side of a burnt pine tree. After being treated at a veterinary hospital in Santa Fe, "Smokey Bear" was kept by Game Warden Ray Bell in his home, where Smokey was said to be somewhat of a ham and a "mite domineering." Smokey was later taken to the National Zoo in Washington DC, where millions visited and marveled at his story.

Remember, "Only YOU can prevent forest fires."

Green Chile Stroganoff

1 medium onion, chopped
1 (4-ounce) can mushrooms, sliced
¼ cup butter or margarine
Garlic to taste
2 pounds lean beef, cubed and rolled in flour

2 cups water
2 beef bouillon cubes
1 (4-ounce) can green chiles, chopped
1 cup sour cream
1 (8-ounce) package noodles

Sauté the onion and mushrooms in butter with the garlic. Brown the cubed beef in this mixture. Drain off the excess fat. Add the water and bouillon cubes. Cover and simmer 2 hours. Add the green chiles and simmer 10 more minutes. Remove from the heat and stir in the sour cream. Cook the noodles according to the package directions. Serve the stroganoff over the noodles. Serves 4.

Green Chile Bible

Beef Fajitas

In the mid-1980s, as Southwestern food spread in popularity faster than a range fire, patrons besieged Rancho de Chimayó with requests for fajitas. A Texas concoction, "fajitas" literally translates from Spanish as "slashes" or "strips." Tender strips of marinated meat are wrapped in warm tortillas and topped with savory vegetables and dollops of a spicy relish. While New Mexicans distrust many Texas imports, this one has won a fair measure of acceptance.

BEEF FILLING:

4 pounds flank steak
1 cup good-quality cold-pressed olive oil
2 tablespoons ground chile pequín, chile de arbol, or cayenne
2 cloves garlic

1 tablespoon lime juice
1 teaspoon white pepper
1 teaspoon salt
Generous dash A-1 Steak Sauce
3 tablespoons clarified butter, or more as needed

Slice the steak against the grain into thin strips and place the strips in a large bowl or pan. Combine the rest of the filling ingredients, except for the butter, and pour them over the steak, tossing to coat. Marinate the beef, refrigerated, for at least 5 hours or overnight.

Pour the marinade and steak into a large skillet and cook over medium-low heat until the strips are cooked through and tender. Drain the liquid from the pan. Add the 3 tablespoons of butter, and heat quickly just until the butter coats the strips and the meat crisps slightly. Turn the meat out on one side of a large serving platter and return the skillet to the stove.

VEGETABLE TOPPING:

1 bell pepper, sliced in vertical strips
1-2 large onions, sliced in strips

2 medium tomatoes, cut into wedges
12 medium mushrooms, sliced thin

Add the vegetables to the skillet, and sauté them briefly over medium heat until they are crisp-tender. If the mixture is too dry, add a little extra butter, scraping up any browned bits from

(continued)

(continued)

the pan's surface. Arrange the mixture beside the beef on the serving platter.

Flour tortillas, 2-3 per person	**Pico de gallo and guacamole, as accompaniments**

Present the meat and vegetables at the table with warm tortillas, pico de gallo, and guacamole. Each guest cups the tortilla and fills it with portions of beef and vegetables, adding spoonfuls of pico de gallo and guacamole according to taste. Tortillas of about 6 inches are a little easier to handle than the larger size, if you have a choice. Serve the fajitas with beans if you like, but they can be a meal in themselves.

The Rancho de Chimayó Cookbook

Green Chile Goulash

1 cup green chiles, chopped	4 cups whole grain corn
1 cup chopped onions	2 (8-ounce) cans tomato sauce
3 tablespoons cooking oil	1 teaspoon salt
1 pound ground beef	

Brown the chiles and onions in oil. Add the ground beef and stir until browned. Drain. Add the remaining ingredients and simmer slowly for 20 minutes. Serves 4.

Variation: Use 1 (16-ounce) can peeled tomatoes instead of the sauce and add ¼ teaspoon cumin and ½ cup chopped celery. Stir in one cup cooked macaroni and lay strips of American cheese over the mixture. Heat until it melts.

Or add ½ teaspoon crushed oregano and ¼ teaspoon garlic powder. Serve over rice or macaroni.

Green Chile Bible

Picadillo

Picadillo is wonderful served over plain boiled rice, but in the Southwest, it is more often a stuffing for tacos, tamales, chicken, or best of all—green chiles.

½ pound ground beef
½ pound ground pork
1 cup chopped onion
2 cloves garlic, minced
1 cup canned tomatoes,
   chopped
1 tablespoon vinegar
Pinch of sugar
½ teaspoon ground cinnamon
Pinch of ground cloves

¼ teaspoon ground cumin
1 teaspoon salt
1 bay leaf
3 drops Tabasco sauce
½ cup seedless raisins
½ cup green olives, chopped
   (optional)
½ cup blanched, slivered
   almonds

Stir meats in a frying pan over high heat. When they begin to release fat, add onion and garlic. As the meat starts to brown, pour off fat and add all other ingredients except raisins, olives, and almonds. Simmer, covered, 30 minutes. Add water or stock if necessary, but not too much, for when done, the picadillo should be moist but not soupy. Finally, add raisins, olives, and almonds and cook 10 more minutes. Serves 4.

The Aficionado's Southwestern Cooking

Chile peppers grow in 2,000 different varieties. The Capsicum species are roasted, fried, stewed, cooked, or just used right off the plant. Chile usually comes in either a red or green sauce. The hotness varies with the variety and growing conditions, but when ordering, your waiter can probably tell you which one is hotter. Many people ask for "Christmas," which is both red and green chiles served side-by-side.

Caldillo

1 pound lean beef round steak,
  cut ½-inch thick
1 tablespoon paprika
2 tablespoons butter or
  margarine
2 cloves garlic, crushed
1½ cups beef broth
1 cup sliced green onions,
  including tops

2 green peppers, cut in strips
3 long green chiles, roasted,
  peeled, and cut lengthwise
2 tablespoons cornstarch
¼ cup water
1 tablespoon soy sauce
2 large fresh tomatoes, cut in
  eights

Pound steak to ¼-inch thickness, cut into ¼ inch wide strips. Sprinkle meat with paprika and allow to stand while preparing other ingredients.

Using a large skillet, brown meat in margarine. Add garlic and broth. Cover and simmer for 30 minutes.

Stir in onions, green peppers, and chiles. Cover and cook for 5 minutes more. Blend cornstarch, water, and soy sauce. Stir into meat mixture. Cook, stirring until clear and thickened, about 2 minutes. Add tomatoes and stir gently. Serve over beds of fluffy rice.

Recipes from Hatch

Son-of-a-Gun Stew

The combination of pork and beef makes a terrific tasting dish. In Billy's day this stew was cooked all day in a cast iron pot hanging from a hook in the back of a fireplace. I've brought this up-to-date and use a two-step method; cooking the meat in a crockpot, and then quickly finishing off the stew on top of the stove. I usually cook enough meat to not only make the stew, but have some left over to make burritos or another dish.

MEAT:

3 pounds chuck or other inexpensive beef roast

2 pounds pork roast or boneless pork ribs

2 bay leaves, broken in half

1 teaspoon dried parsley

2 cloves garlic, chopped

1 tablespoon dried, minced onion flakes

1 tablespoon Worcestershire sauce

1 tablespoon instant beef stock or 1 can beef broth

Water

Cut the meat into chunks small enough to fit in your crockpot. Place the bay leaves, parsley, garlic, onion flakes, and Worcestershire on top of the meat. Mix the instant beef stock with a cup of hot water and pour over the meat, or use the beef broth and pour over the meat. Add enough water to cover the meat, cover and cook on high for one hour, reduce the heat to low and cook for 4-5 hours more or until the meat is tender.

Remove the meat from the crockpot. Divide the meat in half and cut one half of it into bite-size pieces. (Save the other half for another dish such as burritos.) Strain the juice from the crockpot and let cool. Skim off any excess fat and reserve the juice.

VEGETABLES:

2 tablespoons olive oil

1 medium yellow onion, chopped

1 green or red bell pepper, seeded and chopped

2 large carrots, chopped into small bite-size pieces

4 medium potatoes, peeled, cooked and cut into eights

2 tablespoons butter

2 tablespoons all-purpose flour

Juice from the cooked meat

(continued)

(continued)

Heat the oil in a large Dutch oven or heavy pot, stir in the onion, bell pepper, and carrots and cook over medium heat until the onion and bell pepper are tender. Remove the vegetables to a bowl. Melt the butter in the pot, stir in the flour and brown for a minute or so. Whisk in the strained juice from the meat until the consistency of light cream. Add water if you do not have enough juice or want it thinner. Add the vegetables back to the pot. Then add the potatoes, meat, and salt and pepper to taste. Cook for 20-30 minutes over low heat until everything is warmed through and the flavors meld. Serve in large shallow bowls with sourdough or dark, crusty bread. Serves 4-6.

Billy the Kid Cook Book

Bowl of Red

The exact origin of chili is still debated today, but New Mexicans claim it was a chuckwagon cook who ran out of black pepper. Looking for a substitute, he tried the little red peppers commonly used by the local Indians and Mexicans and thus "Bowl of Red" was born.

2 tablespoons vegetable oil
1 large white onion, coarsely
   chopped
3 garlic cloves, finely chopped
3 pounds lean beef, coarse
4 tablespoons ground hot New
   Mexico red chile

4 tablespoons ground mild New
   Mexico red chile
2 teaspoons ground cumin
1½ teaspoons salt
3 cups water

In a 4-quart Dutch oven or heavy pot, heat oil; add onion and garlic. Cook until soft. Add beef, ground chiles, and cumin; cook until meat is evenly browned, breaking any lumps with fork. Add salt and water, bring to a boil; and reduce heat. Simmer uncovered 2-3 hours, stirring occasionally, until meat is very tender and flavors are fully blended. Add more water as necessary. Makes 6 servings.

Sassy Southwest Cooking

Campfire Chili Con Carne

This dish has as many versions as there are campers and cowpokes. In New Mexico, "chile" means a sauce made of chile peppers, either red or green. If you want both, it's called Christmas. Neither has meat, tomatoes, or beans. In Texas, "chili" is made with chunked, not ground, meat. Ours has both kinds of chiles, uses chopped meat, and is beanless. If you keep your eye on the pot and stir from time to time, chili can simmer for several hours either indoors or out. Leftover or frozen and reheated, it just seems to get richer and better tasting.

1 tablespoon oil
1 large onion, chopped
6 cloves garlic, mashed
2½ pounds ground or chopped beef or half pork/half beef
½ - ¾ cup red chile powder
2 (14½-ounce) cans diced tomatoes with roasted garlic
1 (7-ounce) can chopped green chiles

½ cup chopped fresh coriander or 1 tablespoon dried cilantro leaves
2 tablespoons dried oregano
1 tablespoon ground cumin
Cayenne pepper or chipotle pepper sauce to taste
Salt to taste

Heat oil in a large pot over medium heat. Add onions and sauté, stirring until clear and soft. Add garlic and meat. Stir until all pink color is gone. Raise heat to high, add chile powder, tomatoes, and chiles, and bring to a boil. Stir from the bottom up, then add remaining ingredients, except salt. Reduce heat to low, and cover. Simmer at least an hour, stirring from time to time. Salt to taste just before serving. Serves 8-10.

The Happy Camper's Cookbook

Chili purists insist chili is not chili if it has beans in it. In New Mexico there is no such prejudice, and many even say that chili tastes better with beans.

Chili with Avocados

There are probably as many chili recipes as there are chili cooks. This version, without beans and served in avocado halves, is an informally elegant and festive main dish.

3 onions, coarsely chopped
4 cloves garlic, chopped
3 tablespoons vegetable oil
2 pounds beef round, cut in
    small cubes
1 pound lean pork, cut in
    small cubes
⅓ cup chili powder
1 tablespoon flour
1 large can Italian tomatoes,
    cut up, with juice

3 bay leaves
1 tablespoon oregano
2 teaspoons ground cumin
1 tablespoon brown sugar
Salt
1 tablespoon red wine vinegar
1 cup pimento-stuffed green
    olives, drained
3 avocados, peeled, halved

In a medium saucepan sauté onion and garlic in oil until soft. Remove and set aside. Brown meat over high heat in same pan. Stir in onions, garlic, chili powder, flour, tomatoes, bay leaves, oregano, cumin, sugar, salt, and vinegar. Bring to a boil, lower heat and simmer covered for 2 hours, stirring occasionally. Discard bay leaves. Stir in olives, correct seasoning, and serve over avocado halves.

A Little Southwest Cookbook

Barbecued Brisket

1 (8 to 10-pound) beef brisket
1 cup dry white wine
1 cup water
2 tablespoons dried minced onions

Put brisket in a baking pan with wine, water, and onions. Cover with tin foil and bake in 250° oven overnight (10-12 hours), or until meat is tender. Let meat stand while you make the following sauce. (The meat is easier to slice when slightly cooled.)

SAUCE:
1 (14-ounce) bottle ketchup
¾ cup light brown sugar
½ cup red wine vinegar
1½ cups water
½ cup lemon juice
¼ cup prepared mustard
2 tablespoons Worcestershire sauce
1 tablespoon light soy sauce
2 cloves garlic, run through a garlic press
1 teaspoon ground black pepper
½ cup chopped green chile
1 medium-size yellow onion, minced
1 tablespoon chopped cilantro
Tabasco to taste

Mix all ingredients together in a saucepan and simmer over medium heat for 30 minutes. Slice brisket, pour sauce over slices and heat in 325° oven for 30 minutes. Serves 12-15.

New Mexico Cook Book

New Mexico Pot Roast

3-3½ pound boneless chuck
   roast
½ cup all-purpose flour
1 teaspoon paprika
½ teaspoon ground black
   pepper
1 teaspoon garlic salt
2 teaspoons red chile powder

2 tablespoons butter
1 cup water
1 cup dry red wine
4 ounces chopped green chile
   (fresh or canned)
1 clove garlic, peeled, cut in half
2 bay leaves, broken in half

Rinse meat and pat dry with paper towel. Mix flour, paprika, pepper, garlic salt, and 1 teaspoon red chile powder in a plastic or paper bag. Shake meat in the bag to coat it. Melt butter in a Dutch oven or oven-proof dish. Sear roast on all sides over high heat. Remove from heat, add water, wine, green chile, garlic, bay leaves, and 1 teaspoon red chile powder. Cover and bake in 350° oven for 2½ - 3 hours, or until meat tests very tender. Remove bay leaves before serving. Serves 4-6.

New Mexico Cook Book

Baked Fresh Ham with Apple Cider

This is wonderful for a holiday buffet. Slice thinly and serve with a gravy made from the drippings.

1 fresh (10 to 14-pound) ham
1 teaspoon sage
1 teaspoon ground black
   pepper
1 tablespoon marjoram

2 cups apple cider
3 tablespoons butter
3 tablespoons flour
2 tablespoons apple brandy
2 cups chicken broth

Preheat oven to 325°. Score ham with a knife, making a diamond pattern. Mix together sage, black pepper, and marjoram and rub into surface of ham. Place meat on a rack in a large roasting pan. Pour apple cider over meat and roast, uncovered, for 3 hours or until done. Baste about every 30 minutes. Skim fat from the pan drippings. Make a roux by browning butter and flour. Add pan drippings, apple brandy, and chicken broth to make the gravy. Serve on the side. Serves 12-16.

Christmas in New Mexico Cook Book

Ham and Scalloped Potatoes with Green Chile

3 cups cooked ham, cut into
  bite-size cubes
3 green onions, chopped
½ cup diced green chile
6 medium-size potatoes,
  peeled, and thinly-sliced
3 tablespoons butter

3 tablespoons all-purpose flour
2 cups milk
1 teaspoon dried mustard
1 teaspoon salt
1 teaspoon ground black pepper
¼ cup unseasoned bread crumbs
2 teaspoons paprika

Mix together ham, onions, and chile. Put a layer of sliced potatoes in a well-buttered baking dish and sprinkle some of the ham-and-chile mixture over them. Repeat until sliced potatoes and ham and chile mixture are all used.

Melt butter in a frying pan, whisk in flour and then slowly pour in milk, whisking constantly until mixture is smooth and starts to thicken. Whisk in mustard, salt and pepper, and then pour over potato mixture. Top with bread crumbs, sprinkle paprika on top, cover and bake in a 375° oven for one hour. Uncover and bake for 30 more minutes or until potatoes are done. Serves 4.

New Mexico Cook Book

Pork Chops with Mushrooms

2 tablespoons Parmesan
  cheese
2 tablespoons cornmeal
3 tablespoons fine dry bread
  crumbs
½ teaspoon garlic salt
½ teaspoon oregano
6 tablespoons butter or
  margarine

4 lean pork chops, cut ½-inch
  thick
½ pound mushrooms, sliced
1 clove garlic, crushed
¼ teaspoon rosemary
½ cup whipping cream
¼ cup thinly sliced green onions
Salt and pepper to taste

In a paper bag combine Parmesan, cornmeal, bread crumbs, garlic salt, and oregano. Melt butter in a skillet; dip each chop into butter, drain briefly, then shake each chop in the bag. Shake off excess coating and arrange chops on rack of a broiler pan. Bake, uncovered, in 400° oven about 40-50 minutes.

Meanwhile, heat the butter remaining in skillet over medium heat; add mushrooms and garlic and sauté 5 minutes. Stir in rosemary and cream and cook over high heat until liquid is reduced to about ¼ cup. Stir in green onions and salt and pepper to taste. Pour into a bowl and pass at the table with the pork chops. Makes 4 servings.

Simply Simpatico

Chaco Culture National Historical Park in northwestern New Mexico contains the archaeological remains of Anasazi culture (AD 900 - 1275). Pueblo Bonito, one of the major ruins in the park, is believed to have contained 800 rooms.

Harvest Pork Chops

6 loin or rib pork chops, cut
  ¾-inch thick
¼ cup flour
½ teaspoon salt
Dash of pepper

3 orange slices, cut in half
3 lemon slices, cut in half
2 tablespoons brown sugar
½ cup orange juice
¼ cup water

Trim all fat from chops; mix ¼ cup flour, salt and pepper and rub well into both sides of chops. Heat large heavy frying pan with ovenproof handle. Brown chops on both sides in small amount of hot fat. Pour off fat.

Place an orange half slice and lemon half slice on each chop. Sprinkle with brown sugar. Pour orange juice and ¼ cup water mixed together over and around chops. Bake in oven at 325° degrees about one hour, or until chops are tender when tested with fork. Serve on a hot platter and garnish with more lemon and orange slices and parsley, if desired. This is nice served with baked squash or corn.

Cooking with Kiwanis

Pork Tenderloin with Cranberry-Chipotle Sauce

1 tablespoon unsalted butter
1 tablespoon olive oil
1 (½-pound) pork tenderloin

Salt and freshly ground pepper
to taste

Preheat oven to 375°. Melt butter and olive oil in a skillet over medium heat; season pork with salt and pepper, and brown in butter on all sides. Reserve drippings in skillet. Remove pork to a rack in a roasting pan, and cook until a thermometer reaches 155°, about 40 minutes.

CRANBERRY-CHIPOTLE SAUCE:

2 tablespoons minced shallot
2 garlic cloves, minced
2 cups fresh or frozen
   cranberries, thawed
3 tablespoons sugar
1 cup dry red wine
2½ cups chicken stock
1 canned chipotle chile in
   adobo sauce, puréed

1 teaspoon minced fresh sage
   or ½ teaspoon crumbled
   dried sage
3 tablespoons unsalted butter,
   room temperature
Salt and freshly ground pepper
   to taste

Sauté shallot and garlic in reserved drippings 30 seconds; add cranberries and sugar, and cook, stirring constantly, 30 seconds. Add wine to skillet, scraping browned bits loose from pan; boil mixture over high heat until reduced to ¾ cup. Add chicken stock, chipotle purée, and sage to skillet; bring to a boil over high heat until reduced to 2 cups. Strain mixture into a clean saucepan, and bring to a boil. Whisk butter, salt, and pepper into sauce, and keep warm. When pork is done, remove from oven, cover loosely with foil, and let stand 10 minutes. Cut pork into ½-inch slices; place on serving plates, and top with sauce. Makes 6 servings.

Savoring the Southwest Again

Posole

1 pork loin roast, about
   3 pounds
5 cups water
3 cups chicken broth
2 cups chopped onion
2 teaspoons salt
1 whole chicken, about
   2½ pounds
1½ tablespoons bacon grease

2 garlic cloves, crushed
1½ tablespoons chili powder
½ teaspoon paprika
2 (16-ounce) cans white hominy,
   drained
Chopped white onions, sliced
   radishes, sliced avocado, and
   lime wedges (garnish)

In a large Dutch oven, place pork roast and water. Bring to a boil. Add onions and salt. Reduce heat, cover and simmer gently for 30 minutes. Add chicken and bring to a boil, reduce heat, cover and simmer for 45 minutes. Remove pork and chicken from broth and allow to cool. Cover and refrigerate broth. Cut pork and chicken meat into small pieces and discard bones.

In skillet heat bacon grease, add garlic, chili powder, and paprika; stir just until blended. Add small amount of broth and stir. Add mixture and hominy to broth and bring to a boil. Reduce heat, cover and simmer gently for 30 minutes; add pork and chicken pieces and simmer until meat is thoroughly heated, about 15 minutes. Serve in individual bowls with garnishes as side dishes. Makes 8 servings.

Sassy Southwest Cooking

Green Chile Sauce

½ pound lean ground beef, preferably coarse ground
4 cups water
2 cups chopped, roasted green chile, preferably New Mexico green or Anaheim, fresh or frozen
2 medium tomatoes, chopped, or 1 cup canned crushed tomatoes
2 teaspoons minced white onion

1 teaspoon salt
1 clove garlic, minced
¼ teaspoon white pepper
¼ teaspoon Worcestershire sauce
2 tablespoons cornstarch dissolved in 2 tablespoons water
Additional salt and white pepper to taste

Brown the ground beef over medium heat in a high-sided non-reactive skillet until all of the pink color is gone. While continuing to heat the skillet, pour in the water and add the chile, tomatoes, onion, salt, garlic, pepper, and Worcestershire sauce. Bring the mixture to a boil, then lower the heat and simmer for 10-15 minutes. Add the cornstarch, add cook for 5-10 minutes more. The sauce should be thickened, but quite pourable, with no taste of raw cornstarch. Serve warm with burritos, enchiladas, or other dishes.

Green Chile Sauce keeps in the refrigerator for 3-4 days. It freezes well. When reheating, add a little extra water if needed.

Note: If the heat of a chile sauce begins to set your mouth ablaze, don't drink water—it just inflames the heat. Reach for something sweet or creamy, like the honey that accompanies sopaipillas, or a bite of cheese or sour cream.

The Rancho de Chimayó Cookbook

Native American sites in New Mexico include Taos Pueblo, Aztec Ruins National Monument, Chaco Culture National Historical Park, and Gila Cliff Dwellings National Monument.

Carne Adovada

Carne adovada originated as a way to keep meat before the days of refrigeration. The fiery chile both flavored and preserved the fresh pork.

3 pounds boneless pork chops, trimmed of fat and cut into 1 to 2-inch cubes

RED CHILE SAUCE:

8 ounces (about 25) whole dried red chile pods, preferable Chimayó, other New Mexico red, or ancho
4 cups water
1 tablespoon minced white onion

½ teaspoon Worcestershire sauce
½ teaspoon dried oregano
½ teaspoon salt
¼ teaspoon white pepper

Preheat the oven to 300°.

Break the stems off the chile pods and discard the seeds. It isn't necessary to get rid of every seed, but most should be removed. Place the chiles in a sink or large bowl, rinse them carefully, and drain them. Place the damp pods in one layer on a cookie sheet and roast them in the oven for about 5 minutes. Watch the pods carefully so as not to burn them. The chiles can have a little remaining moisture. Remove them from the oven and let them cool. Break each chile into 2 or 3 pieces.

In a blender, purée half the pods with 2 cups of the water. You will still be able to see tiny pieces of chile pulp, but they should be bound in a smooth, thick liquid. Pour the liquid into a large, heavy saucepan. Repeat with the remaining pods and water. Add the remaining sauce ingredients to the chile purée and bring to a boil over medium-high heat. Simmer for 20 minutes, stirring occasionally. The mixture will thicken, but should remain a little soupy. Remove from heat.

While the chile sauce is simmering, oil a large, covered baking dish. When the sauce has completed cooking, layer enough to fully cover the bottom of the baking dish. Top with the pork cubes. Pour the remaining sauce over the pork. There will be more sauce than meat.

(continued)

(continued)

Cover the dish and bake at 300° until the meat is meltingly tender and the sauce has cooked down, about 3½ hours. Check the meat, however, after 3 hours. The Carne Adovada can be left uncovered for the last few minutes of baking, if the sauce seems watery.

Serve garnished with lettuce and tomato on the side, if desired. Rancho de Chimayó accompanies the dish with posole.

The sauce can be made in advance and refrigerated for a day. The completed dish can be refrigerated for up to 3 days. Add a couple of tablespoons of water before reheating in the oven or on the stove. Serves 6-8.

The Rancho de Chimayó Cookbook

Chimayó Red Chile

1 pound coarsely ground pork (optional)	2-3 tablespoons flour
	2 teaspoons salt
1 large onion, chopped	⅔ cup red chile powder
3 cloves garlic, chopped	3 cups chicken/vegetable stock

Sauté the pork, onion, and garlic. (If not using meat, use 1 teaspoon canola oil or olive oil.) Add the flour and salt and stir. Add the red chile and continue to stir for 2-3 minutes. Add the liquid and cook for 20 minutes. Serve alone, over fried potatoes or as a sauce for burritos and enchiladas.

Inn on the Rio's Favorite Recipes

Mark's Red Chile Sauce

This is my variation of the traditional red chile sauce. In this recipe, we combine several types of chile, each with its own taste characteristics and flavor dimensions (one might be fruitier, another smokier or hotter, for example), to create more complex tones and a multi-dimensional sauce. As a result, this if fuller, deeper, and more rounded than most other red chile sauces. The result is comparable to the depth of flavor one experiences in wines composed of several grape varietals. A good accompaniment for most grilled foods. Especially good with red meats, game, such as venison, and tamales and enchiladas.

8 plum tomatoes (about 1 pound)
4 ounces (about 20) dried New Mexico red chiles
2 ounces (about 5) dried ancho chiles
2 ounces (about 20) dried cascable chiles
2 quarts water
1 tablespoon virgin olive oil
1 white onion, peeled and chopped

2 canned chipotle chiles en adobo
1 teaspoon adobo sauce
2 large cloves roasted garlic, peeled and finely chopped
1 teaspoon toasted and finely ground cumin
½ tablespoon toasted and finely ground dried oregano
1 teaspoon salt
2 tablespoons peanut oil, or lard

Cut off ¼ inch of the steam end of the tomatoes. In a skillet over high heat, or under a broiler, blacken the tomatoes (about 5 minutes). Dry-roast the chiles and rehydrate them in the water. Heat the oil in a skillet and sauté the onion over medium heat until browned, about 10 minutes.

Place the blackened tomatoes, rehydrated chiles, onion, chipotle chiles, adobo sauce, garlic, cumin, oregano, and salt in a food processor or blender. If it is not bitter, add one cup of the chile water. Otherwise add one cup plain water. Purée to a fine paste, adding a little more chile water or plain water if necessary.

Heat the oil or lard in a high-sided pan until just smoking. Refry the sauce at a sizzle for 3-5 minutes, stirring continuously. Do not allow the sauce to become too thick; add more liquid if necessary. Serve warm. Keeps in the refrigerator for up to one week; also freezes well. About 4 cups.

Coyote's Pantry

Chile Caribe Rub

Use this hot rub to marinade meats or fish filets for grilling or skillet blackening. If you like, grind 2 teaspoons of rub into a paste with a fresh garlic clove before using—it adds fresh garlic flavor and helps the dry rub adhere to and penetrate the meat. You can also use it to pep up salad dressings and sauces.

1 large very dry New Mexico red chile

2 teaspoons mild Chimayó chile powder

2 teaspoons dried thyme, crushed

2 teaspoons dried Mexican oregano, crushed

2 teaspoons cumin seed, toasted and crushed

1 teaspoon coriander seed, toasted and ground

1 teaspoon ground cloves

1 teaspoon ground cinnamon

1-2 teaspoons turbinado or dark brown sugar

1 teaspoon salt

Wipe the chile with a barely damp cloth to remove any dirt or dust. Remove the stem (but not the seeds) and break up the chile into a mortar or stone bowl. Crush the chile thoroughly. In a deep bowl, gently stir the crushed red chile with the remaining ingredients to blend, taking care not to bring your face close to the bowl or inhale any of the mixture. Carefully spoon the rub into a glass jar, cover tightly, and wash your hands thoroughly. Store the rub away from light in a cool, dry place. It will keep well for years if you have used fresh ingredients and the jar is not exposed to light or moisture (the refrigerator is cool and dark, but full of moisture). If you don't have a cool, dry place to store the jar, try sealing the rub into a plastic freezer bag and keeping it frozen.

Red Chile Bible

Leg of Lamb
Redolent of Garlic and Rosemary

Remember when a roast was the ubiquitous entrée for special occasion? This recipe brings back those days of working kitchens filled with heady aromas.

1 (6-8 pound) leg of lamb
5 cloves garlic, roughly cut
   into thirds
1 tablespoon salt
1 tablespoon freshly ground
   black pepper
2 tablespoons fresh rosemary
   leaves, chopped, or 1
   tablespoon dried rosemary

8 baking potatoes, cut into
   quarters
5 large yellow onions, cut into
   quarters
8 carrots, peeled and cut into
   3-inch lengths

In a large metal roasting pan, place the leg of lamb fat and fleshy side up. To stud the leg with the garlic, using the point of a paring knife, make 15 small x-shaped incisions in the fat sheath of the leg. Insert the garlic pieces into the cuts, burying them. Tuck any remaining garlic in the folds of the meat. Rub the leg with the salt, pepper, and rosemary.

Arrange the prepared vegetables around the roast and place in the oven for 15 minutes. Turn the oven temperature down to 350° and continue to roast until done to your liking, another 16 minutes per pound for medium-rare.

Transfer the roast and vegetables to a warmed carving platter, reserving the juices and fat in the pan for gravy. Let the roast "rest" for at least 15 minutes before carving. This waiting period allows the juices to be reabsorbed and facilitates carving. While the roast is resting, make the gravy.

GRAVY:
Pan juices and fat from roasted
   leg of lamb
4-6 tablespoons all-purpose
   flour

1-2 cups milk
Salt and freshly ground black
   pepper

Put the roasting pan on top of the stove over 2 burners turned to medium heat and begin to heat the juices and fat. As the

(continued)

(continued)

pan heats up, scrape to loosen any crisp, browned bits from the bottom of the pan to incorporate into the gravy. When the liquid is bubbling, make a roux by gently shaking spoonfuls of the flour over the juices, vigorously and continuously stirring with a wire balloon whisk until the mixture becomes slightly browned and nutty in flavor, about 5 minutes. Continuing to stir, slowly add enough milk to achieve the desired consistency for gravy. Season to taste with salt and pepper. Carve the roast and serve the gravy in a bowl on the side. Serves 8.

Cafe Pasqual's Cookbook

Apricot-Prune Stuffed Lamb

½ cup apricots, dried or fresh
½ cup prunes, raisins or
    double amount of apricots
¾ cup rice
½ cup chopped celery
½ cup chopped onion
¼ cup pecans or almonds,
    chopped

½ teaspoon salt
1½ cups water (use 1 cup if
    apricots are fresh)
1 (5-pound) boneless lamb
shoulder roast

Cut apricots and prunes into small pieces (watch for and discard pits). Combine all ingredients except lamb. Simmer, covered, 15-20 minutes or until all water is absorbed. Cool slightly, just enough to handle.

Preheat oven to 325° (slow oven). Unroll lamb shoulder. Sprinkle with salt. Spread stuffing over lamb shoulder, roll and tie (with kitchen twine). Place lamb, fat-side up on a rack in a shallow pan. Roast, uncovered, until internal temperature reaches 180° (about 3-3½ hours). Makes 10-15 servings.

The Joy of Sharing

Burgundy Venison Steak Tips

The best of the best. You must try venison in a rich deep-colored sauce.

3 tablespoons oil
2 pounds venison steak, cut in
    small cubes
2-3 tablespoons dry onion
    soup mix
3 beef-bouillon cubes

2 cups water
1 cup Burgundy wine
1 cup fresh mushrooms or
    1 (4-ounce) can, drained
3 cups cooked rice

In large Dutch oven or heavy pot, heat oil and brown venison. Add remaining ingredients except mushrooms and rice. Cover and simmer for about one hour. Add mushrooms the last 5 minutes. Serve over rice. Makes 6 servings.

Sassy Southwest Cooking

Wok Venison

1½ pounds venison steak
½ cup water, divided
2 tablespoons soy sauce
1 teaspoon vinegar
1 clove garlic, minced
½ teaspoon dry mustard

1 pound fresh broccoli
3 tablespoons peanut oil
1 can tomato sauce
1 cup green onions, sliced
½ cup water chestnuts, sliced
 and rinsed

Thinly slice venison diagonally across the grain (meat will slice better if half frozen.) Combine ¼ cup water, soy sauce, vinegar, garlic, and mustard. Add venison and marinate in refrigerator for one hour. Use a glass container for marinating.

Remove flowerettes from broccoli and break into small pieces. Peel stalk of broccoli and cut into thin strips one inch long. Pour oil into wok or 10-inch skillet. Preheat skillet on high heat about one minute. Add steak and marinade and cook for 5 minutes, stirring often. Push up the side. Add broccoli and cook for 5 minutes, stirring often. Add remaining ingredients plus ¼ cup water. Continue heating and stirring until meat is tender and broccoli is desired doneness.

Cooking with Kiwanis

Marilyn's Everyday Miracle Rub

This is our "house" rub. It goes well with any meat you're grilling or smoking. We use it on everything from turkey burgers to steak. Make a double or triple batch. Store in a cool place.

¼ cup paprika
¼ cup packed brown sugar
1 tablespoon chili powder
1½ teaspoons salt
1 teaspoon minced, dried
   onion

½ teaspoon granulated garlic
   or garlic powder
½ teaspoon black pepper
¼ teaspoon cayenne powder

Makes about ⅔ cup.

The Happy Camper's Cookbook

This traditional gateway near Las Cruces symbolizes the area's heritage and the profound affect of the Spanish explorers who brought their faith and their language to this land over four centuries ago.

Flautas

Flautas resemble rolled tacos. They are a delicate blend of chicken, onion, chile pequín, and seasonings, deep fried and topped with sour cream and guacamole.

3 chicken breasts
1 package corn tortillas
Oil for frying
¼ cup minced onion
¼ cup chile pequín

Onion salt
Garlic salt
Guacamole
1 pint sour cream
Tomato wedges (optional)

Boil chicken until tender, about one hour. Bone chicken; chop; set aside. Fry corn tortillas in one inch of oil for 5 seconds on each side. Drain on paper towel. Place chicken on one side of tortilla, sprinkle with onion, chile pequín, and salts. Roll jelly-roll fashion. Secure with toothpick.

Fry 1-2 minutes until crisp. Drain on paper towel; place in a warm oven until serving time. Serve topped with guacamole and sour cream. Guacamole should be mixed into sour cream for use as topping. Garnish with tomato wedges if you wish. Makes 12.

Variation: Two pounds cooked beef brisket or 2 pounds cooked pork may be substituted for chicken, if desired.

Comida Sabrosa

Pat Garrett, who shot Billy the Kid on July 14, 1881, was the Sheriff of Lincoln County, and a good one, at a time when New Mexico needed such a man. He left his mark on New Mexico in many ways; one of significance is that his daughter, Elizabeth, wrote "O Fair New Mexico," the state song. It begins, "Under a sky of azure, where balmy breezes blow; Kissed by the golden sunshine, is Nuevo Mejico. Home of the Montezuma, with fiery heart aglow, State of the deeds historic, is Nuevo Mejico."

Chicken Tacos with Avocado

1 stewing chicken
2 stalks celery
Salt and pepper, to taste
1 dozen corn tortillas
2 small cans tomato sauce
1 (16-ounce) carton
  half-and-half

Salt and pepper
1 cup grated Italian cheese
4 ripe avocados
½ pint sour cream
¼ teaspoon garlic powder
1 (4-ounce) can chilies

Stew chicken with celery, salt and pepper. After chicken has cooked, remove and bone. Fry tortillas and drain on paper towel, then fill each one with about 2 teaspoons of chicken and keep in place with toothpick. Place in 9x13-inch pan.

Mix tomato sauce with half-and-half and salt and pepper to taste. Pour over tacos and sprinkle with grated cheese. Bake in 350° oven for 25 minutes. Mash ripe avocados and mix with sour cream, garlic powder, and salt. Add can of chilies. This makes a delicious side dish to serve with the tacos.

Beyond Loaves and Fishes

The volcanic monolith Shiprock near Farmington rises to 1,700 feet. Rock climbing is forbidden because it is considered sacred by the Navajos.

Monterey Chicken Rolls

3 whole medium-size chicken
  breasts, skinned, halved,
  and boned
Salt and pepper
1½ ounces Monterey Jack
  cheese cut into pieces to
  match length of chicken

3 tablespoons all-purpose flour
2-3 beaten eggs
6 tablespoons fine dry bread
  crumbs

Place each piece of chicken boned-side up, between 2 pieces of clear plastic wrap. Working from center to edges, pound lightly with meat mallet, forming rectangles about ⅛-inch thick. Remove plastic wrap. Sprinkle each side with salt and pepper. Place one piece of cheese onto each piece of chicken, fold in sides; roll up jelly-roll style. Skewer closed with wooden picks. Roll chicken in flour, then dip in beaten egg. Roll in fine dry bread crumbs to coat evenly.

Place chicken rolls, seam-side down, in a shallow baking dish. Bake, uncovered in 350° oven for 30 minutes.

SAUCE:

6 tablespoons dry white wine
3 tablespoons softened
  margarine
3 teaspoons snipped parsley

½ teaspoon dried oregano
  crushed or dried marjoram
  crushed

In a small saucepan combine the white wine, margarine, parsley, and oregano (or marjoram). Cook and stir over low heat until margarine is melted. Pour the sauce over chicken rolls; continue baking about 10 minutes or until tender. Remove the wooden picks before serving. Makes about 6 servings.

Cooking with Kiwanis

Cheese Tortilla Torta

2 cups cooked turkey or chicken
1 (11-ounce) can Mexican-style corn, drained
2 cups or 2 (4-ounce) cans diced or chopped green chilies, undrained
½ cup chopped red onion (optional)
1 pound container sour cream mixed with 1 tablespoon flour

2 (10-ounce) cans enchilada sauce or same amount of homemade chile sauce
12 corn tortillas, halved
10 ounces shredded sharp Cheddar cheese, or your choice
¼ cup sliced, pitted black olives, if desired

Preheat oven to 350°. Lightly grease a 9x13-inch pan. In medium bowl, combine turkey or chicken, corn, chilies, red onion, and half of the sour cream mixture. Pour enchilada sauce into another medium bowl. Dip 8 tortilla halves, one at a time, in sauce, arrange on bottom of prepared dish. Add half the meat mixture, spreading evenly with spatula to cover. Sprinkle one cup of the cheese over meat layer. Add another layer of 8 dipped tortilla halves, the remaining meat mixture (spread evenly), and one cup of the cheese. Top with remaining 8 tortilla halves, dipped in sauce. Pour any remaining sauce over dish. Spoon remaining sour cream mixture into plastic food storage bag and snip off one corner. With this, make a lattice design over top of the dish. Decorate here and there with green chiles and olives. Sprinkle with cheese and bake 30 minutes or until bubbly. Let stand 15 minutes before serving.

The Eagle's Kitchen

Chicken Enchiladas (Layered)

1 medium onion, chopped
1 stick oleo
1 (4-ounce) can green chilies
2 cans cream of chicken soup
1 large can Pet milk

1 (12-count) package corn
 tortilla's, divided
1 small chicken, cooked and
 boned
½ pound sharp cheese

Sauté onion in margarine, add chilies and cook until clear. Add soup and milk and bring to a bubbling boil. (Be sure and stir the soup mixture until it comes to a boil.) Line casserole with 6 quartered, lightly buttered tortilla's. Layer with chicken, chile sauce and cheese. Top with remaining buttered, quartered tortilla's and more sauce and cheese. Bake at 325° until brown on top, approximately 30 minutes.

Mrs. Noah's Survival Guide

Chicken Enchiladas

4 chicken breasts
1 can cream of chicken soup
1 tablespoon diced onion
1 cup chopped green chile

2 cups grated Longhorn
 cheese
12-20 corn tortillas

Cook chicken breasts in 2-3 cups water. Simmer until done. Shred or dice chicken. Save 1-2 cups of broth. Mix soup, chicken, onion, and green chile into broth. Simmer 5-10 minutes. In a 9x13-inch pan, layer tortillas, chile mixture, and cheese. Should make 3-5 layers. Bake at 300° for ½ hour. Let stand 10-15 minutes. Serves 6-9.

Cooking with Kiwanis

Portales, or "porches" in Spanish, was named for a cowboy campsite where spring water gushed from a string of caves that looked like front porches of a pueblo-style home. The name is fitting, as Portales is considered an entry into New Mexico on the Eastern border.

Chicken Enchilada Casserole

1 (3 to 4-pound) chicken
1 carrot, cut in 1-inch slices
1 sprig parsley
1 stalk celery, cut in 1-inch
   slices

1 1/2 teaspoons salt
1/2 teaspoon pepper

Place chicken in large kettle along with carrot, parsley, celery, and seasonings and add water to cover. Bring to boil, reduce heat and simmer until chicken is tender, 1 - 1 1/2 hours. Cool, remove chicken from bones and cut into bite-size pieces. Discard the carrot, parsley, and celery.

SAUCE:
4 tablespoons olive oil or
   vegetable oil
1 small onion, chopped
1 clove garlic, diced
5 (4-ounce) cans chopped
   green chilies

1/4 teaspoon cumin
1/2 teaspoon salt
1/4 teaspoon pepper
1-1 1/2 cups chicken broth

Heat olive oil in large skillet. Sauté onion and garlic lightly. Add green chilies, cumin, salt, pepper, and chicken broth. Simmer 20 minutes, then set aside.

Cooking oil
18 corn tortillas
1 pound Cheddar cheese, grated
1/2 pound Monterey Jack
   cheese, grated

1 pint (16 ounces) sour cream
1 (2 1/4-ounce) can pitted ripe
   olives, sliced

Heat cooking oil until very hot. Fry tortillas, one at a time, until limp, 1/2 minute on each side, turning with tongs. Drain well on paper towels. Reserving 1/3 of the cheese, layer in a large casserole tortillas, chicken, cheese, and sauce. Spread sour cream over top, sprinkle with remaining cheese and olive slices. Bake in 350° 45 minutes to 1 hour. Serve lettuce and tomatoes in bowls as garnish.

Savoring the Southwest

Enchiladas de Pollo en Cacerola
(Chicken/Tortilla Casserole)

10 ounces mushroom soup
⅓ cup milk
1½ cups shredded chicken
½ teaspoon salt
½ teaspoon garlic salt
¼ cup chopped, green chile
½ cup chopped onion
Shortening
12 corn tortillas

Combine first seven ingredients in a medium-size mixing bowl. Heat ½ inch of shortening in a heavy pan at medium-high heat. Quickly dip each tortilla into the shortening to soften. Drain on absorbent towels. Alternate ingredients in a greased, 2-quart casserole dish, beginning with a tortilla. Cover casserole dish and bake in 350° oven for 25-30 minutes. Freezes well. Yields 4 servings.

Cocinas de New Mexico

Crispy Garlic Chicken

1 (3-pound) broiler-fryer,
  cut up
Salt and pepper
Garlic powder
Paprika
1 large onion

Preheat oven to 350°. Wash chicken pieces and pat dry with paper towels; put chicken on waxed paper. Sprinkle each piece generously on both sides with salt, pepper, garlic powder, and paprika. With fingers, rub seasonings into chicken. Peel and slice onion and arrange on bottom of an ungreased casserole or baking dish. Arrange chicken pieces over onion slices. Slide dish into oven; bake for one hour. To check for doneness, a sharp knife should pierce the meat easily.

Amistad Community Recipes

Curried Chicken

2 tablespoons butter/oil
½ onion, finely diced
1 stalk celery, finely diced
1 tablespoon whole wheat flour
1 cup milk
1 hard-boiled egg, roughly
   chopped
½-1 cup leftover chicken cut
   in ½-inch chunks

1 teaspoon mild curry powder,
   or to taste
Red or green pepper, diced
   (optional)
½ cup green peas (optional)
Herb salt, to taste
Parsley, as garnish

In a medium-sized frying pan, melt one tablespoon of the butter/oil over low heat. Add the onion and celery and sauté until transparent. Remove those vegetables from the pan and set them aside. Add the second tablespoon of butter/oil to the pan. Then add one tablespoon of whole wheat flour. Stir with a whisk until the two ingredients have blended into a roux and are gently bubbling. Slowly add the milk, stirring with the whisk to keep the mixture smooth. When the milk has become the consistency of heavy cream, add the onion, celery, egg, chicken, and curry powder. Add peppers and peas if desired. Let the curry simmer for 5 minutes, or until the ingredients are thoroughly heated. Garnish with fresh parsley. Serves 3.

A Painter's Kitchen

Red Chile Lemon Chicken

Here is a spicy and tasty chicken dish that is wonderful with a summer salad and cornbread or grilled polenta. Summer or winter squash also accompany the chicken nicely.

4 (8-ounce) boneless, skinless
   chicken breasts
⅓ cup lemon juice
1 teaspoon grated lemon zest
½ teaspoon pressed or
   minced garlic
½ teaspoon paprika
½ teaspoon ground New
   Mexico red chile

½ teaspoon crushed red chile
   (chile piquin)
¼ teaspoon black pepper
2 tablespoons light sesame oil
1 tablespoon honey
⅛ teaspoon salt

Wash the chicken in cold water, drain, pat dry, and reserve. Mix together all the other ingredients. Place the chicken in this marinade and coat well. Cover and marinate in the refrigerator for 3-4 hours. Grill or broil the chicken until it is tender but no longer pink inside, 3-5 minutes on each side. Serve immediately. Serves 4.

Cooking at the Natural Cafe in Santa Fe

Lemon Chicken

1¼ cups catsup
1 can frozen lemonade
¾ cup water
¼ cup Worcestershire sauce
¼ cup prepared yellow mustard

¼ cup corn oil
2 tablespoons instant minced
   onion
1 teaspoon Accent (optional)
2 broilers, quartered

In saucepan, stir together catsup, lemonade, water, Worcestershire sauce, mustard, corn oil, onion, and flavor enhancer. Heat to boiling; simmer 5 minutes. Place chicken on grill, skin-side up, about 8 inches from heat. Cook, basting frequently, turning several times for about 1½ hours.

Beyond Loaves and Fishes

Grilled Rosemary Chicken

Chicken is wonderful for a summer barbecue. This dish may also be cooked under an oven broiler.

4 (8 to 10-ounce) boneless, skinless chicken breasts
⅓ cup finely chopped fresh rosemary
⅓ cup dry white wine
⅓ cup extra virgin olive oil

¾ teaspoon black pepper
2-3 cloves garlic, pressed
1½ tablespoons minced green onion
¼ to ½ teaspoon salt

Rinse the chicken in cold water, drain well, and pat dry. Mix together all the remaining ingredients. Add the chicken breasts to the marinade; cover and refrigerate for 1-4 hours. Grill or broil the chicken until tender, about 3-5 minutes on each side. Brush the chicken with the marinade at least once during cooking. Serve hot. Serves 4.

Cooking at the Natural Cafe in Santa Fe

Tequila-Lime-Grilled Chicken

⅔ cup olive oil
½ cup fresh lime juice
1 jalapeño, seeded and
    minced
¼ cup tequila

2 tablespoons triple sec
¼ cup minced fresh cilantro
6 skinned and boned chicken
    breast halves
Salsa

Combine first 6 ingredients; pour into a shallow pan. Add chicken, and turn to coat. Cover and chill chicken 4 hours, turning several times. Prepare grill, or preheat broiler. Remove chicken from refrigerator 30 minutes before cooking, discarding marinade. Cook chicken 4 minutes per side on grill, or 4 inches from broiler. Serve with desired salsa. Makes 6 servings.

Savoring the Southwest Again

The Best Grilled Chicken

Make extra and you'll have a great portable lunch the next day.

**3 pounds chicken parts, with
    skin and bones**

**2 cups Tim's Soy Magic
    Marinade**

Soak chicken in Tim's Marinade for one or more hours covered and refrigerated. Bring to room temperature. Cook over medium fire (about 350°), turning 4 times. Check for doneness with instant-read thermometer (cooking time approximately 50 minutes). Serves 4.

TIM'S SOY MAGIC MARINADE:
Juice of 1 lemon
½ cup soy sauce

2 tablespoons olive oil

Blend well. Makes about ¾ cup.

The Happy Camper's Cookbook

Barbecued Chicken

4 (4-ounce) skinless boneless chicken breast halves

SAUCE:

¼ cup reduced-sodium ketchup

3 tablespoons cider vinegar

1 tablespoon ready-made white horseradish

2 teaspoons firmly packed dark brown sugar

1 clove garlic, minced

⅛ teaspoon dried thyme

¼ teaspoon black pepper

Preheat broiler, heat a charcoal grill until coals form white ash, or preheat a gas grill to medium.

In a small saucepan, combine ketchup, vinegar, horseradish, brown sugar, garlic, and thyme. Mix well. Bring to a boil over medium-low heat. Cook, stirring frequently, until thickened, about 5 minutes. Remove from heat; stir in pepper. Brush tops of chicken pieces lightly with sauce. Place chicken, sauce-side down, on a foil-lined broiler pan or grill rack. Brush other sides lightly with sauce. Broil or grill 3 inches from heat, basting with remaining sauce and turning until no longer pink in center, about 5-7 minutes per side. Let chicken stand for 5 minutes before serving.

What's Cookin' at Casa

Green Chile-Chicken Divan

4 chicken breasts
Salt and pepper to taste
1 onion
2 carrots, peeled
1 celery stalk
2 (10-ounce) packages frozen
  broccoli or 1 large bunch
  fresh broccoli

2 cans cream of chicken soup
1 cup mayonnaise
1 teaspoon lemon juice
½ teaspoon curry powder
¼ cup green chile, chopped
½ cup sharp Cheddar cheese,
  grated

In pot, cover chicken with water, salt, pepper. Add onion, carrots, and celery and simmer until meat is done, about one hour. Remove bones and skin. Cook broccoli according to package directions or, if using fresh, cook in boiling salted water until tender. Drain. Arrange stalks in a greased baking dish and place a portion of chicken on top of each stalk for easy serving. Combine soup, mayonnaise, lemon juice, curry powder, and chile. Pour over chicken. Sprinkle with cheese and bake at 350° for 30 minutes. Serves 4-6.

Fiesta Mexicana

Asparagus Chicken

4 boneless chicken breasts
1 can asparagus, drained
2 cans cream of chicken soup
1 tablespoon mayonnaise

½ tablespoon lemon juice
1 tablespoon curry powder
2 cups shredded Cheddar
  cheese

Sauté chicken to opaque white. Drain. Line casserole dish with asparagus. Top with chicken breasts. Mix soup, mayonnaise, lemon juice, and curry powder. Cover chicken with above sauce and top with shredded cheese. Cover dish with foil (shiny-side down) and bake for 35-40 minutes at 375°.

Good Sam Celebrates 15 Years of Love

Angel Wings

3 whole chicken breasts, split and skinned
3 tablespoons butter or margarine, divided
Salt and pepper
1¼ cups chicken broth, divided
1 onion, chopped
2 (4-ounce) cans diced green chiles
1 clove garlic, minced
1 tablespoon flour
½ cup cream
½ cup shredded Cheddar cheese

Brown chicken lightly in half the butter in skillet, and season with salt and pepper. Lay in single layer in greased shallow baking dish (9x13-inch). Splash with ¼ cup chicken broth. Cover tightly and bake in preheated 350° oven for 20 minutes.

While chicken bakes, sauté onion gently in remaining butter until soft. Add chiles to pan with garlic and flour. Stir and cook a minute or so. Stir in the remaining one cup of broth, and simmer until smooth and slightly thickened. Pour into blender or food processor and whirl until puréed. Put back into skillet and stir in the cream. Heat just to simmering and pour over chicken. Sprinkle with cheese. Bake in 350° oven an additional 30 minutes, or until baked and the cheese is glazed. Serves 6.

Savoring the Southwest

Chicken Breasts
with Raspberry Beurre Blanc

CHICKEN:

2 chicken breasts, boned, skinned and split

Enough heated white wine to make 2 inches in bottom of baking dish

Grill or charbroil breasts until seared. Heat wine in baking dish. Add breasts and bake at 400° for 10-12 minutes. Remove from dish and set aside.

SAUCE:

2 tablespoons minced shallots

1 ounce Chambord (liqueur)

1 tablespoon raspberry vinegar

1 cup fresh raspberries, divided

½ cup cream (optional)

3½ tablespoons softened butter

½ teaspoon true maple syrup

Salt

White pepper

Add shallots to white wine in baking dish. Reduce until almost dry. Add Chambord, raspberry vinegar, ½ cup fresh raspberries, and maple syrup. Heat. Remove from burner and stir in softened butter. Strain out cooked raspberries. Add reserved ½ cup raspberries, plus salt and pepper. Serve sauce over chicken. Serves 4.

Note: A traditional Beurre Blanc does not use cream. Cream may be used as a stabilizer. It should be added to the white wine-shallot reduction.

Contributed by The Range Café, Bernalillo.

Raspberry Enchantment House Tour Cookbook

Gores' Chinese Chicken with Pecans or Walnuts

1½ pounds whole chicken breasts, skinned, boned and split
3 tablespoons soy sauce
2 teaspoons cornstarch
2 tablespoons dry sherry
1 teaspoon sugar
1 teaspoon grated, fresh ginger root
½ teaspoon crushed red pepper

½ teaspoon salt
2 tablespoons cooking oil
2 medium green peppers, cut into ¾-inch pieces
4 green onions, bias-sliced into 1-inch lengths
½ cup walnut halves or New Mexico pecans

Cut chicken into 1-inch pieces; set aside. Blend soy sauce into cornstarch. Stir in sherry, sugar, ginger root, red pepper, and salt; set aside. Preheat wok or large skillet over high heat. Add cooking oil. Stir-fry for 2 minutes. Remove chicken from pan and set aside. Stir-fry remaining chicken for 2 minutes. Return all chicken to wok. Stir soy mixture to evenly blend ingredients, and add to chicken in the pan. Cook and stir until bubbly. Stir in vegetables and nuts. Cover and cook for one minute. Serves 6.
Contributed by Mrs. Al Gore (Tipper Gore).

The Very Special Raspberry Cookbook

Juanita's Special Rio Grande Chicken

Select a very young spring fryer, not over 2½ pounds, for this recipe, and the freshest, top-quality vegetables. The dish almost prepares itself once the chicken is browned and the vegetables are prepared. Use a large heavy skillet, a Dutch oven, or even a deep cast-iron pot, as long as it has a tight-fitting cover. You can cook this to the almost-done stage and then heat just before serving, a technique preferred so that you don't have to watch the clock after your guests have arrived.

2 tablespoons sweet (unsalted) butter

1 young frying chicken (about 2½ pounds) cut into serving pieces

3 zucchini, about 1½ inches in diameter and 6 inches long, cut in ¾-inch slices on the bias

4 ears fresh corn kernels cut off the cob, or 2½ cups frozen, defrosted

2 large, fresh red ripe tomatoes (1 pound each), parched, peeled, and cut into wedges

1 cup thin rounds of small white or yellow Spanish onions

3 garlic cloves, minced

1 jalapeño chile, about 2½ inches long, chopped

½ teaspoon cumin

Melt the butter over medium heat in a large heavy pot. Add the chicken, skin-side down, and turn frequently to brown evenly. When the chicken is browned, add the vegetables in layers—zucchini, corn, tomatoes, and onions. Sprinkle the garlic, jalapeño, and cumin over the top, cover, and steam, reducing heat to just maintain steaming. Check after 30 minutes to be certain all is cooking properly. (If cooking in advance, stop the cooking at this point before the vegetables are completely done.) Then continue to cook for about 30 minutes longer, or until vegetables are done.

To serve, place on a platter with the chicken encircled with the vegetables. For added zip and to suit a mixture of palates, from gringos to chile fire-eaters, serve a side dish of salsa fresca. Or add extra jalapeño to the original dish. Yields 6 servings.

(continued)

(continued)

SALSA FOR POLLO:

1 jalapeño, about 3 inches long,   2 slices (¼ inch thick) red
   finely chopped   Spanish onion, chopped
1 small red ripe tomato, chopped

Combine and serve in a small bowl with the chicken.

Fiestas for Four Seasons

Southwest Orange-Chile Chicken with Black Beans

2 tablespoons olive oil   ¾ cup chicken stock
1 whole chicken (3 to 4 pounds),   3 tablespoons hot chile sauce
   skinned and cut into serving   1¾ cups cooked black beans
   pieces   with 2 tablespoons liquid
1 large purple onion, halved   1 red bell pepper, cut into strips
   and thinly sliced   1 tablespoon dark rum
4 garlic cloves, minced   Salt and pepper to taste
1½ cups freshly squeezed   Chopped fresh cilantro
   orange juice

Heat oil in a large skillet over medium heat. Brown chicken on all sides in oil; remove to a plate lined with paper towels.

Sauté onion in pan drippings until limp and slightly browned, about 8 minutes. Add garlic, and sauté one minute. Return chicken to skillet, and add orange juice, stock, and chile sauce. Cover and simmer over low heat 30 minutes. Add black beans and liquid and bell pepper strips. Simmer, uncovered, 30 minutes. Add rum, salt, and pepper; simmer 15 minutes. Sprinkle with cilantro, and serve immediately. Makes 4-6 servings.

Savoring the Southwest Again

Chicken and Wild Rice

¾ cup Uncle Ben's Wild Rice, uncooked
4 cups chopped, cooked chicken
½ - 1 cup sherry
1 cup chicken broth
1 small onion, chopped
1 (8-ounce) can mushroom slices, drained
¼ cup butter or margarine, melted
1 (10-¾-ounce) can condensed cream of mushroom soup
1 (10-¾-ounce) can condensed cream of chicken soup
2 (10-ounce) packages frozen broccoli or asparagus spears, cooked and drained
1 cup (4 ounces) shredded Cheddar cheese

Cook wild rice according to package directions. Combine rice with chicken, sherry, broth, onion, mushroom slices, margarine, mushroom soup, and chicken soup. Spread half the rice mixture in a 9x13-inch pan. Top with broccoli. Evenly spread remaining rice mixture over all. Bake, uncovered, at 350° for 45 minutes, or until heated through. Sprinkle with cheese and bake an additional 5 minutes, or until cheese is melted.

The Eagle's Kitchen

Northern New Mexico is among the richest places in the world when it comes to culture and tradition. New Mexico has more Native Americans and a higher percentage of Hispanics than any other state. The three major cultural groups of the area are Pueblo, Spanish and Anglo. The original Indian civilization was blended with the Spanish, and this distinctive civilization was, in turn, influenced by the impact of the Anglos in the nineteenth century. This cultural heritage of modern New Mexico is unique among the fifty states and is evident in their unique cuisine.

Chicken Artichoke Casserole

1 (3-pound) chicken, cut into
  serving pieces
1½ teaspoons salt
¼ teaspoon pepper
½ teaspoon paprika
6 tablespoons butter, divided
1 (14-ounce) can artichoke
  hearts, drained

¼ pound fresh mushrooms,
  sliced
2 tablespoons flour
⅔ cup chicken broth
3 tablespoons sherry
¼ teaspoon rosemary

Sprinkle chicken with salt, pepper, and paprika. In skillet, brown chicken in 4 tablespoons of the butter and transfer to a 2-quart casserole. Arrange artichoke hearts between chicken pieces. Melt remaining butter in the skillet and in it, sauté mushrooms until barely tender. Sprinkle flour over mushrooms and stir in broth, sherry, and rosemary. Cook, stirring, until slightly thickened, then pour over chicken and artichoke hearts. Cover and bake in 375° oven for 40 minutes or until tender.

Families Cooking Together

Natural archway made of trees at La Ventana.

Ruidoso Winner

1 (8-ounce) package green
   spinach noodles
¼ cup butter
¼ cup flour
1 cup milk
1 cup chicken stock
1 pint sour cream
⅓ - ½ cup lemon juice
1 (6-ounce) can mushroom
   pieces and juice
2 teaspoons seasoned salt
1 teaspoon MSG (optional)
½ teaspoon nutmeg
2 teaspoons pepper
½ teaspoon cayenne pepper
   (optional)
1 teaspoon paprika
1 tablespoon parsley flakes
4 cups cooked chicken
½ cup toasted bread crumbs
Parmesan cheese

Cook noodles; drain. Melt butter in a large saucepan. Stir in flour. Add milk and chicken stock. Cook over low heat, stirring constantly until sauce thickens. To the cream sauce, add sour cream, lemon juice, mushrooms, seasoned salt, MSG, nutmeg, paprika, pepper, and parsley flakes. Mix well. Cut chicken into large bite-size pieces (4 cups). Butter a 3-quart casserole. Place drained noodles in casserole. Add layer of chicken. Pour some sauce over chicken. Sprinkle with bread crumbs and Parmesan cheese. Repeat layers, ending with cheese on top. Heat in 350° oven until bubbly, about 25 minutes. Can be made the night before and refrigerated. Bake at 325° for one hour. Serves 8-10.

Savoring the Southwest

A snowy mountain stream near Taos. Snowfall averages 30 to 40 inches per year in the northern mountainous areas, which makes skiing a popular sport in the European-style alpine village of Taos Ski Valley.

Crab Quiche Mexicano

Prepare this dish in advance and reheat, or because it can be held uncooked a few hours, assemble the quiche, go to the theater, and bake just before serving.

3 wheat tortillas, 8 to 9 inches in diameter
¼ cup sweet (unsalted) butter or lard
4 fresh green chiles, parched, peeled, and seeds removed
¾ cup each grated Monterey Jack and Cheddar cheeses, mixed
1 (6½-ounce) can flaked crab, or ¾ cup fresh or frozen
3 chopped green onions (scallions), including some of the tops

1 tablespoon chopped cilantro, optional
4 large eggs
1½ cups half-and-half
A few grinds of black pepper
½ teaspoon salt
¾ teaspoon caribe (crushed dried red chile)
2 or more green chiles, parched, peeled, deseeded, and chopped, optional
½ cup sour cream, optional

Select a shallow round cake pan that is the same diameter as the tortillas, so that a whole one will just fit in the bottom. Cut 2 of the tortillas so that the curved outside edge comes to the top of the baking pan. Cut enough to encircle the inside of the pan completely, usually five. Melt the butter or lard in a heavy skillet; fry all the tortillas until lightly browned on each side and drain on paper towels.

Arrange the whole fried tortilla in the bottom of the pan, then stand the cut pieces of tortilla around the rim of the baking pan, creating a crust. Place the whole green chiles in a smooth, uniform layer over the fried tortilla on the bottom of the baking pan. Top with one cup of the grated cheeses, the crab, scallions, and the cilantro (or the cilantro can be served on the side).

Beat the eggs with the half-and-half, pepper, and salt. Pour over the crab mixture, top with the remaining ½ cup of grated cheese, and sprinkle with the caribe. If baking later, cover and refrigerate. When ready to bake, place in a 375° oven for 30-40 minutes, or until puffed and lightly browned. Serve with additional green chiles and sour cream. Yields 6 servings.

Fiestas for Four Seasons

Crab Meat Quesadillas

1 cup fresh crab meat
½ cup sour cream
1 teaspoon lemon juice
3 green onions, chopped
1 (4-ounce) can chopped
  green chilies
1 heaping tablespoon cilantro,
  finely chopped
1 teaspoon chili powder
¼ teaspoon red pepper
1 jalapeño pepper, chopped
  (optional)
12 tortillas
1 cup Cheddar cheese, grated
1 cup Monterey Jack cheese,
  grated
1 egg white
1 tablespoon vegetable oil

In a bowl, combine the crab meat, sour cream, lemon juice, green onions, green chilies, cilantro, chili powder, red pepper, and jalapeño, if desired. Place 2 tablespoons of the mixture on a tortilla (small ones work better, easier to turn), spreading to ¾-inch of the edge. Top with a tablespoon of each of the cheeses. Brush the rim of the tortilla with egg white. Place a second tortilla on top and press to seal. Repeat. Heat vegetable oil in large skillet. Brown the tortillas on both sides to heat and melt the cheese. Cut into wedges. Serve with salsa, sour cream and/or guacamole.

Bon Appétit de Las Sandias

Shrimp Rellenos

Relleno is a Spanish word meaning "stuffed"; chiles rellenos are chiles that have been stuffed. Usually they are filled with cheese, but they can also be stuffed with meat or, as in this recipe, with seafood. This interesting variation on a traditional recipe can be used as an appetizer or as a main dish. Serve Shrimp Rellenos with your favorite salsa or with a fresh tomato and basil sauce.

2 quarts corn oil
4 fresh New Mexico green
　chiles
¾ pound fresh shrimp, in the
　shell
2 ounces Fontina cheese,
　grated
4 ounces Monterey Jack
　cheese, grated
½ cup fresh corn kernels

1 red bell pepper, roasted,
　peeled, and diced
3 tablespoons diced white onion
2 tablespoons chopped fresh
　marjoram
2 tablespoons chopped cilantro
4 eggs, whisked
1 cup medium-grain blue
　cornmeal

Heat oil in a deep-fryer to 375°. Deep-fry chiles for about 3 minutes, or until skin blisters. Place in a stainless steel bowl, cover with plastic wrap, and sweat for 20 minutes. Reserve oil and keep warm.

Grill or dry-roast the shrimp. (To dry-roast, cook briefly on a comal or in a heavy-bottomed skillet without any liquid or fat.) Peel shrimp and chop into large pieces. Combine in a large bowl with the cheeses, bell pepper, corn, onion, herbs, and mix well. Divide mixture into 4 portions. Gently peel chiles, cut a lengthwise slit in each, and carefully remove seeds. Stuff with shrimp mixture and roll gently between the fingers to close the opening.

Reheat oil to 375°. Dip the chiles in the whisked egg and then roll in the cornmeal. Deep-fry until exterior is dark blue, about 4-5 minutes.

For a lighter version, you can make the rellenos without frying them. Just heat the stuffed chiles in a 400° oven for about 20 minutes, taking care not to overcook the shrimp. Yields 4 servings.

The Great Chile Book

Spiedino Di Mare

1 pound medium shrimp
   (50 count)
½ cup virgin olive oil (or less)
Salt and pepper to taste

Seasoned bread crumbs
Lemon Butter Sauce
1 pound cooked pasta of your
   choice

Lightly brush peeled shrimp with oil and season with salt and pepper. Cover all sides with bread crumbs. Skewer shrimp and grill for about 3 minutes per side. Divide shrimp and pasta among 6 plates. Cover with Lemon Butter Sauce.

LEMON BUTTER SAUCE:

2 teaspoons finely chopped
   garlic
2 teaspoons finely chopped
   onion
1 ounce clarified butter

½ cup white wine
¼ cup lemon juice
½ cup (1 stick) cold unsalted
   butter
Salt and white pepper to taste

Sauté garlic and onion in clarified butter over medium heat until onions are soft. Add wine and lemon juice; turn the flame to high and reduce by three-fourths. Lower flame and slowly add cold butter one small pat at a time. Shake the pan continuously to blend the sauce. Add salt and pepper to taste.

Raspberry Enchantment House Tour Cookbook

Jerry's World Famous Baked Trout Recipe

Start by catching one monster trout, preferably fly-fishing. Clean the trout in the normal way. Lay the trout on aluminum foil and cut the trout on one side of the spine the whole length of the fish. This will allow you to lay the trout so both sides of the meat are laying flat. Now put 4 or 5 pats of butter on the trout. Next, sprinkle garlic powder, spike (an herbal blend), parsley, and basil on the fish. Last, squeeze fresh lemon all over the trout. Seal up the foil and bake the trout in the oven (350° for 35-50 minutes) or on the grill until done. Cooking time depends on the size of the trout and the temperature of the grill. If cooked on the grill, when the fish is almost done, open the foil and let the fish absorb the hickory or mesquite flavor from the coals.

Red River's Cookin'

Pan-Fried San Juan Trout

Sportsmen from around the world travel to northern New Mexico's San Juan River to fly-fish for trophy trout. This recipe will transform any fresh trout into award-winning dinner fare.

½ cup all-purpose flour, sifted
1 teaspoon Chimayó chile
   powder, or to taste
1 teaspoon salt
1 pinch freshly ground black
   pepper
8 small trout fillets, 3-4 ounces
   each, rinsed and dried

2 tablespoons vegetable oil
3-4 tablespoons unsalted butter,
   softened
¼ cup fresh parsley, chopped
1 tablespoon cilantro leaves,
   chopped
Juice of 2 lemons

Mix the sifted flour with the chile powder, salt, and pepper and spread out on a flat plate. Dredge the trout fillets in the flour, and lay out on a flat dish or baking rack.

Heat the vegetable oil to hot, but not smoking, in a heavy nonstick skillet. Pan fry the fillets in the hot oil for about one minute on each side, then add the softened butter and cook until the fillets are golden, another minute on each side. With a slotted spatula, remove the filets to 4 warmed plates. Toss the parsley, cilantro, and lemon juice into the skillet and whisk together 1 or 2 minutes until hot. Pour the sauce over the trout fillets, garnish with parsley and lemon wedges and serve. Serves 4.

Red Chile Bible

Salmon Loaf

1 large can red salmon
1½ cups cracker crumbs
1 can cream of celery soup

2 eggs, slightly beaten
1 small onion, minced

SAUCE:
½ cup milk

1 can celery soup

Mix all ingredients except sauce. Place in greased loaf pan and bake at 350° for 25-30 minutes until set. Cover with heated sauce before serving.

The Joy of Sharing

Soy Glazed Salmon with Orange Sauce

MARINADE:
½ cup soy sauce
Juice of 2 limes
Juice of 2 oranges

½ cup brown sugar
1 teaspoon fresh minced
   ginger

Whisk all ingredients together.

4 (6 to 8-ounce) salmon filets
1 pound fresh spinach leaves
   washed and stemmed

1 pint fresh raspberries
1 orange, sliced

Marinate salmon filets for 1-2 hours. Roast in 400° oven for 10-15 minutes. Divide spinach leaves onto 4 plates. Surround with Orange Sauce. Place roasted salmon on spinach. Garnish with orange slice and fresh raspberries.

ORANGE SAUCE:
¼ cup champagne vinegar
½ cup fresh orange juice
1 cup olive oil

1 teaspoon minced shallots
Salt and pepper to taste

Whisk together.
Contributed by The Artichoke Café, Albuquerque.

Raspberry Enchantment House Tour Cookbook

Lime Marinated Grilled Salmon

LIME MARINADE:

⅓ cup freshly squeezed
   lime juice
2 cups coarsely chopped
   onion
1½ teaspoons coarsely
   chopped garlic

2 large jalapeños, minced
1 bunch cilantro, coarsely
   chopped
1 tablespoon honey
1 teaspoon salt

Combine marinade ingredients in the work bowl of a food processor and pulse for 30 seconds. Taste and adjust seasoning.

2 pounds salmon fillets,
   cut in 4 to 5-ounce portions

Salt and pepper to taste

Pour half the marinade over the bottom of a glass or stainless steel baking dish. Place the fillets on the marinade and pour the remaining marinade to cover the fillets. Marinate for at least one hour at room temperature or refrigerate overnight.

Wipe the marinade from the salmon, sprinkle the fish with salt and pepper to taste, and grill the salmon to desired doneness. Yields 6-8 servings.

The Santa Fe School of Cooking Cookbook

A highway snakes lazily around rocky buttes toward northern New Mexico's haunting horizon.

Mexico City Earthquake Cake

The finished cake will have cracks and crevices.

1 cup coconut
1 cup chopped pecans
1 box German chocolate cake mix
½ cup soft margarine

1 (8-ounce) package cream cheese
1 teaspoon vanilla
1 (16-ounce) package powdered sugar

Spray a 9x13-inch baking pan. Layer coconut and pecans. Prepare cake mix according to package directions; pour over coconut and nut mixture. Mix margarine, cream cheese, vanilla, and powdered sugar. Spoon over cake batter. Bake in preheated 350° oven for 40-50 minutes.

Good Sam Celebrates 15 Years of Love

Elephant Butte is the state's largest lake with 35-40,000 surface acres and a length of about 40 miles.

Cherry-Pineapple Cake

1 large can cherry pie filling
1 large can crushed pineapple
and juice

¾ box yellow cake mix
1 stick oleo, chipped
Walnuts, if desired

Layer ingredients as listed. Sprinkle walnuts on top and bake in a well greased 9x13-inch pan for 30 minutes at 350°.

Amistad Community Recipes

Norwegian Apple Pie Cake

1 cup sugar
½ cup butter, room
temperature
1 egg
1 cup flour
¼ teaspoon salt
1 teaspoon baking soda

1 teaspoon nutmeg
1 teaspoon cinnamon
2½ cups diced, unpeeled
apples
½ cup chopped pecans
2 tablespoons hot water

Preheat the oven to 325°. Combine the sugar and butter in a large mixing bowl. Add the egg and beat until well blended. Next, add the dry ingredients. Mix in the apples and nuts, then stir in the hot water. Bake in a greased 9-inch pie pan for 40 minutes. Serve warm with Rum Sauce. Serves 6-8.

RUM SAUCE:
½ cup brown sugar
½ cup cream (or half-
and-half)

¼ cup rum
½ cup whipped, heavy cream
(optional)

In a small saucepan, combine the brown sugar and cream over low heat. Stir constantly. Add the rum slowly when the cream mixture begins to thicken. This sauce should be the consistency of heavy cream. Drizzle over warm Apple Pie Cake. For added richness, whip ½ cup heavy cream and spoon the whipped cream on top of the cake before drizzling the Rum Sauce.

A Painter's Kitchen

Bavarian Apple Torte

CRUST:

½ cup butter
⅓ cup sugar

¼ teaspoon vanilla
1 cup flour

Combine butter, sugar, vanilla, and flour; cut with a pastry blender until crumbly. Pat firmly onto bottom and 1½ inches up sides of 9-inch springform pan.

FILLING:

1 (8-ounce) package cream
  cheese
¼ cup sugar

1 egg
½ teaspoon vanilla

Beat cheese and sugar till smooth. Add egg and vanilla; blend well. Pour onto crust; spread to edges.

TOPPING:

4 cups thinly sliced apples,
  peeled, cored
¼ cup slivered almonds

⅓ cup sugar
½ teaspoon cinnamon

Combine apples and almonds; mix in sugar and cinnamon; toss well to coat apples. Pour over cheese mixture. Bake at 450° for 10 minutes. Reduce heat to 400° and bake 25 minutes more. Loosen torte from rim of pan; cool before removing from pan. Serves 8-10.

Recipes from the Cotton Patch

Applesauce Cake

¼ cup butter
2 cups sugar
2 eggs
2½ cups all-purpose flour
2 teaspoons baking soda
1 teaspoon salt
1 teaspoon ground cinnamon

½ teaspoon ground nutmeg
¼ teaspoon ground allspice
1½ cups Homemade
  Applesauce
½ cup raisins
½ cup chopped pecans

Preheat oven to 350°. Cream butter and sugar together. Lightly beat the eggs and add to the sugar mixture. Mix dry ingredients together and stir into the mixture. Add Homemade Applesauce, raisins and nuts and stir well. Pour into a well-greased 9x13-inch baking pan and bake for 45 minutes or until the cake tests done.

In Billy the Kid's day, they didn't run to the store to buy applesauce, they made it at home. It's easy to do and tastes better.

HOMEMADE APPLESAUCE:
12 medium tart apples
Water
1 tablespoon lemon juice

½ cup sugar
1 tablespoon grated orange peel
½ teaspoon salt

Wash, peel and core apples. Coarsely chop apples and place in a large nonreactive saucepan. Barely cover apples with cold water, add lemon juice, and bring to a boil. Cover and cook over low heat about 45 minutes or until the apples are tender. Add sugar, orange peel and salt, and stir well. Cook for another 5 minutes. Let mixture cool and then mash or blend in a blender. Store in the refrigerator until ready to use or serve. Yields approximately 3 cups.

Billy the Kid Cook Book

Strawberry Meringue Cake

1 package yellow cake mix
1⅓ cups orange juice
4 egg yolks
1½ teaspoons grated orange
   peel
4 egg whites

¼ teaspoon cream of tartar
1 cup sugar
1 quart fresh strawberries,
   divided
2 tablespoons sugar
2 cups heavy whipping cream

Combine cake mix, orange juice, egg yolks, and orange peel; beat 4 minutes at medium speed of electric mixer. Pour into 2 greased and floured 9-inch round pans. Beat egg whites with cream of tartar to soft peaks; gradually add the one cup sugar, beating to stiff peaks. Spread meringue over batter evenly. Bake at 350° for 35 minutes. Cool. Remove from pans, meringue side up.

Mash ½ cup strawberries with 2 tablespoons sugar; add cream, whip till stiff. Add sugar to whipped cream as desired. To assemble cake, spread ½ of cream mixture over bottom meringue. Reserve 2 cups whole berries; slice remainder and place over cream mixture. Add top layer; garnish with remaining cream mixture and reserved berries.

Recipes from the Cotton Patch

During the Albuquerque International Balloon Fiesta, most flights last from one to two hours, and flight distances are generally 3 to 12 miles. Hot air balloons have flown as high as 53,000 feet (occupants, of course, require oxygen), but Balloon Fiesta flights rarely exceed 2,000 feet above ground level.

Rum Cake

4 eggs, beaten until frothy
½ cup oil
½ cup water
½ cup light rum

1 white or yellow cake mix
1 package instant vanilla
   pudding
½ cup pecans

Mix eggs, oil, water, and light rum. Add cake mix and pudding. Mix well. Put pecans in bottom of greased and floured bundt pan; pour mixture on top. Bake in 325° oven for 55 minutes.

ICING:

1 stick butter
1 cup sugar

¼ cup water
¼ cup rum

Boil butter, sugar, and water until thickened. Add rum. Pour over cake as it comes out of oven (poke holes in top, if desired). Let stand 15 minutes. Invert and serve.

Recipes for Rain or Shine

Eclair Cake

1 cup water
1 stick margarine
1 cup flour
4 eggs
1 large package vanilla instant
   pudding

1 (8-ounce) package cream
   cheese
1 (8-ounce) tub Cool Whip
Hershey's syrup

Heat water and margarine. Add flour, stir. Add eggs, one at a time; beat well. Spread in a 9x13-inch greased pan. Bake at 400° for 30 minutes. (Don't mind how it looks); cool. Fix instant pudding according to directions on box, then add cream cheese and beat thoroughly. Pour on cake. Top with Cool Whip. Drizzle with Hershey's syrup. Cut in 16-20 servings.

Saint Joseph's Really Grande Cookbook

Blueberry Sour Cream Pound Cake

1 cup butter or margarine
2½ cups sugar
6 eggs or egg substitute
  equivalent
3¼ cups flour
¼ teaspoon baking soda

⅔ cup light sour cream or
  plain yogurt
½ teaspoon vanilla
½ cup milk
1 cup blueberries

Let all ingredients reach room temperature, if possible. Preheat oven to 325°. Grease and flour 2 large or 3 medium loaf pans. Cream butter and sugar. Add eggs one at a time, beating well after each. Sift flour with baking soda. Add 2 cups of the flour and mix alternately with sour cream. Add vanilla, remaining flour mixture and milk. Fold in blueberries. Pour batter into prepared pans. Bake large loaf pans for 1 hour and 15 minutes, or medium loaf pans for 1 hour.

Families Cooking Together

Durgin-Parks Blueberry Tea Cake

3 cups sifted flour
¾ teaspoon salt
4 teaspoons baking powder
¾ cup sugar
2 eggs, well blended

2 tablespoons melted butter
1½ cups milk
½ cup blueberries
¼ to ⅓ cup flour

Butter a 9x13-inch pan. Dust with flour. Resift the 3 cups of flour with salt and baking powder. Mix sugar and eggs well. Add flour mixture, melted butter, and milk. Mix only enough to moisten all ingredients. Batter will be slightly lumpy. Sprinkle the ¼ to ⅓ cup flour over the berries. Immediately add the floured berries to the batter. Mix lightly. Pour into pan and bake about 30 minutes in 350° oven.

The Eagle's Kitchen

Los Alamos has the distinction of being the site of the world's first atomic bomb explosion (1945). The Bradbury Science Museum there allows visitors to look into the history of nuclear energy.

22-Minute Cake

CAKE:

2 cups flour
2 cups sugar
1 stick margarine, softened
1 cup water
½ cup shortening
3½ tablespoons cocoa

½ cup buttermilk
2 eggs
1 teaspoon baking soda
1 teaspoon vanilla
1 heaping teaspoon instant
   coffee

Do not use mixer. Combine flour and sugar in large bowl. In a saucepan, combine and bring to a boil the margarine, water, shortening, and cocoa; pour over flour and sugar mixture. Combine buttermilk, eggs, soda, vanilla and coffee and add to the mixture and mix all together. Pour into a 12x7-inch greased pan and bake 20 minutes at 400°.

ICING:

1 stick margarine
3½ tablespoons cocoa
⅓ cup milk
1 pound powdered sugar

1 cup chopped pecans
1 heaping tablespoon instant
   coffee

When cake has baked for 18 minutes, combine in saucepan the margarine, cocoa, and milk. Bring to a boil. Add the powdered sugar, nuts, and coffee. Pour over cake when removed from oven.

Recipes for Rain or Shine

Heavenly Chocolate Cake

2 squares unsweetened
  chocolate
¼ cup boiling water
¼ cup tequila
2 eggs, well beaten
1½ cups sugar
½ cup butter, room temperature

Pinch salt
1 teaspoon vanilla
¾ cup buttermilk
1 teaspoon baking soda
1½ cups all-purpose flour

Preheat oven to 375°. Put chocolate, water, and tequila in a saucepan and cook over low heat until chocolate is melted. Let cool, then stir the eggs into the chocolate mixture. Cream sugar and butter together and stir into the chocolate and egg mixture. Add salt, vanilla, buttermilk, baking soda, and flour and stir until blended, but do not over beat. Pour into 2 lightly greased and floured 8-inch-round cake pans. Bake in a 375° oven for 45 minutes or until a toothpick comes out clean when inserted in the center. Let the cake cool in the pans on a wire rack. Remove from the pans and frost with Tequila Frosting.

TEQUILA FROSTING:
½ cup butter or margarine,
  room temperature
½ teaspoon salt
2½ cups powdered sugar

½ teaspoon vanilla
1 tablespoon Grand Marnier
3-4 tablespoons tequila

Cream butter, salt, and sugar together. Add vanilla and Grand Marnier. Then slowly add tequila until the frosting is a spreadable consistency. Spread smoothly over cake.

The Tequila Cook Book

Gallup is the only large settlement in the Southwest that still hosts, in any significant number, the unique mercantile tradition of trading post. Located between the Navajo and Zuni reservations, the town has 110 trading posts, shops and galleries, making it the undisputed Southwestern center for original, authentic Native American arts and crafts. In August of each year the Inter-Tribal Ceremony attracts upwards of 50,000 visitors, making it one of the largest annual events in the Southwest. Permanent grandstands built against towering red rock formations create an unforgettable amphitheater for the event.

Decadent Chocolate Cake

¾ cup butter, softened
2 cups sugar
2 eggs, separated
1 teaspoon vanilla
1 cup sour cream
1 teaspoon baking soda
1 package powdered whipped
    topping mix

2 cups flour
¾ cup cocoa
1 teaspoon baking powder
1 (3-ounce) package chocolate
    fudge pudding mix
1¼ cups half-and-half

Cream butter and sugar; add egg yolks and vanilla. Beat one minute on high speed; set aside. Beat egg whites until soft peaks form; fold into sour cream; add baking soda and whipped topping mix. Add sour cream mixture to butter mixture. Mix flour, cocoa, baking powder, and pudding mix. Add alternately with half-and-half and butter mixture. Beat two minutes on high. Pour into two greased and lightly floured 8-inch pans. Bake at 350° for 35-40 minutes.

CREAMY CHOCOLATE FROSTING:

6 tablespoons butter,
    softened
¾ cup cocoa

3 cups powdered sugar
⅓ cup half-and-half
1 teaspoon vanilla

Cream butter; add cocoa and sugar alternately with cream and vanilla. With electric mixer, beat until smooth. When cake is done, cool in pans for 10 minutes. Remove to wire rack to complete cooling. Frost.

Beyond Loaves and Fishes

Cinnamon Carob Tunnel Cake

A moist carob n' cinnamon center makes this bundt cake irresistible!

½ cup vegetable oil
½ cup butter or margarine,
  room temperature
1 teaspoon vanilla extract
1 teaspoon lemon extract
1⅔ cups sugar
3 eggs
1½ cups all-purpose flour
1 cup whole wheat flour

½ teaspoon ground
  cinnamon
¾ teaspoon baking soda
½ teaspoon baking powder
Dash salt
1 cup buttermilk
½ cup raisins
1 cup Carob Syrup

Preheat oven to 350°. In large mixing bowl cream oil and butter till smooth. Blend in extracts, sugar, and eggs; beat till light. In separate bowl combine dry ingredients; stir dry mixture together to mix. Add ½ of dry mixture to the creamed mixture in mixing bowl; blend mixtures together while adding ½ the buttermilk. Repeat with remaining dry ingredients and buttermilk. Beat one minute. Stir in raisins. Grease and flour 10-inch bundt pan. Remove 1½ cups of batter; reserve. Pour remaining batter into prepared pan.

Prepare Carob Syrup. Add syrup to reserved batter; stir to mix. Carefully pour over cake batter in pan. Using a knife or handle of wooden spoon, slice through top of batter in center. Go around pan twice. Do not marble. Bake in 350° oven 55-65 minutes or till test done in center. Cool in pan 10-15 minutes. Remove to rack to cool. Drizzle with thin lemon icing, or sprinkle top with powdered sugar. Yields 1 (10-inch) bundt cake.

CAROB SYRUP:
½ cup carob powder
¼ cup maple syrup
¼ cup water

½ teaspoon ground cinnamon
¼ teaspoon ground cloves
¼ teaspoon baking soda

Mix all ingredients together with fork till smooth.

Carob Cookbook

Pumpkin Cheesecake

The use of pumpkins and squash is centuries old in New Mexico, and this recipe gives a new twist to an old favorite.

CRUST:

¾ cup graham cracker crumbs
2 tablespoons sugar

2 tablespoons melted butter

Preheat the oven to 350°. Combine the cracker crumbs, sugar, and butter thoroughly. Press the mixture into the bottom of a 9-inch springform pan. Chill in the refrigerator for 15 minutes.

CHEESECAKE:

1½ pounds cream cheese, at
   room temperature
1½ cups sugar
4 large eggs
¾ cup canned solid-pack
   pumpkin

2 teaspoons ground cannèlla, or
   1 teaspoon ground cinnamon
1 tablespoon Mexican vanilla
Whipped cream for garnish

In a mixer with a paddle attachment, whip the cream cheese and sugar until light and fluffy. Add the eggs and the pumpkin, and continue beating until the mixture is smooth. Add the cannèlla and vanilla and incorporate thoroughly. Pour the cream cheese mixture into the prepared crust and bake for approximately one hour, or until the cheesecake is set all the way through. Turn off the oven and let the cake sit for 15 minutes. Remove the cake from the oven and chill. Top with whipped cream. Yields 10-12 servings.

The Santa Fe School of Cooking Cookbook

The yucca is the state flower of New Mexico. Early settlers called the yucca "our Lord's candles." Another flower seems to be more popular, however. The colorful hollyhock, seen around most New Mexico homes, is more so the flower of the people.

Mexican Cake

1 (20-ounce) can crushed
   pineapple, undrained
1 cup flour
1 teaspoon baking soda

2 eggs
2 cups sugar
Pinch of salt
1 cup chopped pecans

Put all ingredients into mixing bowl. Mix with spoon. Pour into 9x13-inch pan and bake at 350° for 35-45 minutes.

FROSTING:
4 (3-ounce) packages cream
   cheese

1 stick melted oleo
1 teaspoon vanilla

Frost cake while still hot. Cover with foil.

Our Best Home Cooking

Chocolate-Chocolate Cake

1 (8-ounce) package cream
   cheese
1 cup sour cream
½ cup coffee flavored liqueur
2 eggs

1 (2-layer) chocolate cake mix
1 (4-ounce) package chocolate
   Jell-O instant pudding mix
1 cup semisweet chocolate chips
Sifted powdered sugar

Beat cream cheese and blend in sour cream, liqueur and eggs. Add cake mix and pudding mix. Fold in chocolate chips. Bake for 1 hour and 5 minutes at 325°. Cool completely and then sprinkle with powdered sugar. Serves 8-10.

Good Sam Celebrates 15 Years of Love

For nine days each October, the New Mexico skies are painted brilliant colors as hundreds of hot-air balloons participate in the Albuquerque International Balloon Fiesta. It has become the world's most photographed event.

Adobe Bars

Delicious warm or cold, these chewy bars have a rich brown topping that looks like New Mexico adobe.

¼ cup shortening
¼ cup butter
1 cup sugar
1 whole egg
2 eggs, separated
1½ cups flour
1 teaspoon baking powder

¼ teaspoon salt
1 cut nuts, chopped
½ cup semisweet chocolate
  pieces
1 cup miniature marshmallows
1 cup light brown sugar, packed

Preheat oven to 350°. Cream shortening, butter and sugar. Beat in the whole egg and 2 egg yolks. Sift flour, baking powder, and salt together; combine the 2 mixtures and blend thoroughly. Spread batter in a greased 9x13-inch pan. Sprinkle nuts, chocolate pieces and marshmallows over the batter. Beat 2 egg whites stiff; fold in brown sugar. Spread over top of cake. Bake 35 minutes. Cool and then cut into bars. Makes 32 bars.

Simply Simpatico

Favorite Decadence Layer Bars

"What takes minutes to make, combines my guests' favorite cookie ingredients and disappears in seconds? Why, Decadence Layer Bars, of course," comments innkeeper Julie Cahalane.

½ cup butter
2 cups graham cracker crumbs
1 cup (7-ounces) coconut
1 (12-ounce) package
   semisweet chocolate chips

2 cups chopped pecans
1 (14-ounce) can sweetened
   condensed milk

Preheat oven to 350°. While the oven preheats, melt the butter in a 9x13-inch pan. One layer at a time, sprinkle the graham cracker crumbs, coconut, chocolate chips, and pecans over the melted butter. Pour sweetened condensed milk over all. Bake for 30 minutes. Cool and cut into squares. Makes 18 large bars.

Inn on the Rio's Favorite Recipes

Pumpkin Squares

1 cup flour
½ cup quick oats
½ cup brown sugar
½ cup margarine
1 (1-pound) can pumpkin
1 (12-ounce) can evaporated
   milk

2 eggs
¾ cup sugar
½ teaspoon salt
1 teaspoon cinnamon
½ cup chopped nuts
½ cup brown sugar
2 tablespoons margarine

Combine the first 4 ingredients in a mixing bowl. Mix until crumbly. Press into an ungreased 9x13x2-inch pan. Bake at 350° for 15 minutes. Combine pumpkin, milk, eggs, sugar, salt, and cinnamon. Mix well and pour into crust. Bake at 350° for 20 minutes. Combine nuts, brown sugar, and margarine; sprinkle over pumpkin filling. Return to oven for 15-20 minutes. Serve with a scoop of Cool Whip.

Amistad Community Recipes

Lemon Squares

CRUST:

2 cups flour
½ cup powdered sugar

1 cup oleo, softened

Mix well and spread in a 9x13-inch pan.

FILLING:

4 eggs, beaten (do not overbeat)
3 tablespoons flour
1 teaspoon baking powder

Grated rind and juice of 2 lemons
2 cups sugar
Powdered sugar

Mix all ingredients except powdered sugar together and pour over crust. Bake 20 minutes at 350°. Sprinkle with powdered sugar. While still warm, cut into squares.

Recipes for Rain or Shine

Carob Cherry Bon Bons

Crunchy nut coating and a cherry in the middle; these cookies are great after dinner with coffee.

1 cup softened butter or margarine
¾ cup brown sugar
1 egg
1 teaspoon vanilla extract
½ teaspoon almond extract
1 cup all-purpose flour

¾ cup whole wheat flour
⅓ cup carob powder
¾ teaspoon baking soda
Dash salt
33 maraschino cherries, cut in half
1 cup finely chopped almonds

Preheat oven to 350°. Beat butter and sugar till light. Add egg and extracts; blend in. Stir in flours, carob powder, soda, and salt. Cover and chill one hour.

Wrap teaspoons full of chilled dough around each cherry half. Place finely chopped almonds in shallow dish; roll each cookie ball in nuts to coat. Place on lightly greased cookie sheet, 2 inches apart. Bake in 350° oven 10-12 minutes or till very lightly browned. Yields 65 cookies.

Carob Cookbook

Nanaimo Bars

½ cup butter	1 egg
¼ cup sugar	2 cups graham cracker crumbs
5 tablespoons cocoa powder	1 cup flaked coconut
1 teaspoon vanilla	½ cup chopped nuts

Place ½ cup butter, sugar, cocoa, vanilla, and egg into top of double boiler. Place over hot water; cook, stirring, until mixture is of custard consistency. Remove from heat and stir in crumbs, coconut, and nuts; blend well. Pack mixture into a buttered 9-inch square pan.

ICING:

½ cup butter	2 cups powdered sugar
3 tablespoons milk	
2 tablespoons vanilla pudding mix (instant)	

Cream butter; blend milk and pudding powder and stir in. Add powdered sugar; mix until smooth and creamy. Spread over cookie base. Refrigerate until firm, about 15 minutes.

TOPPING:

4 squares semisweet chocolate	1 tablespoon butter

Melt chocolate and butter. Spread over vanilla layer. Refrigerate until firm; cut in squares.

A Fork in the Road

Gypsy Raspberry Brownies

¾ cup melted butter
1½ cups sugar
2 teaspoons vanilla
3 eggs, slightly beaten

¾ cup flour
½ cup unsweetened cocoa
½ teaspoon baking powder
½ teaspoon salt

Cream butter, sugar, and vanilla. Beat in eggs. In another bowl, stir together flour, cocoa, baking powder, and salt with fork. Blend dry ingredients into egg mixture. Do not over beat. Spread batter into ungreased 8-inch square baking pan.

FILLING:

1 (8-ounce) package cream
   cheese, softened
1 egg
½ teaspoon baking powder

1 tablespoon sugar
1 (12-ounce) jar raspberry
   preserves
Powdered sugar

Combine cream cheese, egg, baking powder, and sugar thoroughly. Swirl (use back of spoon to make trenches) cream cheese mixture and raspberry preserves through chocolate batter before baking. Bake 50-60 minutes in oven preheated to 350° until brownie pulls away from edges of pan. Cool completely. Dust with powdered sugar and cut into squares.

Raspberry Enchantment House Tour Cookbook

Polvorones
(Crumb Cookies)

1 cup soft margarine
½ cup powdered sugar
2¼ cups flour

¼ teaspoon salt
1 teaspoon vanilla
Powdered sugar

Cream margarine and sugar in a medium-size mixing bowl. Add flour, salt, and vanilla, and work mixture into moderately thick dough. Cover and chill dough for approximately 2 hours. Shape dough into balls approximately 1 inch in diameter. Bake Polvorones on a greased baking sheet in a 400° oven for 15-20 minutes, or until cookies are lightly browned. Roll baked cookies in powdered sugar while still warm. Freezes well. Yields 5 dozen.

Cocinas de New Mexico

Biscochitos

This is New Mexico's traditional cookie.

6 cups flour
3 teaspoons baking powder
¼ teaspoon salt
1 pound (2 cups) lard
1½ cups sugar

2 teaspoons anise seeds
2 eggs
¼ cup brandy
¼ cup sugar
1 tablespoon cinnamon

Sift flour with baking powder and salt. Cream lard with sugar and anise seeds until fluffy. Beat in eggs one at a time. Mix in flour and brandy until well blended. Turn dough out on floured board and pat or roll to ¼ or ½-inch thickness. Cut into shapes. (The fleur-de-lis is traditional.) Dust with mixture of sugar and cinnamon. Bake 10 minutes at 350° or until browned.

The Best from New Mexico Kitchens

Orange Biscotti

The addition of orange juice and tequila to this classic Italian cookie makes this a perfect pastry to serve with after-dinner coffee or at teatime.

1 cup sugar
½ cup butter, at room
   temperature
2 eggs, lightly beaten
2 tablespoons tequila
2 tablespoons orange juice

1 teaspoon grated orange peel
2½ cups all-purpose flour
2 teaspoons baking powder
¼ teaspoon salt
⅓ cup slivered almonds

Mix sugar and butter together, then add eggs, tequila, orange juice, orange peel and beat. Stir in flour, baking powder and salt. Then stir in the almonds. Place the mixture on a lightly floured pastry board and knead until the dough makes a ball—approximately 5-6 minutes. Divide dough into two halves and roll the halves into a rope about the length of a cookie sheet. Place each rope on an ungreased cooking sheet and bake in a 325° oven for 20-30 minutes or until golden brown. Remove from the baking sheet and let cool for 6-7 minutes. Slice diagonally to ½-inch pieces, lay the pieces flat on the cookie sheet and bake in a 325° oven for 5 minutes. Turn over and bake for 5 more minutes. Let cool to room temperature and store in a covered container. Makes approximately 3 dozen.

The Tequila Cook Book

Viennese Crescents

¼ cup unsalted butter (room temperature)
¼ cup sugar
¼ cup skim milk
1 tablespoon vanilla extract
1 teaspoon almond extract
1½ cups flour
1 cup (4 ounces) ground almonds
Confectioners' sugar

Heat oven to 325°. Have cookie sheets ready. Beat butter and sugar in a medium-sized bowl with electric mixer until light in color. Beat in milk and extracts (mixture will look curdled). Gradually add flour until blended. With fingers, knead in almonds. Shape rounded teaspoonfuls of dough into 1½-inch long logs. Taper ends then bend into crescent shapes. Place 1 inch apart on ungreased cookie sheets. Bake 20-25 minutes until cookies are golden brown. Remove to rack to cool completely. Sprinkle warm cookies with confectioners' sugar sifted through strainer. Store in airtight container.

The Eagle's Kitchen

Clouds

A light, practically fat free, meringue cookie. Clouds make excellent use of extra egg whites and are loved for their delicate texture and just the right amount of chocolate.

4 egg whites, room temperature
¼ teaspoon cream of tartar
1 cup sugar
Dash salt
½ teaspoon vanilla extract
1 (12-ounce) package chocolate chips

Preheat oven to 325°. With an electric mixer, beat the egg whites and cream of tartar until stiff. Gradually add the sugar, salt, and vanilla extract. Fold in the chocolate chips. Drop dough by tablespoonfuls onto brown paper bag which has been placed on a standard cookie sheet. Bake for 20 minutes. Turn oven off and keep cookies in the oven for another 20 minutes. Store in an airtight container. Makes 4 dozen "Clouds."

Inn on the Rio's Favorite Recipes

Mandazis

6½ cups flour
2 tablespoons baking powder
¾ cup sugar

½ cup water
2 eggs

Combine flour and baking powder. Dissolve sugar in water. Mix with dry ingredients. Add eggs and knead. Let rise at least 30 minutes (overnight is fine). Make about 3 balls and roll out to desired thinness (the thinner they are, the more they puff up). Cut up like sopapillas. Fry in deep oil until golden brown.

Mrs. Noah's Survival Guide

Mexican Honey Dainties

⅓ cup cooking oil
½ cup unsalted butter, softened
⅓ cup sugar
1 tablespoon orange juice
1 teaspoon baking powder

½ teaspoon baking soda
1¾ - 2 cups all-purpose flour
¾ cup sugar
½ cup water
⅓ cup honey
⅓ cup pecans, finely chopped

In mixer bowl, beat together cooking oil and butter until blended. Beat in the sugar. Add orange juice, baking powder, and baking soda. Mix well. Add enough of the flour, a little at a time, to make a medium-soft dough. Shape dough into 2-inch ovals and place on an ungreased baking sheet. Bake in 350° preheated oven for 20-25 minutes or until cookies are golden.

Meanwhile, in a saucepan, combine sugar, water, and honey. Boil gently uncovered for 5 minutes. Cool. Dip face of cookies into warm syrup and then press into chopped nuts. Let dry. Store in covered container or freeze for later use. Yields 2½ - 3 dozen.

Fiesta Mexicana

Peanut Butter Cookies

1 cup sifted flour
½ teaspoon soda
¼ teaspoon salt
½ cup shortening
½ cup packed brown sugar

½ cup granulated sugar
1 egg
½ cup peanut butter
1 tablespoon water
½ teaspoon vanilla

Sift together flour, soda, and salt. Set aside. Beat for 2 minutes shortening, brown sugar, granulated sugar, egg, peanut butter, water, and vanilla. Add sifted flour mixture; beat one minute. Drop by teaspoonfuls on a greased cookie sheet and press lightly with a fork dipped in flour. Bake at 325° for 15-20 minutes. Makes 3½ dozen cookies.

Peanut Palate Pleasers from Portales

Four Corners Monument is the only point in the US where four states touch: New Mexico, Arizona, Colorado and Utah.

Mexican Wedding Cakes

This traditional holiday cookie is rich and delicious. "Nothing makes the inn smell as warm and wonderful as a batch of Mexican Wedding Cakes baking in the oven," comments innkeeper Julie Cahalane. "My guests can't wait to enjoy them."

2 cups butter, softened
1 cup powdered sugar
2 teaspoons vanilla extract
4½ cups flour

½ teaspoon salt
2 cups chopped pecans
Additional powdered sugar

Preheat oven to 325°. Grease cookie sheets.

With an electric mixer, cream the butter, powdered sugar, and vanilla. Beat in the flour, salt, and pecans. Roll stiff dough into bite-sized balls. Place 8 across and 9 down on a cookie sheet. Bake for 20 minutes. After cooling for 5 minutes, roll still-warm cookies in a bowl of powdered sugar. Allow to cool. Roll again to cover completely. Makes 6 dozen cookies.

Inn on the Rio's Favorite Recipes

Mexican Pecan Candy

¾ cup milk
2 cups sugar
½ teaspoon soda

1½ teaspoons vanilla
1½ cups nuts
1 tablespoon butter

Mix milk, sugar, and soda in large saucepan. Cook until soft ball stage. Add vanilla, nuts, and butter. (Will turn golden brown while cooking.) Beat until creamy. Drop to form patties on salted waxed paper.

Recipes for Rain or Shine

Georgia O'Keeffe, renowned artist, fell in love with New Mexico on her first visit and remained there until her death at the age of 98. The Georgia O'Keeffe Museum in Santa Fe features the largest repository of her work in the world.

Chocolate Pecan Toffee

1 cup (2 sticks) butter
1⅓ cups granulated sugar
3 tablespoons water
1 tablespoon corn syrup

1 cup pecans
8 ounces semisweet or
   bittersweet chocolate

Butter a 9x13-inch pan and set aside. Melt the butter in a heavy saucepan. Add sugar, water, and corn syrup; place a candy thermometer in the pan. Cook at a low boil, stirring occasionally. When the mixture reaches 300°, quickly add the pecans. Swirl the pan vigorously, and pour the mixture into the buttered pan. Spread the candy out when cool, invert onto waxed paper and wipe away any excess butter from the bottom side.

   Melt the chocolate over hot water. Spread on the smooth bottom side of toffee and let harden. Break candy into pieces and refrigerate. Can also be made with coarsely chopped macadamia nuts. Yields 2 pounds.

The Very Special Raspberry Cookbook

Best in the World Peanut Brittle

Oh! So good!

1 cup white corn syrup
2 cups white sugar
½ cup water
2 cups raw peanuts

2 teaspoons margarine
2 teaspoons vanilla
2 teaspoons soda
½ teaspoon salt

Place syrup, sugar, and water in iron skillet and cook to soft ball stage (230°). Add raw peanuts. Stir and cook these ingredients on medium-high to the crack stage (301° - 302°), stirring constantly. Turn off heat. Stir in margarine, vanilla, soda, and salt until well blended. This will want to foam over. Keep stirring fast until well blended. Pour into large platter that is well buttered. As soon as possible, start pulling over the edges of platter. Work on Formica or tile counter. You can't pull this out thin until it reaches the right temperature. (If it's too hot, it will not be clear, so just keep working with it.) You can make it as thin as you like, and break it into pieces.

Peanut Palate Pleasers from Portales

Torreon, a tower built in the 1850s, is one of Lincoln's earliest structures. Its thick walls protected Spanish-American sharpshooters against the Apaches during the Lincoln County War.

Red Hot Apple Crepes

½ cup sugar
2 cups water
½ cup red hot cinnamon
   candies
4 large apples, peeled, cored
   and sliced thin
2 (3-ounce) packages cream
   cheese, softened

¼ cup finely chopped
   walnuts
¼ cup milk
12 prepared crepes
2 tablespoons cornstarch
2 tablespoons water

In saucepan, bring sugar and water to boil. Add candies and stir until completely melted. Add apples. Cover and simmer for 5-10 minutes or until tender. Let apples stand in syrup until deep pink, turning if necessary until uniform in color. Meanwhile, mix cream cheese, walnuts, and milk until blended. Spread on crepes. With slotted spoon, remove apples from syrup and lay apples over cream cheese mixture and roll up. Stir blended cornstarch and water into remaining syrup. Cook and stir until thickened and translucent. Return any leftover apple slices to syrup and spoon over crepes. Serve warm or cold. Yields 12 servings.

Bon Appétit de Las Sandias

Pear-Raspberry Cobbler

½ cup sugar or Sugar Twin
2½ tablespoons flour
⅛ teaspoon cinnamon
⅛ teaspoon nutmeg

2½ pounds firm pears,
   sliced (5 or 6)
1 tablespoon lemon juice
1 cup raspberries, fresh or frozen

Preheat oven to 350°. Halve and core pears. Combine sugar, flour, spices, and sliced pears in this mix. Add lemon juice and raspberries. Mix and spoon into 2-quart baking dish.

TOPPING:

¾ cup flour
1 tablespoon plus 1 teaspoon
   sugar or Sugar Twin
¾ teaspoon baking powder

¼ teaspoon soda
¼ teaspoon salt
3 tablespoons cold butter
¼ cup non-fat buttermilk

Combine flour, one tablespoon sugar, baking powder, soda, and salt. Cut butter into small pieces and blend with pastry cutter with flour mixture until coarse meal texture, then add buttermilk. Stir, roll between waxed paper sprayed with Pam. Peel off waxed paper and place over fruit and sprinkle with remaining teaspoon sugar. Bake for 45 minutes. Serves 8.

Beyond Loaves and Fishes

Impossible Pie

2 cups milk
⅔ cup sugar
½ stick margarine
½ teaspoon salt

4 eggs
1 teaspoon vanilla
½ cup flour
1 cup coconut

Place all ingredients in blender and spin for 20 seconds. Pour into greased deep 10-inch pie plate. Bake 40 minutes at 350°. Best when served the day it is made.

Rehoboth Christian School Cookbook

Mile-High Raspberry Pie

ALMOND PASTRY:

¼ cup butter
¼ teaspoon salt
2 tablespoons sugar

1 egg yolk
¾ cup sifted flour
¼ cup finely chopped almonds

Cream butter, salt, and sugar until light and fluffy. Add egg yolk; beat well. Stir in flour and almonds to make a stiff dough. Press into a 9-inch pan. Refrigerate 30 minutes, then bake for 10 minutes at 400°, until golden.

FILLING:

1 (10 to 12-ounce) package
   frozen raspberries; or 2½
   cups fresh raspberries
1 cup sugar for frozen and 1⅓
   cups sugar for fresh
   raspberries

1 tablespoon lemon juice
Dash of salt
2 egg whites, room
   temperature
1 cup heavy cream, whipped
½ teaspoon almond extract

Thaw raspberries if frozen. Place raspberries in large bowl of mixer. Add sugar, lemon juice, salt, and egg whites. Beat 15 minutes, or until stiff. Fold in whipped cream and almond extract. Mound in baked pastry shell. Freeze until firm. Serve. Makes 8 servings.

The Very Special Raspberry Cookbook

Las Cruces Pecan Pie

1 (9-inch) pie shell, frozen
3 eggs, beaten
1 cup sugar
1 cup dark karo syrup

1 teaspoon vanilla extract
3 tablespoons melted butter
   (cooled)
1½ cups pecans

Slightly thaw pie shell. Combine eggs and sugar, mixing together slightly. Add karo syrup, vanilla, and melted butter to egg mixture. Fold into pie shell. Gently top with pecans. Preheat oven to 350°. Place pie pan on cookie sheet and bake at 350° for 10 minutes. Reduce heat to 325° and bake for 40-45 minutes. Cool and serve.

Fiery Appetizers

Millionaire Pie

2 cups powdered sugar
1 stick butter or margarine
¼ teaspoon salt
¼ teaspoon vanilla
1 large egg

1 (8-inch) pie shell, baked
1 cup heavy whipped cream
1 cup crushed pineapple,
  drained
½ cup nuts

Cream together powdered sugar and butter; add salt, vanilla, and egg; mix until light and fluffy. Spoon mixture evenly into pie crust. Chill. Whip cream until stiff. Blend in pineapple and nuts. Spread on top of other mixture and chill.

Mrs. Noah's Survival Guide

Pietown, New Mexico. The first merchant in town had such a demand for homemade pies, and they were of such quality that they became justly famous. Local folks as well as travelers began to refer to the community as "Pie Town." And that's how it got its name.

Carob Cream Pie

A delicious version of an old favorite!

½ cup sugar
⅓ cup flour
Dash salt
¼ cup powdered milk
1½ cups milk
3 egg yolks, lightly beaten
(reserve whites)
2 tablespoons butter

2 teaspoons vanilla extract
½ cup carob syrup (⅓ cup
carob powder and ⅓ cup
water beaten together till
smooth)
1 (9-inch) baked and cooled
pastry shell
Meringue

Preheat oven to 375°. In saucepan mix together sugar, flour, salt, and powdered milk. Gradually stir in the milk to dissolve dry ingredients to make smooth, lump-free mixture. Place over medium heat; stir constantly with wire whisk till mixture thickens. Remove from heat. Stir 3 tablespoons of hot mixture into beaten yolks, rapidly. Stir back into hot mixture, stirring quickly. Return mixture to heat. Cook just till mixture thickens to pudding consistency, stirring constantly. Remove from heat and turn burner off. Still using wire whisk, add butter, vanilla, and carob syrup. Whisk till smooth and creamy. Pour into prepared pastry shell. Top with Meringue.

MERINGUE:
3 egg whites
¼ teaspoon cream of tartar

⅓ cup sugar
1 teaspoon vanilla extract

Beat egg whites in large mixing bowl, on high speed, till frothy. Add cream of tartar, beat in. Gradually add sugar, beating to stiff peaks. Beat in vanilla. Spread meringue over carob filling in shell. Seal meringue to edges of crust. Bake 375° 10 minutes or till lightly browned. Let pie stand about one hour before serving. Yields 1 (9-inch) pie.

Note: Add one tablespoon cocoa powder to carob syrup, if desired.

Carob Cookbook

New Mexico Peanut Pie

½ cup sugar
¼ cup firmly packed brown
   sugar
¼ cup flour
2 tablespoons cornstarch
¼ teaspoon salt
3 cups milk

½ cup peanut butter chips
4 egg yolks
3 tablespoons butter or
   margarine
1½ teaspoons vanilla
1 (7¼-ounce) bag chocolate
   covered peanuts, chopped

Combine sugar, brown sugar, flour, cornstarch, and salt in saucepan. Add milk and peanut butter chips gradually. Cook and stir on medium heat until thick and bubbly. Reduce heat; cook and stir 2 minutes. Beat egg yolks lightly in small bowl. Stir one cup hot mixture into yolks gradually and return egg mixture to saucepan. Bring to gentle boil. Cook and stir on low heat 2 minutes. Remove from heat and stir in butter and vanilla. Pour mixture into baked pie shell and sprinkle with peanuts. Bake at 350° for 12 minutes. Cool to room temperature before serving.

Peanut Palate Pleasers from Portales

Chocolate-Piñon Pie

8 ounces piñons (pine nuts)
7 ounces unsweetened
   chocolate squares
1 cup unsalted butter,
   softened

1 cup plus 1 tablespoon sugar
4 large egg yolks
Zest of 1 orange
4 large egg whites

Preheat oven to 300°. Process piñons and chocolate in a food processor until ground. Beat butter at medium speed with an electric mixer until creamed; add sugar, and beat until sugar dissolves. Add egg yolks to butter mixture; add zest and piñon mixture, and beat until blended. Beat egg whites at high speed until stiff peaks form. Fold egg whites, one-third at a time, into butter mixture. Pour batter into a buttered, floured 8-inch round cake pan lined with parchment paper. Bake for 45 minutes or until pie shrinks away from edges of pan. Cool and slice with a wet knife. Makes 10 servings.

Savoring the Southwest Again

New Mexico's distinctive insignia is the Zia Sun Symbol which originated with the Indians of the Zia Pueblo in ancient times. According to their tribal philosophy which taught the basic harmony of all things in the universe, the sacred number four is embodied in the earth with its four main directions; in the four seasons; the four times of day (sunrise, noon, evening, night); and life (childhood, youth, manhood, old age). Everything is bound together in a circle of life and love, without beginning, without end. They believed man has four sacred obligations: to develop a strong body, a clear mind, a pure spirit, and a devotion to the welfare of his people. Guided by this historic background, the flag of New Mexico was wisely chosen, with the ancient Zia Sun Symbol in red on a field of Spanish yellow.

Piñon Nut Torte

CRUST:*

1¼ cups all-purpose flour
1½ teaspoons sugar
¼ teaspoon salt
1 tablespoon grated orange
   peel

½ cup chilled butter-flavored
   solid vegetable shortening,
   cut into small pieces
2 tablespoons ice water

In a food processor combine the flour, sugar, salt, and grated orange peel. Turning the food processor on and off, cut in the vegetable shortening until coarsely blended. Add enough ice water to form moist clumps. Mold the dough into a ball; then flatten it into a disk. Wrap it in plastic wrap and refrigerate for one hour.

Bring the dough to room temperature and roll it out on a lightly floured surface to a size that will cover the torte pan (about 12 inches). Press the dough into the pan with your fingers and trim the edges. Place the crust in the freezer for 15 minutes. Pour in the filling and bake.

*A frozen pie crust works well if you need to save time.

FILLING:

1 cup light corn syrup
3 whole eggs, lightly beaten
⅔ cup granulated sugar

2 tablespoons butter, melted
1 teaspoon vanilla
2 cups piñon nuts, roasted**

Preheat the oven to 350°. Combine the corn syrup, eggs, sugar, melted butter, and vanilla in a medium-sized bowl. Whisk until the mixture is well blended and fold in the piñon nuts. Pour the filling into the torte shell and bake for about one hour.

Let it cool completely. Cut into wedges and serve with vanilla ice cream with candied orange strips (available at most candy stores) and Spanish Coffee. Serves 6-8.

**To roast Piñon nuts, preheat the oven to 400°. Spread the nuts in a single layer on a baking sheet and roast for 7-12 minutes, or until they are a rich golden brown. The nuts burn easily, so keep an eye on them and shake the pan occasionally to avoid scorching.

Christmas Celebration: Santa Fe Traditions

Raspberry Pizza

CRUST:

1 cup flour

1 stick butter or margarine, softened

½ cup powdered sugar

Blend and knead into dough. Spread on pizza pan and bake 10 minutes at 350°.

FILLING:

1 (8-ounce) package cream cheese

1 can condensed milk

1 teaspoon vanilla

⅓ cup lemon juice

1 pint fresh raspberries

Combine cream cheese, milk, vanilla, and lemon juice. Spread over cooled crust. Top with raspberries and cover with raspberry glaze.

GLAZE:

1 cup raspberries

1 cup sugar, divided

1 cup water

2½ tablespoons cornstarch

In a saucepan, combine raspberries, ¾ cup sugar, and water. Cook until berries are soft. Add ¼ cup sugar mixed with cornstarch. Cook until thick and glazed.

Contributed by The Honorable Joe Skeen, congressman from New Mexico.

The Very Special Raspberry Cookbook

Capirotada

Many cultures have some variation of bread pudding. The traditional recipes in northern New Mexico usually differ from those elsewhere in the lack of eggs and the addition of cheese. Because Capirotada originated as a special holiday dessert, sugar was used liberally to make a very sweet dish. This is the Jaramillos' favorite version.

SYRUP:

2½ cups water
1 cup brown sugar

2 cloves
1 stick cinnamon

Combine all of the ingredients in a small saucepan and simmer over medium heat for about 15 minutes, until the mixture has cooked down by about one quarter. Remove the cloves and cinnamon. Set the syrup aside to cool.

PUDDING:

Butter
8 slices white bread
1 cup grated mild Cheddar cheese

½ cup raisins
½ cup piñon nuts

Preheat the oven to 350°. Butter a shallow medium-sized baking dish and set it aside.

Tear the bread into bite-size pieces, and spread the pieces on a baking sheet. Toast the bread in the oven for 10-15 minutes, turning occasionally, until dry and slightly browned.

Layer ½ of the toast pieces, cheese, raisins, and piñon nuts, then repeat for a second layer. Slowly ladle the reserved syrup over the layers, making sure that the toast pieces are soaked well. Gently press the toast into the syrup. Bake for 30-40 minutes, or until the syrup is absorbed and the Capirotada has a creamy, almost custard-like consistency.

Serve warm. Capirotada can be assembled up to 6 hours in advance and refrigerated. Bring the dish back to room temperature before proceeding with baking. Leftovers can be refrigerated for a couple of days and gently reheated. Makes 6 servings.

Variation: Chimayó residents often add some of their noted apples to Capirotada. Pare one of your favorite apples, slice it into small chunks, and sauté it lightly in a tablespoon of butter. Add the sautéed apple to the layers of bread and other ingredients.

The Rancho de Chimayó Cookbook

Black Forest Trifle

This is one of my favorite "party" recipes, because it looks so festive and elegant.

1 (19.8-ounce) package fudge
   brownie mix
1 (3.5-ounce) package instant
   chocolate pudding mix
¼ cup coffee or chocolate-
   flavored liqueur (optional)
1 can cherry pie filling (you will
   use only about ⅔ of can)

1 (12-ounce) carton frozen
   whipped topping, thawed
Garnish: Chocolate curls,
   mini-chocolate morsels, or
   maraschino cherries

Prepare brownie mix according to package directions for cake-like brownies in a 9x13x2-inch pan. Cool, divide in half and crumble.

Prepare chocolate pudding according to package directions. Chill and divide in half.

Place ½ crumbled brownies in bottom of a 3-quart trifle bowl; drizzle ½ of the liqueur over the brownies in the bowl. Dot with ⅓ of the cherry pie filling (make sure some of them show through the sides of the bowl), layer with ½ pudding, then ½ the whipped topping. Repeat layers: Brownies, liqueur, cherries, pudding, and whipped topping. Garnish with 1-2 of the items listed for garnishing. Chill 8 hours. Yields 16-18 servings.

Recipes from the Cotton Patch

Four-Layer Chocolate Dessert

2 cups vanilla wafers, crushed
½ - 1 cup pecans, chopped
  (optional)
1 stick margarine, melted
1 (8-ounce) package cream
  cheese
1 large carton Cool Whip

1 cup powdered sugar
2 small packages chocolate
  instant pudding
3 cups milk
1 teaspoon vanilla
Shaved chocolate

Mix vanilla wafer crumbs, pecans, and margarine together. Line bottom of 9x13-inch glass dish and bake for 10 minutes at 350°. Mix cream cheese, one cup Cool Whip, and powdered sugar together; spread on cooled crust.

Mix chocolate instant pudding, milk, and vanilla until thick; spread over layer of cream cheese mixture. On top of chocolate pudding layer, spread balance of Cool Whip. On top of this, use chocolate shavings. Keep refrigerated. Makes approximately 15 servings.

Red River's Cookin'

Methodist Pudding
(Lemon Fluff)

2 cups vanilla wafers, crushed
1 package lemon Jell-O
1 cup boiling water
1 cup sugar

5 tablespoons lemon juice
1 large can evaporated milk,
  chilled* and whipped

Cover bottom of buttered 9x13-inch dish with half of crumbs. Dissolve Jell-O in water and add sugar and lemon juice. Chill until slightly congealed. Whip, then fold evaporated milk into lemon mixture. Pour over crumbs. Sprinkle remaining crumbs. Chill until firm.

*Put evaporated milk into freezer 30-45 minutes. Use cool bowl and beaters.

The Joy of Sharing

Flan Café

3 eggs, slightly beaten
6 tablespoons sugar
¼ teaspoon salt
3 tablespoons instant coffee
    granules

1 teaspoon vanilla extract
3 cups milk, scalded
6 tablespoons coffee-flavored
    liqueur
½ cup whipped cream

In a mixing bowl, combine eggs, sugar, salt, coffee and vanilla. Mix thoroughly. Gradually add scalded milk, stirring vigorously. Pour mixture into 6 custard cups. Place in pan of hot water and bake at 375° for 25 minutes or until firm. Chill thoroughly. To serve, spoon liqueur over flan and top with whipped cream.

Simply Simpatico

The town of Lincoln is filled with memories of Billy the Kid. Though his legend bears only remote resemblance to the Billy the Kid of history, the outlaw of sunny disposition and deadly trigger finger still rides boldly across America's mental landscape. In 1881 Sheriff Pat Garrett shot Billy the Kid (alias Henry McCarty, alias Kid Antrim, alias William H. Bonney) near Ft. Sumner. La Mesilla, the onetime Mexican border town that witnessed the signing of the Gadsden Purchase in 1853, is also the site of the trial and murder conviction of Billy the Kid in 1881. His jail cell is in the nearby Gadsden Museum.

Berry-Pecan Flan

This is a good dessert after a hot and spicy meal, as the cream cheese diminishes any heat lingering in the mouth.

CRUST:

¾ cup unsalted butter, softened   1½ cups flour
½ cup powdered sugar   ¼ cup ground pecans

Preheat oven to 325°. Mix all ingredients and pat into greased flan pan. Bake 10-12 minutes until lightly browned. Cool.

FILLING:

1 (8-ounce) package cream   ½ cup sugar
   cheese, softened   1 teaspoon Mexican vanilla

Mix all ingredients together and spread on the bottom of the cooled flan shell.

TOPPING:

½ pint strawberries, sliced, or   ½ cup pecan halves
   whole raspberries

Arrange decoratively on top of cream cheese spread, covering evenly.

SAUCE:

1 cup cranberry juice   1 teaspoon lemon juice
   (unsweetened)   ½ cup sugar
2 tablespoons cornstarch   1 cup raspberry jam

Combine all ingredients in a small, heavy saucepan and cook over low heat, stirring constantly, for about 2 minutes. Sauce will thicken slightly. Cool to room temperature and spread over the fruit and pecans on the flan. Chill before serving.

The Santa Fe School of Cooking Cookbook

Ibarra Chocolate Flan
with Crispy Phyllo Crust

Flan is a traditional, even quintessential, Southwestern dessert in the Spanish and Mexican tradition. It is the one dessert item you'll find on most menus between Mexico City and Santa Fe. Flan makes a great medium for assertive flavors—like oranges, lemons, cinnamon, pine nuts, berries, anise, and licorice. Steeped vanilla beans, mint, and even basil can also be used. Don't plan on making these flans at the last minute, because the caramel takes time to set, and be sure to cook them slowly so the egg doesn't curdle. This recipe gives the flan a completely different dimension with the addition of the light, flaky crust.

PHYLLO CRUST:

¼ cup ground almonds
1 teaspoon ground cinnamon
¼ cup sugar
4 sheets phyllo dough, covered
   with a damp towel

6 tablespoons unsalted butter,
  melted

Preheat the oven to 425°. Mix together the almonds, cinnamon, and sugar in a bowl. Cut the phyllo sheets in half vertically and horizontally, creating 4 equal rectangles per sheet. Brush each rectangle with a little melted butter and sprinkle with some of the almond mixture. Take 4 of the rectangles and layer them on top of each other. Repeat for the other 3 phyllo sheets. Work quickly while cutting and coating phyllo, always keeping the resting sheets covered with a damp towel, to prevent them from drying out. Place four 6-ounce (¾ cup) ramekins upside down on a cookie sheet. Carefully mold the phyllo crusts over and around the ramekins so they form an inverted "nest." Bake in the oven for about 15 minutes, or until crispy and browned. Set "the nests" aside and wash the ramekins.

CARAMEL:

1 cup sugar
½ cup water

1 teaspoon fresh lemon juice

Place the sugar, water, and lemon juice in a saucepan. Bring to a boil, and cook until the mixture reaches a deep amber color.

(continued)

(continued)

Remove from the heat and immediately ladle 2 tablespoons into each of the 4 clean ramekins. Let the caramel set.

FLAN:

1 cup heavy cream
1 cup milk
6 tablespoons sugar
2 sticks canela, each about
    4 inches long, or 1 stick
    cinnamon

½ cup chopped toasted
    almonds
2½ ounces good-quality
    bittersweet chocolate, finely
    chopped (about ½ cup)
1 egg plus 3 egg yolks

Bring the cream, milk, sugar, canela, and almonds to a boil in a heavy saucepan. Turn off the heat and let steep for 30-45 minutes. Strain into a clean saucepan and return to a boil. Turn off the heat and stir in the chocolate to melt. Place the egg and yolks in a bowl and temper by slowly pouring in the hot chocolate mixture, while whisking constantly. Strain again and pour into the ramekins on top of the hardened caramel.

Reheat the oven to 325°. Place the ramekins in a water bath, by putting enough water in a large baking pan to reach half-way up the sides of the ramekins when they are sitting in the pan. Cover the water bath with foil and bake for about 30 minutes or until the flans are set. Let cool and chill for at least 3 hours before serving.

To serve, loosen the flans by running a knife around the inside edges of the ramekins. Invert the ramekins and carefully drop the flans into the phyllo "nests." Yields 4 servings.

Mark Miller's Indian Market Cookbook

Mexican Pecan-Toffee Tartlets in Chocolate Chip Cookie Crust

Who doesn't like chocolate chip cookies? When combined with pecan-stuffed coffee-toffee ice cream, the result is a rich blend of flavors that no dessert lover can resist.

24 small or 12 medium-size chocolate chip cookies
4 tablespoons sweet (unsalted) butter, melted
1 pint coffee ice cream
1 toffee candy bar, 4-ounce
½ cup very coarsely chopped pecan halves

½ pint heavy whipping cream
3 tablespoons vanilla-scented sugar (made by storing sugar with a broken piece of vanilla bean)
½ cup thick, rich chocolate fudge sauce

Using a food processor, blender, or a rolling pin, crush the cookies until finely crumbled. Meanwhile, melt the butter. Butter the insides of 6 small soufflé cups, or any other suitable small serving dishes. Combine remaining butter with the cookie crumbs in a bowl. Divide the mixture evenly among the 6 cups, and then press it firmly into them. Freeze.

Soften the ice cream by scooping it into a mixing bowl and letting it set a few minutes, then process in a food processor or mixer. Crush the toffee bar in the processor or with a rolling pin, until it is in chunks about ½ inch across, not too fine. Add to the ice cream along with ⅓ cup of the pecans. Process or mix until just combined so as not to overly crush the candy and the nuts. Divide among the cookie crusts, leaving the surface of each somewhat uneven and interesting looking as you would frosting. Whip the cream with the vanilla sugar.

Divide the chocolate fudge sauce among each of the tarts, drizzling it in a swirl in the center of each, allowing some of the ice cream filling around the edges to show. Top each with a dollop of the whipped cream. If you have too much, place the extra in dollops on a cookie sheet covered with wax paper and freeze for later garnishing for drinks or desserts. Sprinkle reserved pecan pieces over the top of the cream. Freeze until serving time.

Fiestas for Four Seasons

Blueberry Ice Cream Dessert Squares

½ cup butter or margarine
1 cup whole wheat flour
½ teaspoon salt
½ teaspoon nutmeg
½ cup brown sugar
⅓ cup carob powder

2 eggs
½ cup honey
¼ cup flour
1 cup frozen blueberries, undrained
1 quart vanilla ice cream

Preheat oven to 350°. In medium bowl combine butter, whole wheat flour, salt, nutmeg, sugar, and carob powder. Cut together with pastry blender to fine crumbly texture. Set aside.

Place eggs, honey, ¼ cup flour and blueberries into a blender container. Process till thoroughly blended, about 30 seconds. Pour into a 12x8-inch well buttered baking dish or pan. Sprinkle crumb mixture over top and slightly press crumbs into blueberry mixture, leaving top crumbly. Bake in 350° oven 25-30 minutes; center will be set when done. Cool completely. Cut into 4-inch squares.

To serve, place blueberry squares on top of ice cream squares on serving plates. To make ice cream squares, remove ice cream from freezer for 30 minutes. When slightly softened, press all of ice cream into 12x8-inch baking dish. Refreeze for at least one hour. Cover for longer freezing time. Cut ice cream into 4-inch squares. Yields 6 servings.

Variations: Raspberry Ice Cream Squares—substitute one cup frozen raspberries for the blueberries.

Cherry Ice Cream Squares—substitute one cup frozen cherries for the blueberries.

Carob Cookbook

Twila's Eggless Fruit Ice Cream

1 can Eagle Brand milk
1 cup sugar
1 (3-ounce) Jell-O (any flavor)
   or 1 (3-ounce) instant
   pudding mix

1 (8-ounce) Cool Whip
Milk

Mix the first 4 ingredients; pour into a 1½-gallon ice cream freezer and finish filling it with milk. Add chopped fruit and freeze.

This can be made any flavor; depending on what flavor Jell-O you use; or if you want chocolate or vanilla, add pudding mix.

Amistad Community Recipes

Avocado Sherbet

If you can resist serving avocados or guacamole in your meal, then count on this velvety delight to end it.

1 cup sugar
1½ cups water
3 medium avocados

⅔ cup lemon juice (or lime)
1 teaspoon lemon rind, grated
   (or lime)

Put sugar and water in a saucepan and stir over high heat until the sugar is dissolved. Turn heat low and simmer 5 minutes. Place in a jar and refrigerate till cool.

Peel and pit the avocados and purée in a blender or food processor. Add lemon juice and rind, and the syrup. Freeze in ice cream machine according to manufacturer's directions, or freeze in ice trays, whirling in a blender or processor 30 minutes before serving, and placing back in the freezer to firm. Serves 4.

The Aficionado's Southwestern Cooking

The multi-storied Taos Pueblo was over 400 years old when Coronado's forces arrived in 1541.

Mexican Cream with Strawberries

A delicious cooling dessert, not too sweet, after a hot spicy meal. It is the ideal choice for company, when you want something pretty and easy to prepare ahead.

1 tablespoon plain gelatine	2 cups sour cream
2 cups cream	1 teaspoon vanilla
½ cup sugar	Strawberries

Put gelatine, cream, and sugar in a saucepan. Cook over medium-low heat, stirring until gelatine and sugar are dissolved—don't let it boil. Place in a bowl, cover, and refrigerate an hour, or until thickened to the consistency of egg whites. Stir in sour cream and vanilla. Lightly oil a 1½-quart ring mold, add the cream mixture, cover, and chill until firm—about 6 hours.

To serve, run a knife around the mold, dip outside of mold in hot water a few seconds, and invert on a serving plate. Garnish with plenty of fresh strawberries in the center, and around the cream. Serves 8-10.

The Aficionado's Southwestern Cooking

Log Cabin Pudding

When sugar was limited during the war, this was our dessert.

1 cup milk
1 tablespoon Knox gelatine
¼ cup cold water
1 cup Log Cabin syrup

1 cup pecans, chopped fine
1½ cups whipped cream
Vanilla wafers (about 25)

Bring the milk to a boil. Soak the gelatine in cold water and add to milk; stir until dissolved. Add Log Cabin syrup; set it aside to partly congeal. Add pecans and stiffly whipped cream. Butter a 9x13-inch pan. Line it with crushed vanilla wafers. Pour in the pudding and top with crushed wafers. Refrigerate for several hours.

Red River's Cookin'

The beautiful Jemez (pronounced Hay-mes) River flows through the canyons of the Jemez Mountains—a volcanic field in north central New Mexico famous for its natural hot springs.

Ancho: Dried form of the green Poblano. Anchos vary in pungency from almost mild to medium, with smoky flavors reminiscent of coffee, prunes, and tobacco.

Cascabel Chile: A dried, dark reddish-brown chile with smooth, tough skin and a round shape about 1½ inches in diameter.

Chile Caribe: Crushed form of New Mexican dried red chile pods along with the seeds.

Chipotles: Dried and smoked form of a fresh jalapeño chile which is dusty brown in color. It is ridged, with wrinkly skin, measuring about 2 to 2½ inches long and about ¾ to 1 inch wide. The chipotle has a rich, smoky, tobacco-like flavor with a very pronounced heat.

Chipotles in Adobo: Canned chipotle chiles in a sauce of tomatoes, vinegar, garlic, onion, and spices.

De Arbol: A dried, bright red chile measuring 2-3 inches long and related to the cayenne chile. It is very hot with intense flavor.

Guajillo: Dried red chile pod similar in look to a dried New Mexican pod but smaller and smoother in texture. It has an earthy flavor.

Jalapeno: Fresh, small, thick-fleshed green chile approximately 2 inches long and 1 inch wide. It is the most popular hot green chile.

Moritals: Another type of dried, smoked jalapeno chile which is deep red to red-brown in color. It measures 1 to 2 inches long and about ⅜ inch wide.

New Mexico Green Chile: Fresh New Mexican variety of chile in its green form, measuring about 4-6 inches long. There are a variety of types of New Mexican chiles distinguished by heat level from mild to hot. When New Mexican green chile is called for, it is assumed the chile has been roasted and peeled.

New Mexico Red Pods: The form of the green chile that has ripened to its red state and dried. The traditional method for storing these chiles is to tie them in a long bunch called a ristra.

New Mexico or Chimayó Chile Powder: Dried version of the New Mexican green chile which has been ripened (turned red) and ground into powder without additional ingredients.

Mulato: A type of poblano chile, dried, browner in color than the ancho chile and slightly smokier, but without the depth. It is one of the three chiles (ancho, mulato, pasilla) used in traditional Mole Poblano.

Pasilla: Also called Chile Negro. Pasilla, a dried chile, translated as "little raisin." It is brownish-black in color, wrinkled, long, and tapered.

Poblano: Fresh form of the ancho chile measuring 3-4 inches. This is a good chile for chile rellenos due to its size and the thickness of its flesh. A dark green color, the poblano is usually charred and peeled to enhance its full flavor.

Serrano: Fresh, small green chile, cylindrical in shape and measuring approximately 1 to 2 inches long and ½ to ¾ inch in width. It is a crisp, hot chile used extensively in salsas.

The Silver City Museum embodies southwestern history—the house was built by a man who struck it rich with a silver mine. It now houses a priceless archive and historical collection as well as a local history research library.

Adobo: A vinegary sauce that may also be used for pickling.

Albondigas: Meatballs.

Arroz: Rice.

Atole: Hot, thick corn cereal.

Bizcochito: State cookie made from flour, sugar and anise seeds.

Bolillos: Small, long rolls of bread; hard rolls.

Burritos: Rolled flour tortillas with a variety of fillings.

Calabacitas: Vegetable side dish, usually containing a mix of corn, chiles, zucchini, onions and spices.

Caldillo: A kind of gravy or sauce.

Capirotada: Dessert bread pudding with raisins, cinnamon and cheese.

Carne Adovada: Cubes of pork, marinated in red chile and baked until tender.

Carne Asada: Beef or pork cut into strips and barbecued or roasted.

Carnitas: Beef or pork cut into strips and marinated in green chile and spices.

Chalupas: Flat corn tortillas fried and topped with refried beans, onion, cheese, lettuce, tomato, guacamole and sour cream.

Chile (green): A long mild green pepper.

Chile (red): A green chile allowed to ripen, usually dried and used as a basic in seasoning Mexican food.

Chile con Carne: Chile with meat.

Chile con Queso: Chile mixed in melted cheese served as a dip with corn chips.

Chile Rellenos: Whole green chiles stuffed with cheese, wrapped in a flour mixture, dipped in egg batter, fried until golden brown.

Chili Powder: Dried, crumbled chiles combined with other dried spices (onion, garlic, coriander, oregano, cloves).

Chimichanga: Meat or bean burritos, deep fried and topped with chile or salsa.

Chorizo: Spicy pork sausage, usually used in breakfast dishes.

Cilantro: Fresh coriander leaf resembling parsley; the same as Chinese parsley.

Coriander: Round, pale yellow to brown seed of coriander plant; may be used to grow fresh plants for cilantro.

Cumin: An herb plant whose seeds are used as a flavoring; a member of the parsley family.

Empanadas: Rich mincemeat turnovers.

Enchiladas: White or blue corn meal tortillas that are stacked or rolled and made with any combination of meat, cheese, onion, tomato, lettuce, sour cream and chili sauce.

Ensalada: Salad.

Fajitas: Skirt steaks.

Flan: Baked caramel cream custard.

Flautas: Crisp rolled corn tortillas filled with meat.

Frijoles: Beans, usually pinto.

Frijoles Refritas: Refried beans. First cooked with tomatoes, onions, chile and other seasonings, then mashed and fried.

Fry Bread: Native American flour pastries, deep fried in oil, usually served with honey or powdered sugar and cinnamon.

Garbanzos: Chick peas.

Gazpacho: A cold vegetable soup.

Green chile stew: Vegetables, meat and green chile.

Guacamole: Avocado salad or dip, usually mashed avocado with seasoning.

Huevos: Eggs.

Heuvos Rancheros: Corn tortillas covered with fried eggs, frijoles, chile and cheese.

Hornos: Adobe ovens used for making bread. Shaped like domed beehives, they are about six feet tall and ten feet in circumference at the base. Made out of clay and straw, they are still a familiar sight in New Mexico.

Indian Taco: Fresh lettuce, tomato, refried beans, meat, guacamole, sour cream and red or green chile, piled open-faced onto puffy tortillas or fry bread.

Jicama: A large root vegetable with gray-brown skin; the crisp white meat has the appearance of a potato, texture of a water chestnut and the flavor of a mild radish; usually served peeled and raw.

Masa: Corn meal used to make tortillas and tamales.

Menudo: Soup made of chile and tripe.

Mole: Hot sauce of chiles, spices, and sometimes chocolate.

Nachos: Fried tortilla chips topped with melted cheese and chile slices.

Picadillo: A dish made of chopped or ground pork and veal cooked together and then mixed with tomatoes, garlic, onion, olives, and other ingredients.

Pico de Gallo: Salsa made with cilantro, fresh chiles, onions and tomatoes.

Piñon Nuts: Pine nuts.

Pollo: Chicken.

Posole: Corn kernels that have been treated with lime; hominy. Meat is often added with a little bit of red chile.

Quesadillas: Two flour tortillas laid flat with cheese and/or meat inside and baked until the cheese is melted.

Queso: Cheese.

Ristra: A string of red chiles.

Salsa: Sauce.

Salsa Picante: A very hot sauce made from fresh chiles and tomatoes.

Sopa: Soup.

Sopaipillas: Pillow-shaped flour pastries, deep fried in oil until they fill with air, usually served with honey or honey butter.

Stuffed Sopaipillas: With cheese, beans and meat, smothered in red or green chiles.

Tamales: Thick ground corn meal wrapped around a spicy meat filling, enclosed in corn husks and steamed.

Tomatillo: A bright green fruit covered with a papery husk that looks like a small green tomato and is used in many Mexican dishes.

Tortillas: Round, flat bread made from either corn or flour. Tortillas complement nearly every New Mexican dish.

Tostada: A crisp, fried tortilla topped with all kinds of garnishes.

Probing the farthest reaches of the universe, the largest array of radio telescopes in the world are near Sorocco.

All recipes in this book have been selected from the cookbooks shown on the following pages. Individuals who wish to obtain a copy of any particular book may do so by sending a check or money order to the address listed by each cookbook (not Quail Ridge Press). Please note the postage and handling charges that are required. State residents add tax only when requested. Prices and addresses are subject to change, and the books may sell out and become unavailable. Retailers are invited to call or write to same address for discount information.

THE AFICIONADO'S SOUTHWESTERN COOKING
by Ronald Johnson
Living Batch Press
3721 Spirit Drive SW
Albuquerque, NM 87106-5631

Fax 800-622-8667
800-249-7737
http://unmpress.unm.edu
E-mail unmpress@unm.edu

In almost 300 pages, Ronald Johnson not only introduces us to the Southwestern classics, but develops magnificent, though simple, recipes to tempt the palate. This is true regional haute cuisine. The book concludes with explanations of ingredients and suggested menus.

$13.95   Retail price   Visa/MC accepted
$ .70   Tax for New Mexico residents
$ 4.00   Postage and handling
Make check payable to UNM Press
ISBN 0-945953-06-2

AMISTAD COMMUNITY RECIPES
c/o Sheila Miller
Amistad Community Members
P. O. Box 224
Amistad, NM 88410   505-633-2258

A collection of 486 recipes and household tips from the early 1900s to the present day. These include, but are not limited to, old homesteader's recipes, ranching and branding dishes, and Southwest cuisine. All proceeds benefit our tiny one-room-type Amistad grade school.

$10.00   Retail price
$ 2.35   Postage and handling
Make check payable to Amistad Association

THE BEST FROM NEW MEXICO KITCHENS

by Sheila MacNiven Cameron
New Mexico Magazine
495 Old Santa Fe Trail   Fax 505-827-6496
Santa Fe, NM 87501   505-827-7447

Recipes from New Mexico restaurants, homes, and hotels. Multicultural compilation of New Mexico cooking with chile as a specialty. 148 pages, over 100 recipes.

$ 9.95   Retail price   Visa/MC accepted
$ 2.50   Postage and handling
Make check payable to *New Mexico Magazine*
ISBN 0-936206-00-8

BEYOND LOAVES AND FISHES

St. Paul's Episcopal Churchwomen
706 W. Quay
Artesia, NM 88210   505-746-3183

Two hundred seventy-five pages of favorite recipes from the women of St. Paul's, our friends and families. This is a cookbook you'll keep on your counter. It includes recipes for kids and some wonderful stories.

$15.00   Retail price
$ 3.00   Postage and handling
Make check payable to St. Paul's Episcopal ECW

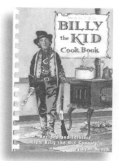

BILLY THE KID COOK BOOK

by Lynn Nusom
Golden West Publishers
4113 N. Longview Avenue   Fax 602-279-6901
Phoenix, AZ 85014-4949   800-658-5830
                    E-mail goldwest@goodnet.com

Southwestern recipes with a flair for the dramatic! More than 100 tempting recipes combined with history, legends and folklore from Billy the Kid Country.

$ 7.95   Retail price   Visa/MC accepted
$ 3.00   Postage and handling
Make check payable to Golden West Publishers
ISBN 1-885590-32-6

BON APPÉTIT DE LAS SANDIAS

Aleen Freeman
3424 Calle Suenos
Rio Rancho, NM 87124   505-896-1516

Bon Appétit de Las Sandias contains 247 recipes contributed by members of the Woman's Club of West Mesa in Rio Rancho. Half of the recipes were featured at ten "theme" luncheons that were held during the year, and the other half are members' "tried-and-true" favorites.

$10.00   Retail price
$ 2.50   Postage and handling
Make check payable to Woman's Club of West Mesa

CAFE PASQUAL'S COOKBOOK: SPIRITED RECIPES FROM SANTA FE

by Katharine Kagel
Chronicle Books
85 Second Street   Fax 800-858-7787
San Francisco, CA 94105   800-722-6657

Enticing, easy-to-follow recipes for every meal of the day, featuring a wide variety of chiles and other favorite New Mexican and Old World ingredients. Includes lovely hand-tinted photographs by Barbara Simpson, colorful Mexican popular art, and a source list for special ingredients. Brings home the true spirit of Sante Fe.

$19.95   Retail price
$ 1.00   Tax for New Mexico residents
$ 3.50   Postage and handling
Make check payable to Chronicle Books
ISBN 0-8118-0293-0

CAROB COOKBOOK

Sunstone Press
P. O. Box 2321   Fax 505-988-1025
Santa Fe, NM 87504-2321   800-243-5644
www.sunstonepress.com

Here's a cookbook for anyone who loves the taste of chocolate but doesn't want the caffeine, fat or the fear of allergic reaction to chocolate. Enjoy over 90 recipes that use carob instead of chocolate and get a flavor that mimics it almost exactly.

$10.95   Retail price   Visa/MC accepted
$ .69   Tax for New Mexico residents
$ 3.50   Postage and handling
Make check payable to Sunstone Press
ISBN 0-86534-135-4

CHRISTMAS CELEBRATION: SANTA FE TRADITIONS

by Richard Clawson/Jann Arrington Wolcott
Clear Light Publishers
823 Don Diego   Fax 505-989-9519
Santa Fe, NM 87501   800-253-2747
E-mail ordercl@aol.com

This lavishly illustrated book captures the ambience and mix of cultural traditions—Indian, Spanish, and Frontier American—that lend pure magic to the Christmas season in Santa Fe. A feast for the eye and mind, it also presents recipes, party plans, decoration and gift crafts to inspire readers and bring fresh enjoyment to their Christmas celebrations.

$39.95   Retail price   Visa/MC accepted
$ 2.50   Tax for New Mexico residents
$ 3.00   Postage and handling .50 each add'l copy
Make check payable to Clear Light Publishers
ISBN 0-940666-68-5

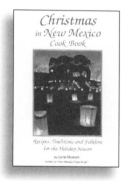

CHRISTMAS IN NEW MEXICO COOK BOOK

by Lynn Nusom
Golden West Publishers
4113 N. Longview Avenue   Fax 602-279-6901
Phoenix, AZ 85014-4949   800-658-5330
E-mail goldwest@goodnet.com

Recipes, traditions and folklore for the Holiday Season—or all year long. Try "Three Kings Bread," "Posole de Posada," "Christmas Pumpkin Pie, "Christmas Turkey with White Wine Basting Sauce," and many more taste tempters! Makes an excellent gift!

$ 8.95   Retail price   Visa/MC accepted
$ 3.00   Postage and handling
Make check payable to Golden West Publishers
ISBN 0-914846-59-0

COCINAS DE NEW MEXICO

Attn: Gina Martinez
Public Service Company of New Mexico
Alvarado Square MS 1110   Fax 505-241-4386
Albuquerque, NM 87158   505-241-4514
E-mail gmartin2@pnm.com

Cocinas, Spanish for "kitchen," describes one of the most important places in New Mexico households. Between these pages you'll find a rich history of unique New Mexican cooking. Now in its ninth edition, with 79 pages of mouth-watering recipes, you'll discover the rich flavor of New Mexico.

$11.95   Retail price (shipping included)
Make check payable to PNM
ISBN 0-9649-0260-5

COMIDA SABROSA: HOME-STYLE SOUTHWESTERN COOKING
by Irene Barraza Sanchez and Gloria Sanchez Yund
University of New Mexico Press
3721 Spirit Drive SW   Fax 800-622-8667
Albuquerque, NM 87106-5631   800-249-7737
http://unmpress.unm.edu
E-mail unmpress@unm.edu

A cookbook for everyone who wants to prepare the kind of food for which New Mexico is famous, from chile con queso through burritos and sopaipillas to biscochitos. Using their mothers' recipes, the authors make Southwest cooking simple and appealing, using traditional and microwave variations where applicable. 145 pages.

$11.95 Retail price   Visa/MC accepted
$ .60 Tax for New Mexico residents
$ 4.00 Postage and handling
Make check payable to UNM Press
ISBN 0-8263-0664-0

COOKING AT THE NATURAL CAFE IN SANTA FE
by Lynn Walters
The Crossing Press
P. O. Box 1048   Fax 800-549-0020
Freedom, CA 95019   800-777-1048
www.crossingpress.com   E-mail crossing@aol.com

The Natural Cafe in Santa Fe, New Mexico, was one of the most creative natural food restaurants in the United States. "Will spice up any collection of innovative vegetarian cookbooks"—*Vegetarian Times*.

$14.95 Retail price   Visa/MC accepted
$ 4.00 Postage and handling .50 each add'l item
Make check payable to The Crossing Press
ISBN 089594-560-6

COOKING WITH KIWANIS
Kiwanis Club of Los Alamos
822 Camino Acoma   Fax 505-986-0195
Santa Fe, NM 87501   505-986-1897
E-mail landry@lanl.gov

Cooking with Kiwanis published by the Kiwanis Club of Los Alamos, the "Atomic City," presents recipes that reflect the unique culture of the town. From Green Chile Stew to Jambalaya, the recipes will tantalize your palate. We know you will enjoy them all. 255 pages with 275 recipes.

$10.00 Retail price
$ 2.00 Postage and handling
Make check payable to Kiwanis Club of Los Alamos

COYOTE'S PANTRY: SOUTHWEST SEASONINGS AND FLAVORINGS

by Mark Miller and Mark Kiffin
Ten Speed Press
P. O. Box 7123
Berkeley, CA 94707

Fax 510-524-4588
800-841-2665
E-mail order@tenspeed.com

This book collects the best of Mark's gourmet pantry basics, with over 125 recipes for marinades, glazes, rubs, oils, vinegars, sauces, dressing, salsas, chutneys, and more—all the secret ingredients for making great tasting Southwestern food at home. 144 pages, full color.

$19.95   Retail price
Make check payable to Ten Speed Press
ISBN 0-89815-930-X

THE EAGLE'S KITCHEN

Belen Middle School M.E.S.A.
314 South 4th Street
Belen, NM 87002

505-864-7453 ext. 13
E-mail cami343@aol.com

The Eagle's Kitchen is a cookbook with 188 pages and 350 favorite recipes from the kitchens of homes in beautiful Belen, NM. Belen is located in a valley nestled against the Manzano Mountains on the east, Measas on the west.

$15.00   Retail price
Make check payable to BMS MESA

FAMILIES COOKING TOGETHER

Georgia O'Keeffe Elementary Friends of the Library
11701 San Victorio N.E.
Albuquerque, NM 87111

505-293-4259
E-mail families-cooking@keeffe.aps.edu

Over 450 family favorite recipes submitted by the staff and parents at Georgia O'Keeffe Elementary. Included are a favorites section from the sold-out *Storybook Cookbook* and local restaurant recipes. The cookbook is infused with delightful student poetry.

$12.95   Retail price
$ 2.50   Postage and handling
Make check payable to Georgia O'Keeffe Friends of the Library

FIERY APPETIZERS
by Dave DeWitt and Nancy Gerlach
The Crossing Press
P. O. Box 1048   Fax 800-549-0020
Freedom, CA 95019   800-777-1048
www.crossingpress.com   E-mail crossing@aol.com

This sizzling collection offers easy-to-follow recipes for seventy spicy-hot appetizers guaranteed to satisfy the most discerning of heat-seeking palates. From Dangerous Dips to Simply Scorching Sandwiches.

$ 8.95   Retail price   Visa/MC accepted
$ 4.00   Postage and handling .50 add'l item
Make check payable to The Crossing Press
ISBN 089594785-4

FIESTA MEXICANA
by Toby Arias and Elaine Frassanito
1412 Stagecoach Road   Fax 505-299-0264
Albuquerque, NM 87231   505-299-7502
                           E-mail frass@bigfoot.com

Fiesta Mexicana, a collection of favorite recipes combining exotic tastes of the old world with new world innovations, represents the most delectable, exciting dishes in the Southwest. With 90 pages and 163 concisely written, easy to follow recipes. *Fiesta Mexicana* is a must for both experienced and novice cooks.

$ 7.95   Retail price
$ .46   Tax for New Mexico residents
$ 1.50   Postage and handling
Make check payable to T & E Enterprises
ISBN 0-9609942-0-3

FIESTAS FOR FOUR SEASONS
by Jane Butel
Clear Light Publishers
823 Don Diego   Fax 505-989-9519
Santa Fe, NM 87501   800-253-2747
                           E-mail ordercl@aol.com

Long before southwestern cuisine became so popular, Jane Butel transformed a local culinary tradition into a national favorite. Readers rely on her creativity, knowledge of cooking, and skill in designing nutritious meals that are also aesthetically pleasing. With *Fiestas for Four Seasons*, she triumphs once again. Thirty-five color photographs. 192 pages.

$14.95   Retail price   Visa/MC accepted
$ .93   Tax for New Mexico residents
$ 3.00   Postage and handling .50 each add'l copy
Make check payable to Clear Light Publishers
ISBN 0-940666-72-3

A FORK IN THE ROAD

Mimbres Region Arts Council
P. O. Box 1830   Fax 505-538-9209
Silver City, NM 88062   505-538-2505
E-mail arts@mrac.cc

A tasty treat for both the eyes and palate. Local artists donated artwork that highlights the unique recipes in this cookbook. Recipes range from Chile 'N Cheese Roll-Ups to Aunt Ruth's Pickles. Desserts are simple, practical, but delicious. There is also a section on Vegetarian Main Dishes.

$10.00   Retail price
$ 5.00   Postage and handling
Make check payable to Mimbres Region Arts Council

GOOD SAM CELEBRATES 15 YEARS OF LOVE

Socorro Good Samaritan Village
P. O. Box 1279   Fax 505-835-4378
Socorro, NM 87801   505-835-2724
E-mail gsscenter576@worldnet.att.net

A compilation of recipes from the Middle Rio Grande Valley featuring favorites from the best cooks in New Mexico. The cookbook features over 300 recipes published to help celebrate our 15th anniversary of providing "a new wrinkle in caring" to the 62 men and women who call Socorro's Good Sam "home."

$ 7.50   Retail price   Visa/MC accepted
$ 2.50   Postage and handling
Make check payable to Socorro Good Samaritan Village

THE GREAT CHILE BOOK

by Mark Miller with John Harrison
Ten Speed Press
P. O. Box 7123   Fax 510-524-4588
Berkeley, CA 94707   800-841-2665
E-mail order@tenspeed.com

A wonderful—and useful—full-color handbook showcasing 100 chiles (50 each of fresh and dried) with color photographs of each, along-side a brief description, including cooking tips and heat scale. 160 pages, full color.

$14.95   Retail price
Make check payable to Ten Speed Press
ISBN 0-89815-428-6

THE GREAT SALSA BOOK
by Mark Miller with Mark Kiffin
Ten Speed Press
P. O. Box 7123   Fax 510-524-4588
Berkeley, CA 94707   800-841-2665
E-mail order@tenspeed.com

This sparkling full-color cookbook features 100 widely varied recipes—tomato and tomatillo, chile, tropical, fruit, corn, bean, garden, ocean, exotic, and nut, seed, and herb. Includes hints on handling volatile peppers, suggested accompaniments, and of course, a heat scale. 160 pages, full color.

$14.95   Retail price
Make check payable to Ten Speed Press
ISBN 0-89815-517-7

GREAT SALSAS BY THE BOSS OF SAUCE
by W.C. Longacre and Dave DeWitt
The Crossing Press
P. O. Box 1048   Fax 800-549-0020
Freedom, CA 95019   800-777-1048
www.crossingpress.com   E-mail crossing@aol.com

Longacre brings a creative collection of recipes from the Southwest, Mexico, Asia and the Caribbean into your kitchen. This book is 128 pages and contains 82 delightful recipes.

$12.95   Retail price   Visa/MC accepted
$ 4.00   Postage and handling .50 each add'l item
Make check payable to The Crossing Press
ISBN 089594-817-6

GREEN CHILE BIBLE
Compiled by *Albuquerque Tribune*
Clear Light Publishers
823 Don Diego   Fax 505-989-9519
Santa Fe, NM 87501   800-253-2747
E-mail ordercl@aol.com

The Albuquerque Tribune proudly presents 200 prize-winning family recipes from throughout New Mexico, home of the fabulous long green chile. A treasury of the best green chile recipes in the world, drawn from a long tradition notable for variety, subtlety, and the incomparable New Mexican chile flavor preferred by true aficionados.

$12.95   Retail price   Visa/MC accepted
$ .81   Tax for New Mexico residents
$ 3.00   Postage and handling .50 each add'l copy
Make check payable to Clear Light Publishers
ISBN 0-940666-35-9

THE HAPPY CAMPER'S COOKBOOK
by Marilyn Abraham and Sandy MacGregor
Clear Light Publishers
823 Don Diego
Santa Fe, NM 87501

Fax 505-989-9519
800-253-2747
E-mail clpublish@2l.com

Delicious grill classics plus hot and cold sides, what to cook on a rainy day, intentional leftovers for fabulous lunches, and great desserts. After quitting their big city jobs, the authors spend half the year at their home in New Mexico and the rest traveling all over the continent in their home on wheels.

$14.95   Retail price
$ 1.25   Tax for New Mexico residents
$ 3.00   Postage and handling
Make check payable to Clear Light Publishers
ISBN 1-57416-024-9

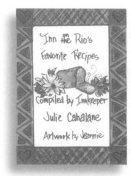

INN ON THE RIO'S FAVORITE RECIPES
by Julie Cahalane
6529 NDCBU
Taos, NM 87571

Fax 505-751-1816
505-758-7199
E-mail innonrio@laplaza.org

After spending each morning after breakfast sitting at the computer printing out copies of recipes for my guests, I decided it was time for a keepsake cookbook! Thus, *Inn on the Rio's Favorite Recipes* was born. The book contains favorite recipes, anecdotes, and a history of the recipe. Enjoy!

$ 7.95   Retail price
$ .51   Tax for New Mexico residents
$ 1.50   Postage and handling
Make check payable to Inn on the Rio

THE JOY OF SHARING
First United Methodist Women Artesia
P. O. Box 1492
Artesia, NM 88211-1492

Fax 505-746-1624
505-746-3535
E-mail pvtnetworks.net/-clarkfamily

The Joy of Sharing is a heavenly collection of over 375 recipes gathered by the United Methodist Women group of Artesia. If you want to add the "zing" of green chile to your cuisine or new ways to fix lamb, a southwestern favorite, this is the cookbook for you.

$10.00   Retail price
$ 5.00   Postage and handling
Make check payable to United Methodist Women Artesia

LICENSE TO COOK NEW MEXICO STYLE

Penfield Press
215 Brown Street
Iowa City, IA 52245-5842   800-728-9998

License to Cook New Mexico Style introduces the spicy cooking of the Southwest with traditional dishes, fast and easy recipes, and new creations using traditional ingredients. Plus some highlights of "The Land of Enchantment."

$ 6.95   Retail price (2 for $12; 3 for $18)
$ .35   Tax for New Mexico residents
Make check payable to Penfield Press
ISBN 0-941016-58-7

A LITTLE SOUTHWEST COOKBOOK

by Barbara Karoff
Chronicle Books
85 Second Street   Fax 800-858-7787
San Francisco, CA 94105   800-722-6657

A delightful collection of southwestern dishes from Blue Corn Bread and Green Chili Stew to Avocado Soup and Old Southwest Spoon Bread. Delicious classics such as Huevos Rancheros, Chili-Corn Souffle, Bischochios and more capture the rich heritage of Southwest cuisine. Every outstanding recipe is accompanied by a charming full-color illustration.

$ 7.95   Retail price
$ .46   Tax for New Mexico residents
$ 3.50   Postage and handling
Make check payable to Chronicle Books
ISBN 0-8118-0381-3

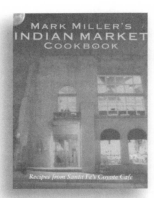

MARK MILLER'S INDIAN MARKET COOKBOOK: RECIPES FROM SANTA FE'S COYOTE CAFE

by Mark Miller
Ten Speed Press
P. O. Box 7123   Fax 510-524-4588
Berkeley, CA 94707   800-841-2665
                          E-mail order@tenspeed.com

Every year, the Coyote Cafe celebrates Santa Fe's Indian Market Week with a special array of dishes highlighting a wide range of ingredients drawn from farmers throughout the region (but reproducible just about anywhere). 224 pages, full color.

$39.95   Retail price
Make check payable to Ten Speed Press
ISBN 0-89815-620-3

MEN'S GUIDE TO BREAD MACHINE BAKING
by Jeffrey Gerlach
Prima Publishing/ Attn: Customer Service
P. O. Box 1260   Fax 916-632-1232
Rocklin, CA 95677   800-632-8676
                     E-mail sales@primapub.com
This 208-page book features over 100 unique recipes including bagels, specialty breads, pretzels and sourdough. In addition to the recipes themselves, Gerlach includes sections on how to choose and fix a machine as well as how to troubleshoot bread recipes. A must have for any bread machine owner.

$15.00   Retail price   Visa/MC/AM.EX accepted
$ 4.00   Postage and handling
Make check payable to Prima Publishing
ISBN 0-7615-0652-7

MRS. NOAH'S SURVIVAL GUIDE
New Mexico Christian Children's Home Ladies Associates
1356 N.M. Hwy 236   Fax 505-356-0760
Portales, NM 88130   505-356-5372
A delicious collection of over 300 favorite recipes from members of the New Mexico Christian Children's Home Ladies Associates that will take you from Appetizers to Desserts with words of wisdom and humorous quotes from children to spice up your journey. Proceeds help the children at the New Mexico Christian Children's Home.

$10.00   Retail price
$ 2.00   Postage and handling
Make check payable to NM Christian Children's Home

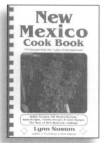

NEW MEXICO COOK BOOK
by Lynn Nusom
Golden West Publishers
4113 N. Longview Avenue   Fax 602-279-6901
Phoenix, AZ 85014-4949   800-658-5330
                     E-mail goldwest@goodnet.com
History and foods of New Mexico. Includes Indian heritage, chile as a way of life, Mesilla Valley, Santa Fe, Albuquerque, and Taos style recipes. By noted food columnist, Lynn Nusom.

$ 5.95   Retail price   Visa/MC accepted
$ 3.00   Postage and handling
Make check payable to Golden West Publishers
ISBN 0-914346-48-5

OUR BEST HOME COOKING

Roosevelt County Family and Community Educators
P. O. Box 455   Fax 505-359-1322
Portales, NM 88130   505-356-4417
                      E-mail roosevelt@nmsu.edu

The Roosevelt County Family and Community Education cookbook consists of 198 pages with over 400 delicious recipes which reflect our southwest and agricultural heritages from the homemakers of Central Eastern New Mexico. Recipes include practical everyday ingredients for that fresh-from-the-farm flavor including canning and microwave dishes.

$ 8.00   Retail price
$ 3.50   Postage and handling
Make check payable to Roosevelt County FCE

A PAINTER'S KITCHEN: RECIPES FROM THE KITCHEN OF GEORGIA O'KEEFFE

by Margaret Wood
Red Crane Books
2008 Rosina, Ste. B   Fax 505-989-7476
Santa Fe, NM 87505   800-922-3392
                      E-mail publish@redcrane.com

The meals served in O'Keeffe's household focused on homegrown and natural foods. Meals were always tasty, nutritious, modest, and beautifully presented. Includes photographs of O'Keeffe. 110 pages, 8 color and 8 b/w photos.

$14.95   Retail price   Visa/MC accepted
$ 4.00   Postage and handling
Make check payable to Red Crane Books
ISBN 1-878610-61-9

PEANUT PALATE PLEASERS FROM PORTALES

Portales Woman's Club
P. O. Box 564
Portales, NM 88130

Peanut Palate Pleasers from Portales is an appropriate cookbook from New Mexico, since Portales is the home of Valencia peanuts. This 159-page book contains 320 delicious, nutritional peanut recipes. There are irresistible, favorite peanut recipes for all occasions.

$10.00   Retail price
Make check payable to Portales Woman's Club

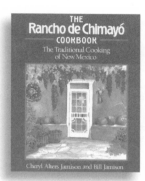

RANCHO DE CHIMAYÓ COOKBOOK

Cheryl Alters Jamison and Bill Jamison
Harvard Common Press
535 Albany Street   Fax 617-695-9794
Boston, MA 02118   888-657-3755
               E-mail adwinell@harvardcommonpress.com

Traditional New Mexican fare from one of the nation's most acclaimed restaurants. The 66 vibrant recipes and innumerable fascinating sidebars of the *Rancho de Chimayó Cookbook* are an inspired insight into this fascinating cuisine and culture. This 144-page gem represents the best of the Southwest.

$10.95   Retail price   Visa/MC accepted
$ 3.00   Postage and handling
Make check payable to The Harvard Common Press
ISBN 1-55832-035-0

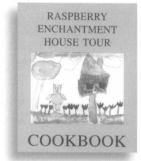

RASPBERRY ENCHANTMENT HOUSE TOUR COOKBOOK

Carrie Tingley Hospital Foundation
2711 University Boulevard NE   Fax 505-243-7232
Albuquerque, NM 87102   505-243-6626
               E-mail helpkids@unm.edu

Never before published chef recipes, in menu form, from Albuquerque's finest restaurants. Recreate the outstanding meals served over the past four years at the Foundation's signature event, The Raspberry Enchantment House Tour and Brunch. Includes chef bios and house descriptions. Quality looseleaf notebook; annual recipe updates available for $5.00.

$15.00   Retail price   Visa/MC accepted
$ 3.50   Postage and handling
Make check payable to CTHF

RECIPES FOR RAIN OR SHINE

First Christian Church
1006 W. Bullock Avenue
Artesia, NM 88210   505-746-9895

We have such wonderful cooks that bring delicious dishes to our fellowship dinners. It is with this thought in mind that we compiled these recipes. Some of the recipes are treasured family keepsakes and some are new; all reflect the love of good cooking. 273 recipes; 98 pages; spiral binding.

$10.00   Retail price
$ 1.50   Postage and handling
Make check payable to First Christian Church

RECIPES FROM HATCH: CHILE CAPITOL OF THE WORLD

Hatch FHA
P. O. Box 38
Hatch, NM 87937   505-267-5050

Composed of about 460 award-winning recipes from people who entered our Chile cook-off, plus helpful hints on how to make a chile ristra, roast green chile, and prepare red chile sauce. Recipes range from the very simple to whole meals in one recipe. If you are a chile-head (or know one), this cookbook is for you.

$10.00   Retail price
$ 1.50   Postage and handling
Make check payable to Hatch Chamber of Commerce

RECIPES FROM THE COTTON PATCH

c/o Joan Giordano
St. Luke's Episcopal Church
6736 Southwind Drive
El Paso, TX 79912

Our cookbook features 496 recipes; 238 pages with spiral-binding for easy use. We are a country parish with a very diverse congregation which enhances our recipe collection. The watercolor on the cover was painted by an award-winning artist who is a member of our parish.

$12.95   Retail price
$ 3.00   Postage and handling
Make check payable to St. Luke's Cookbook

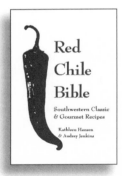

RED CHILE BIBLE

by Kathleen Hansel and Audrey Jenkins
Clear Light Publishers
823 Don Diego   Fax 505-989-9519
Santa Fe, NM 87501   800-253-2747
                                 E-mail ordercl@aol.com

Santa Fe chefs Kathleen Hansel and Audrey Jenkins share festive creations for casual and formal entertaining, plus selected recipes from the finest home cooks and professional chefs throughout the Southwest. Save time without sacrificing quality or flavor with the author's shortcuts and ingredient substitutions. Emphasizes fresh, healthy ingredients and dishes "made from scratch."

$12.95   Retail price   Visa/MC accepted
$ .81   Tax for New Mexico residents
$ 3.00   Postage and handling .50 each add'l copy
Make check payable to Clear Light Publishers
ISBN 0-94666-93-6

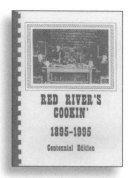

RED RIVER'S COOKIN': CENTENNIAL EDITION

Red River Women's Club
P. O. Box 261   Fax 505-754-3234
Red River, NM 87558   505-754-6114
                    E-mail tmbrline@newmex.com

Red River's Cookin' Centennial Edition was compiled to honor the first settlers who came to Red River in 1895. This cookbook has recipes that have endured 100 years of Red River living, and it also includes historical information and pictures from our founding fathers and mothers of Red River.

$12.00   Retail price
$ .83   Tax for New Mexico residents
$ 3.00   Postage and handling
Make check payable to Red River Women's Club

REHOBOTH CHRISTIAN SCHOOL COOKBOOK

Tse Yaaniichii Promoters
P. O. Box 41
Rehoboth, NM 87322   505-863-4412

This cookbook reflects the history of Rehoboth Mission. The recipes blend the local cultures of Native America and Hispanic cooking with the home cooking and Dutch treats of the Anglo missionaries who came to the Southwest in the early 1900s. Also includes modern recipes for family meals and potluck occasions. 177 pages.

$ 5.00   Retail price
$ 2.95   Postage and handling
Make check payable to Rehoboth Christian School

SAINT JOSEPH'S REALLY GRANDE COOKBOOK

Saint Joseph Parish
4080 St. Joseph Road NW   Fax 505-831-8264
Albuquerque, NM 87120   505-831-8265
                    E-mail sjrgl@juno.com

This cookbook is a parish project that doesn't take itself too seriously. Its 214 pages contain 186 recipes in 8 sections that include recipes by kids, appetizers, breads, desserts, main dishes, salads, soups and vegetables. The largest sections are the desserts and main dishes.

$10.00   Retail price
$ .58   Tax for New Mexico residents
$ 3.00   Postage and handling
Make check payable to Saint Joseph on the Rio Grande Parish

THE SANTA FE SCHOOL OF COOKING COOKBOOK

by Susan Curtis
Gibbs Smith, Publisher
P. O. Box 667   Fax 800-213-3023
Layton, UT 84041   800-748-5439
                              E-mail info@gibbs-smith.com

The Santa Fe School of Cooking continually draws many top Southwestern chefs, in addition to thousands of other students. Over 120 recipes from the school are presented in this extraordinary cookbook, featuring step-to-step instructions for making everything from appetizers and soups, to beverages, breads, and desserts.

$19.95   Retail price   Visa/MC accepted
$ 4.00   Postage and handling
Make check payable to Gibbs Smith, Publisher
ISBN 0-87905-873-0

SASSY SOUTHWEST COOKING: VIBRANT NEW MEXICO FOODS

by Clyde Casey
Pecos Valley Pepper Company
608 W. McCune
Roswell, NM 88201   505-622-8561
                              E-mail lazykc@dfn.com

Sassy Southwest Cooking offers unforgettable easy-to-prepare dishes that are the best the Land of Enchantment has to offer. Clyde Casey goes beyond the boundaries of his popular *New Mexico Cooking—Southwestern Flavors of the Past and Present*. Here he shares the best of almost 400 years of New Mexico food and its zesty unforgettable cuisine.

$ 9.95   Retail price
$ .65   Tax for New Mexico residents
Make check payable to Pecos Valley Pepper Company
ISBN 0-9659234-0-1

SAVORING THE SOUTHWEST

Roswell Symphony Guild Publications
P. O. Box 3078   Fax 505-627-0936
Roswell, NM 88202   800-457-0302
                                          505-623-7477

More than a cookbook, *Savoring the Southwest* reflects not only the rich and colorful heritage and mystique of New Mexico, but the dedication of those who believe beautiful music should be a part of the cultural legacy of a community.   Benefits Roswell Symphony. Hardcover; 329 pages; 400 recipes.

$18.95   Retail price   Visa/MC accepted
$ 1.23   Tax for New Mexico residents
$ 3.00   Postage and handling
Make check payable to RSP
ISBN 0-96-24660-X

SAVORING THE SOUTHWEST AGAIN

Roswell Symphony Guild Publications
P. O. Box 3078   Fax 505-627-0936
Roswell, NM 88202   800-457-0302
                                                    505-623-7477

Savoring the Southwest Again through the eyes of some of our most talented artists. Delight your taste buds with exceptional recipes from this "land of enchantment." Experience the tongue-in-cheek fun of the UFO Section (Unusual and Ungourmet Food Offerings). Hardcover; 318 pages; nearly 400 recipes. Recipient of the Tabasco Community Cookbook Award.

$22.50   Retail price   Visa/MC accepted
$ 1.46   Tax for New Mexico residents
$ 3.00   Postage and handling
Make check payable to RSP
ISBN 0-9612466-1-8

SIMPLY SIMPATICO

The Junior League of Albuquerque
P. O. Box 8858   Fax 505-881-0393
Albuquerque, NM 87198   800-753-7731

Considered "The Authority" for *authentic* New Mexican cuisine. Its "Comida Simpatica" section offers a history of this intriguing cuisine—a unique blend of Indian, Spanish, Mexican and Anglo cultures which flourished under our brilliant turquoise skies.

$14.95   Retail price
$ 3.20   Postage and handling
Make check payable to *Simply Simpatico*
ISBN 0-9609278-0-8

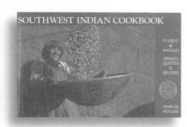

SOUTHWEST INDIAN COOKBOOK

by Marcia Keegan
Clear Light Publishers
823 Don Diego   Fax 505-989-9519
Santa Fe, NM 87501   800-253-2747
                                             E-mail ordercl@aol.com

This richly descriptive book includes recipes and folklore about the preparation of food by Southwest Indians. A bestselling favorite that delights the palate and the eye, this cookbook ventures beyond mere recipes into the hearts and souls of the Pueblo and Navajo Indians. Forty-four full-color photographs. 120 pages.

$12.95   Retail price   Visa/MC accepted
$ .81   Tax for New Mexico residents
$ 3.00   Postage and handling .50 each add'l copy
Make check payable to Clear Light Publishers
ISBN 0-940666-03-0

THE TEQUILA COOK BOOK

by Lynn Nusom
Golden West Publishers
4113 N. Longview Avenue   Fax 602-279-6901
Phoenix, AZ 85014-4949   800-658-5830
                     E-mail goldwest@goodnet.com

More than 150 recipes featuring tequila as an ingredient. Appetizers, soups, salads, main dishes, breads, desserts and drinks. Includes fascinating tequila trivia. A unique cook book!

$ 7.95   Retail price   Visa/MC accepted
$ 3.00   Postage and handling
Make check payable to Golden West Publishers
ISBN 0-914846-89-2

THE VERY SPECIAL RASPBERRY COOKBOOK

Carrie Tingley Hospital Foundation
2711 University Boulevard NE   Fax 505-243-7323
Albuquerque, NM 87102   505-243-6626
                     E-mail helpkids@unm.edu

Four hundred recipes using raspberries, raspberry products and other New Mexico produce—peanuts, pinons, apples, pistachios and chiles. Menus contributed by prominent New Mexicans, heart healthy recipes and decadent desserts. Includes tips for planting, growing and eating raspberries. Illustrated with children's artwork. 275 pages, hard cover, hidden comb binding.

$18.50   Retail price   Visa/MC accepted
$ 3.50   Postage and handling
Make check payable to VSRC
ISBN 0-9646119-0-2

WHAT'S COOKIN' AT CASA

Casa Arena Blanca
205 Moonglow Avenue   Fax 505-434-4513
Alamogordo, NM 88310   505-434-4510

What's Cookin' at Casa is a unique cookbook made up of 102 favorite recipes submitted by residents, family members and staff. The proceeds from sales of the cookbook will benefit the resident aviary project.

$10.00   Retail price
$ 1.65   Postage and handling
Make check payable to Casa Arena Blanca Resident Council Fund

*Visiting Steins Railroad Ghost Town will transport you back to the 1880s.
The unique collection of buildings is filled with history and wild west artifacts,
as its final residents left many of their belongings behind.*

A

Adobe Bars 216
Albuquerque Delight 33
Angel Wings 185
Anne's Quiche 127
Appetizers
  Albuquerque Delight 33
  Armadillo Eggs 30
  Baked Caramel Goodstuff 20
  Broccoli-Hamburger Dip 34
  Carnitas Caliente 36
  Chile Cheese Roll 29
  Chile Con Queso 28
  Chunky Guacamole 21
  Cilantro Mousse 31
  Cocktail Meatballs 37
  Green Apple Serrano-Cilantro Salsa 25
  Green Chile Pinwheels 29
  Green Chile Won Tons 28
  Harlequin Dip 34
  Heavy-Duty Nacho Sauce 32
  Indian Nut Mix 18
  Indienne Cashew Spread 31
  Jiffy Chile con Queso 27
  Mango Salsa 26
  Many Layered Nacho Dip 33
  Marinated Mexican Mushrooms 24
  Mexican Deviled Eggs 23
  Mexican Hot Nuts 18
  Mexican Peanuts 19
  Mushroom Turnovers 35
  New Mexico Cherry Bombs 23
  Party Peanut Ball 20
  Pico de Gallo Salsa 26
  Rajas Salsa 24
  Shrimp Cheese Ball 30
  Stuffed Jalapeño Chile Peppers 22
  Stuffed Jalapeños 21
  Tangy Chicken Tidbits 38
  Texas Gunpowder Salsa 27
  Valley-of-Fire Pecans 19
Apple Bread, Mom's 55
Apple Crepes, Red Hot 230
Apple Pie Cake, Norwegian 203
Apple Torte, Bavarian 204
Applesauce Cake 205
Applesauce Loaf, Easy 58
Apricot-Prune Stuffed Lamb 168
Armadillo Eggs 30
Asparagus Chicken 184

Autumn Soup 72
Avocado, Chicken Tacos with 173
Avocado Salad 85
Avocado Sherbet 248

B

Baked Caramel Goodstuff 20
Baked Fresh Ham with Apple Cider 155
Banana Walnut Buttermilk Bread 53
Barbecued Brisket 154
Barbecued Chicken 183
Bart's Barbecue Green Beans 114
Bavarian Apple Torte 204
Beans
  Bart's Barbecue Green Beans 114
  Bean Salad 88
  Black Beans with Garlic and Chipotle
    Chiles 112
  Hearty Black Bean Soup 78
  Indian-Style Pinto Beans 113
  Sausage and Bean Burritos 135
Beef
  Barbecued Brisket 154
  Beef Fajitas 146
  Beef Tortilla Pizza 141
  Bowl of Red 151
  Caldillo 149
  Campfire Chili Con Carne 152
  Chile Rellenos Bake 140
  Chiles Rellenos Dulces 138
  Chili with Avocados 153
  Chimichangas 132
  Easiest-Yet Tortilla Casserole 140
  Green Chile Goulash 147
  Green Chile Sauce 161
  Green Chile Stroganoff 145
  Jalapa Hamburgers 142
  Meatballs Diablo 139
  New Mexico Pot Roast 155
  Picadillo 148
  Six Layer Dinner 138
  Son-of-a-Gun Stew 150
  Southwestern Stuffed Flank Steak 144
  Southwestern Tamale Pie 141
  Sweet Chile Meat Balls 138
  Tyrone Steak 143
Beer Biscuits 44
Bell Peppers, Hungarian Stuffed 118
Berry-Pecan Flan 243
Best Grilled Chicken, The 182

Best in the World Peanut Brittle 228
Beverages
   My Kinda Cocoa 17
   Perfect Margaritas 16
Biscochitos 221
Biscotti, Orange 222
Black Beans with Garlic and Chipotle
   Chiles 112
Black Forest Trifle 240
Bloody Mary Soup 70
Blue Corn Meal Dumplings 79
Blue Corn Meal Pancakes 43
Blue Corn Muffins 40
Blueberry Ice Cream Dessert Squares
   247
Blueberry Sour Cream Pound Cake 208
Blueberry Tea Cake, Durgin-Parks 208
Biscuits, Beer 44
Biscuits, Ranch 44
Bon Bons, Carob Cherry 218
Bowl of Red 151
Bread
   Banana Walnut Buttermilk Bread 53
   Beer Biscuits 44
   Blue Corn Muffins 40
   Broccoli Cheese Cornbread 41
   Cocas 56
   Cranberry-Orange Bread 52
   Door Knobs 43
   Easy Applesauce Loaf 58
   Empanadas de Fruta 48
   Garlic Focaccia 47
   Ginger Bread 51
   Green Chile Muffins 41
   Hush Puppies 43
   Irish Soda Bread 48
   Mom's Apple Bread 55
   Navajo Fry Bread with Cilantro Butter
      and Raspberry Honey 49
   Peanut-Carrot-Pineapple Holiday
      Bread 52
   Ranch Biscuits 44
   Skillet Corn Bread 42
   Sopaipillas 50
   Sour Cream Bread 45
   The Ultimate Sandwich Bread 46
Breakfast
   Blue Corn Meal Pancakes 43
   Breakfast Burritos 64
   Breakfast Pear Loaf 55

Chile Egg Puff 64
Company Eggs and Cheese 59
Early Morning Casserole 65
Farmer's Breakfast Casserole 65
Green Chilaquiles Omelet 63
Grits and Cheese Casserole 59
Huevos Rancheros 60, 61
Mexican Omelet 62
Mom's Streusel-Filled Coffee Cake 54
Spicy Southwest Bake 66
Brisket, Barbecued 154
Broccoli Cheese Cornbread 41
Broccoli-Hamburger Dip 34
Burgundy Venison Steak Tips 168
Burritos, Sausage and Bean 135

C

Cabbage Salad with Apple and Walnuts
   91
Cakes
   Applesauce Cake 205
   Bavarian Apple Torte 204
   Blueberry Sour Cream Pound Cake
      208
   Cherry-Pineapple Cake 203
   Chocolate-Chocolate Cake 214
   Cinnamon Carob Tunnel Cake 212
   Decadent Chocolate Cake 211
   Durgin-Parks Blueberry Tea Cake 208
   Eclair Cake 207
   Heavenly Chocolate Cake 210
   Mexican Cake 214
   Mexico City Earthquake Cake 202
   Norwegian Apple Pie Cake 203
   Pumpkin Cheesecake 213
   Rum Cake 207
   Strawberry Meringue Cake 206
   22-Minute Cake 209
Candies
   Best in the World Peanut Brittle 228
   Chocolate Pecan Toffee 227
   Mexican Pecan Candy 226
Calabacitas 105
Caldillo 149
Caldo de Queso con Calabacitas 75
Calico Corn 101
Campfire Chili Con Carne 152
Capirotada 239
Carne Adovada 162
Carnitas Caliente 36

Carob Cherry Bon Bons 218
Carob Cream Pie 234
Carob Tunnel Cake, Cinnamon 212
Cashew Spread, Indienne 31
Casseroles
    Chicken Artichoke Casserole 191
    Chicken Enchilada Casserole 177
    Chile Relleno Casserole 135
    Early Morning Casserole 65
    Easiest-Yet Tortilla Casserole 140
    Enchiladas de Pollo en Cacerola 178
    Farmer's Breakfast Casserole 65
    Fiesta Casserole 136
    Governor King's Chicken Enchilada
        Casserole 134
    Green Chile Corn Casserole 101
    Grits and Cheese Casserole 59
    Hominy Cheese Casserole 100
    Spicy Southwest Bake 66
    Sweet Potato and Apple Casserole 121
    Zucchini Casserole 107
    Zucchini Casserole, Diabetic 107
Cattle King Potatoes 119
Cheesecake, Pumpkin 213
Cheese Ball, Shrimp 30
Cheese Roll, Chile 29
Cheese Tortilla Torta 175
Cherry-Pineapple Cake 203
Chicken (see Poultry)
Chiles
    Chile Caribe Rub 165
    Chile Cheese Roll 29
    Chile Con Queso 28
    Chile Egg Puff 64
    Chile Pie 126
    Chile Relleno Casserole 135
    Chile Rellenos Bake 140
    Chile Rice Navidad 129
    Chiles Rellenos Dulces 138
    Green Chile Corn Casserole 101
    Green Chile Cream Chicken
        Enchiladas 133
    Green Chile Goulash 147
    Green Chile Muffins 41
    Green Chile Pinwheels 29
    Green Chile Sauce 161
    Green Chile Stew 81, 82
    Green Chile Stroganoff 145
    Green Chile Won Tons 28
    Green Chile-Chicken Divan 184
    Green Enchilada Casserole 134

Chili
    Bowl of Red 151
    Campfire Chili Con Carne 152
    Chili with Avocados 153
Chimayó Red Chile 163
Chimichangas 132
Chocolate
    Adobe Bars 216
    Black Forest Trifle 240
    Chocolate-Chocolate Cake 214
    Chocolate Flan, Ibarra 244
    Chocolate Pecan Toffee 227
    Chocolate-Piñon Pie 236
    Decadent Chocolate Cake 211
    Favorite Decadence Layer Bars 217
    Four-Layer Chocolate Dessert 241
    Heavenly Chocolate Cake 210
Christmas Eve Salad 92
Chunky Guacamole 21
Cilantro Mousse 31
Cinnamon Carob Tunnel Cake 212
Clouds 223
Cobbler, Pear-Raspberry 231
Cocas 56
Cocoa, My Kinda 17
Cocktail Meatballs 37
Coffee Cake, Mom's Streusel-Filled 54
Cole Slaw, Mexican 90
Company Eggs and Cheese 59
Cookies and Bars
    Adobe Bars 216
    Biscochitos 221
    Carob Cherry Bon Bons 218
    Clouds 223
    Crumb Cookies 221
    Favorite Decadence Layer Bars 217
    Gypsy Raspberry Brownies 220
    Lemon Squares 218
    Mandazis 224
    Mexican Honey Dainties 224
    Mexican Wedding Cakes 226
    Nanaimo Bars 219
    Orange Biscotti 222
    Peanut Butter Cookies 225
    Polvorones 221
    Pumpkin Squares 217
    Viennese Crescents 223
Corn
    Calico Corn 101
    Corn Cakes with Calabacitas 102
    Corn Soup 74

Corn Casserole, Green Chile 101
Hopi Corn Stew 79
Corn Bread, Skillet 42
Cornbread, Broccoli Cheese 41
Corn Cakes with Calabacitas and Queso
   Blanco Salsa 102
Crab Meat Quesadillas 195
Crab Quiche Mexicano 194
Cranberry-Orange Bread 52
Cream with Strawberries, Mexican 249
Crepes, Red Hot Apple 230
Crescents, Viennese 223
Crispy Garlic Chicken 178
Curried Chicken 179

D

Dainties, Mexican Honey 224
Decadent Chocolate Cake 211
Desserts
   Avocado Sherbet 248
   Berry-Pecan Flan 243
   Black Forest Trifle 240
   Blueberry Ice Cream Dessert Squares
      247
   Capirotada 239
   Flan Café 242
   Four-Layer Chocolate Dessert 241
   Ibarra Chocolate Flan with Crispy
      Phyllo Crust 244
   Lemon Fluff 241
   Log Cabin Pudding 250
   Methodist Pudding 241
   Mexican Cream with Strawberries 249
   Mexican Pecan-Toffee Tartlets in
      Chocolate Chip Cookie Crust 246
   Pear-Raspberry Cobbler 231
   Raspberry Pizza 238
   Red Hot Apple Crepes 230
   Twila's Eggless Fruit Ice Cream 248
Door Knobs 43
Durgin-Parks Blueberry Tea Cake 208
Dutch Lasagna 125

E

Early Morning Casserole 65
Easiest-Yet Tortilla Casserole 140
Easy Applesauce Loaf 58
Eclair Cake 207
Eggplant Mexicano 109

Eggs
   Anne's Quiche 127
   Armadillo Eggs 30
   Breakfast Burritos 64
   Chile Egg Puff 64
   Chile Pie 126
   Company Eggs and Cheese 59
   Crab Quiche Mexicano 194
   Early Morning Casserole 65
   Green Chilaquiles Omelet 63
   Huevos Rancheros 60, 61
   Mexican Deviled Eggs 23
   Mexican Omelet 62
   Southwestern Quiche 126
Empanadas de Fruta 48
Enchiladas
   Chicken Enchilada Casserole 177
   Chicken Enchiladas 176
   Chicken Enchiladas (Layered) 176
   Enchiladas de Pollo en Cacerola 178
   Governor King's Chicken Enchilada
      Casserole 134
   Green Chile Cream Chicken
      Enchiladas 133
   Green Enchilada Casserole 134
   Vegetable Enchilada 100

F

Fajitas, Beef 146
Farmer's Breakfast Casserole 65
Favorite Decadence Layer Bars 217
Fettucine with Zucchini-Basil Sauce 124
Fiesta Casserole 136
Fish (see Seafood)
Flan, Berry-Pecan 243
Flan, Ibarra Chocolate 244
Flan Café 242
Flautas 172
Focaccia, Garlic 47
Four-Layer Chocolate Dessert 241
Fresh Fruit Salad with Spicy Avocado
   Dressing 84
Fry Bread, Navajo 49

G

Garlic Focaccia 47
Garlic Potatoes 120
Gazpacho 69
Ginger Bread 51
Ginger Yams 121

Gores' Chinese Chicken with Pecans or Walnuts 187
Goulash, Green Chile 147
Governor King's Chicken Enchilada Casserole 134
Green Apple Serrano-Cilantro Salsa 25
Green Chilaquiles Omelet 63
Green Chiles (see Chiles)
Grilled Polenta with Red Chile Sauce and Black Beans 110
Grilled Rosemary Chicken 181
Grits and Cheese Casserole 59
Gypsy Raspberry Brownies 220

H

Ham, Baked Fresh with Apple Cider 155
Ham and Scalloped Potatoes 156
Hamburgers, Jalapa 142
Harlequin Dip 34
Harvest Pork Chops 158
Hearty Black Bean Soup 78
Heavenly Chocolate Cake 210
Heavy-Duty Nacho Sauce 32
Holiday Squash 108
Holiday Tortilla Stew 80
Hominy Cheese Casserole 100
Hopi Corn Stew with Blue Corn Meal Dumplings 79
Huevos Rancheros 60, 61
Hungarian Stuffed Bell Peppers 118
Hush Puppies 43

I

Ibarra Chocolate Flan with Crispy Phyllo Crust 244
Ice Cream Dessert Squares, Blueberry 247
Ice Cream, Twila's Eggless Fruit 248
Impossible Pie 231
Indian Nut Mix 18
Indian-Style Pinto Beans 113
Indienne Cashew Spread 31
Irish Soda Bread 48

J

Jalapa Hamburgers 142
Jalapeño Chile Peppers, Stuffed 22
Jalapeños, Stuffed 21
Jambalaya, Chicken and Sausage 128
Jerry's World Famous Baked Trout 197

Jicama Salad with Watercress, Radishes, and Chiles 92
Jiffy Chile con Queso 27
Juanita's Special Rio Grande Chicken 188

K

Kale, Sautéed with Garlic and Vinegar 116

L

Lamb, Apricot-Prune Stuffed 168
Lamb Redolent of Garlic and Rosemary, Leg of 166
Las Cruces Pecan Pie 232
Lasagna, Dutch 125
Lemon
   Lemon Chicken 180
   Lemon Squares 218
   Methodist Pudding (Lemon Fluff) 241
Lime Marinated Grilled Salmon 200
Log Cabin Pudding 250

M

Macaroni Salad, Tuna 94
Make-a-Meal Soup 76
Mandazis 224
Mango Salsa 26
Many Layered Nacho Dip 33
Margaritas, Perfect 16
Marilyn's Everyday Miracle Rub 170
Marinated Mexican Mushrooms 24
Mark's Red Chile Sauce 164
Meat Balls, Sweet Chile 138
Meatballs, Cocktail 37
Meatballs Diablo 139
Methodist Pudding (Lemon Fluff) 241
Mexican Cake 214
Mexican Cole Slaw 90
Mexican Cream with Strawberries 249
Mexican Deviled Eggs 23
Mexican Honey Dainties 224
Mexican Hot Nuts 18
Mexican Omelet 62
Mexican Peanuts 19
Mexican Pecan Candy 226
Mexican Pecan-Toffee Tartlets in Chocolate Chip Cookie Crust 246
Mexican Salad 87
Mexican Wedding Cakes 226

Mexico City Earthquake Cake 202
Mile-High Raspberry Pie 232
Millionaire Pie 233
Minestrone Soup 77
Mom's Apple Bread 55
Mom's Streusel-Filled Coffee Cake 54
Monterey Chicken Rolls 174
Mousse, Cilantro 31
Muffins, Blue Corn 40
Muffins, Green Chile 41
Mushrooms, Marinated Mexican 24
Mushrooms, Pork Chops with 157
Mushroom Turnovers 35
My Kinda Cocoa 17

N

Nacho Dip, Many Layered 33
Nacho Sauce, Heavy-Duty 32
Nanaimo Bars 219
Navajo Fry Bread with Cilantro Butter
   and Raspberry Honey 49
New Mexico Burning Salad 88
New Mexico Cherry Bombs 23
New Mexico Peanut Pie 235
New Mexico Pot Roast 155
Norwegian Apple Pie Cake 203
Nuts
   Baked Caramel Goodstuff 20
   Indian Nut Mix 18
   Indienne Cashew Spread 31
   Mexican Hot Nuts 18
   Mexican Peanuts 19
   Party Peanut Ball 20
   Peanut Salad 96
   Piñon Nut Torte 237
   Valley-of-Fire Pecans 19

O

Old Town Soup 73
Orange Biscotti 222
Orange-Almond Salad 85

P

Pan-Fried San Juan Trout 198
Pancakes, Blue Corn Meal 43
Party Peanut Ball 20
Pasta
   Dutch Lasagna 125
   Fettucine with Zucchini-Basil Sauce
      124

Pat's Pasta Salad 93
Peanut Ball, Party 20
Peanut Butter Cookies 225
Peanut Brittle, Best in the World 228
Peanut Pie, New Mexico 235
Peanut Salad 96
Peanuts, Mexican 19
Pear Loaf, Breakfast 55
Pear-Raspberry Cobbler 231
Pecans
   Berry-Pecan Flan 243
   Chocolate Pecan Toffee 227
   Las Cruces Pecan Pie 232
   Mexican Pecan Candy 226
   Mexican Pecan-Toffee Tartlets 246
   Valley-of-Fire Pecans 19
Perfect Margaritas 16
Picadillo 148
Pico de Gallo Salsa 26
Pies
   Carob Cream Pie 234
   Chocolate-Piñon Pie 236
   Impossible Pie 231
   Las Cruces Pecan Pie 232
   Mile-High Raspberry Pie 232
   Millionaire Pie 233
   New Mexico Peanut Pie 235
   Piñon Nut Torte 237
Pinwheels, Green Chile 29
Pizza
   Beef Tortilla Pizza 141
   Cocas (Little Spanish Pizzas) 56
Polenta, Grilled 110
Polvorones 221
Pork
   Carne Adovada 162
   Carnitas Caliente 36
   Chimayó Red Chile 163
   Ham and Scalloped Potatoes with
      Green Chile 156
   Baked Fresh Ham with Apple Cider
      155
   Harvest Pork Chops 158
   Pork Chops with Mushrooms 157
   Pork Tenderloin with Cranberry-
      Chipotle Sauce 159
   Posole 160
Pot Roast, New Mexico 155
Potatoes
   Cattle King Potatoes 119
   Garlic Potatoes 120

Ham and Scalloped Potatoes 156
Roasted Scarlet Potatoes 119
Tiny Green Beans and Baby Red
  Potatoes in Salsa Vinaigrette 95
Twice Baked Chile Potatoes 120
Poultry
  Angel Wings 185
  Asparagus Chicken 184
  Barbecued Chicken 183
  Best Grilled Chicken, The 182
  Cheese Tortilla Torta 175
  Chicken and Wild Rice 190
  Chicken Artichoke Casserole 191
  Chicken Breasts with Raspberry Beurre
    Blanc 186
  Chicken Enchilada Casserole 177
  Chicken Enchiladas 176
  Chicken Enchiladas (Layered) 176
  Chicken Tacos with Avocado 173
  Chicken/Tortilla Casserole 178
  Crispy Garlic Chicken 178
  Curried Chicken 179
  Enchiladas de Pollo en Cacerola 178
  Flautas 172
  Gores' Chinese Chicken with Pecans or
    Walnuts 187
  Green Chile-Chicken Divan 184
  Grilled Rosemary Chicken 181
  Juanita's Special Rio Grande Chicken
    188
  Lemon Chicken 180
  Monterey Chicken Rolls 174
  Red Chile Lemon Chicken 180
  Ruidoso Winner 192
  Southwest Orange-Chile Chicken with
    Black Beans 189
  Tequila-Lime-Grilled Chicken 182
Posole 160
Prairie Soup 73
Pudding, Log Cabin 250
Pudding, Methodist 241
Pumpkin Cheesecake 213
Pumpkin Squares 217

Q

Quesadillas, Crab Meat 195
Queso
  Caldo de Queso con Calabacitas 75
  Chile Con Queso 28
  Jiffy Chile con Queso 27

Queso Blanco Salsa 102
Quiche
  Anne's Quiche 127
  Chile Pie 126
  Southwestern Quiche 126

R

Rajas Salsa 24
Ranch Biscuits 44
Randy's Raspberry Vinaigrette 90
Raspberry
  Raspberry Green Salad 89
  Raspberry Pie, Mile-High 232
  Raspberry Pizza 238
  Raspberry Vinaigrette, Randy's 90
Relish, Zucchini 122
Red Chile Lemon Chicken 180
Red Hot Apple Crepes 230
Red Hot Salad 94
Rice
  Chicken and Sausage Jambalaya 128
  Chicken and Wild Rice 190
  Chile Rice Navidad 129
  Rice and Chile Bake 130
  Sherried Orange Rice 130
Rub, Chile Caribe 165
Rub, Marilyn's Everyday Miracle 170
Roasted Scarlet Potatoes 119
Ruidoso Winner 192
Rum Cake 207

S

Salads
  Avocado Salad 85
  Bean Salad 88
  Cabbage Salad with Apple and
    Walnuts 91
  Christmas Eve Salad 92
  Fresh Fruit Salad with Spicy Avocado
    Dressing 84
  Jicama Salad with Watercress,
    Radishes, and Chiles 92
  Mexican Cole Slaw 90
  Mexican Salad 87
  New Mexico Burning Salad 88
  Orange-Almond Salad 85
  Pat's Pasta Salad 93
  Peanut Salad 96
  Randy's Raspberry Vinaigrette 90
  Raspberry Green Salad 89

Red Hot Salad 94
Strawberry Spinach Salad 86
Tiny Green Beans and Baby Red
  Potatoes in Salsa Vinaigrette 95
Tuna Macaroni Salad 94
24-Hour Vegetable Salad 86
Wilted Lettuce Salad 87
Salmon, Lime Marinated Grilled 200
Salmon Loaf 199
Salmon, Soy Glazed 199
Salsas and Dips
  Albuquerque Delight 33
  Broccoli-Hamburger Dip 34
  Chile Con Queso 28
  Chunky Guacamole 21
  Green Apple Serrano-Cilantro Salsa 25
  Harlequin Dip 34
  Heavy-Duty Nacho Sauce 32
  Jiffy Chile con Queso 27
  Mango Salsa 26
  Many Layered Nacho Dip 33
  Mark's Red Chile Sauce 164
  Pico de Gallo Salsa 26
  Rajas Salsa 24
  Salsa Rancherita 66
  Salsa Vinaigrette 95
  Texas Gunpowder Salsa 27
Santa Fe Soup, A 68
Sauce, Mark's Red Chile 164
Sausage Jambalaya, Chicken and 128
Sausage and Bean Burritos 135
Sautéed Kale with Garlic and Vinegar
  116
Seafood
  Crab Meat Quesadillas 195
  Crab Quiche Mexicano 194
  Jerry's World Famous Baked Trout
    Recipe 197
  Lime Marinated Grilled Salmon 200
  Pan-Fried San Juan Trout 198
  Salmon Loaf 199
  Shrimp Cheese Ball 30
  Shrimp Rellenos 196
  Soy Glazed Salmon with Orange
    Sauce 199
  Spiedino Di Mare 197
Secret Soup 76
Sherried Orange Rice 130
Shrimp Cheese Ball 30
Shrimp Rellenos 196
Sinister Stew 78

Six Layer Dinner 138
Skillet Corn Bread 42
Son-of-a-Gun Stew 150
Sopaipillas 50
Soups
  Autumn Soup 72
  Bloody Mary Soup 70
  Caldo de Queso con Calabacitas 75
  Corn Soup 74
  Gazpacho 69
  Green Chile Stew 81, 82
  Hearty Black Bean Soup 78
  Holiday Tortilla Stew 80
  Hopi Corn Stew with Blue Corn Meal
    Dumplings 79
  Make-a-Meal Soup 76
  Minestrone Soup 77
  Old Town Soup 73
  Prairie Soup 73
  Santa Fe Soup,, A 68
  Secret Soup 76
  Sinister Stew 78
  Taco Soup 72
  Tortilla Soup 71
Sour Cream Bread 45
Southwest Orange-Chile Chicken with
  Black Beans 189
Southwestern Quiche 126
Southwestern Spinach 115
Southwestern Stuffed Flank Steak 144
Southwestern Tamale Pie 141
Soy Glazed Salmon with Orange Sauce
  199
Spicy and Saucy Stir-Fry 99
Spicy Southwest Bake 66
Spiedino Di Mare 197
Spinach Bake 115
Spinach Salad, Strawberry 86
Spinach, Southwestern 115
Squash, Holiday 108
Steak, Southwestern Stuffed Flank 144
Steak, Tyrone 143
Stew
  Green Chile Stew 81, 82
  Holiday Tortilla Stew 80
  Hopi Corn Stew 79
  Sinister Stew 78
Stir-Fry, Spicy and Saucy 99
Strawberry Meringue Cake 206
Strawberry Spinach Salad 86
Stuffed Jalapeño Chile Peppers 22

Stuffed Jalapeños 21
Stuffed Sweet Peppers 117
Stroganoff, Green Chile 145
Succotash, Zuñi 98
Sweet Potato and Apple Casserole 121

T

Taco Soup 72
Tacos, Shed Style 131
Tamale Pie, Southwestern 141
Tangy Chicken Tidbits 38
Tartlets, Mexican Pecan-Toffee 246
Tequila-Lime-Grilled Chicken 182
Texas Gunpowder Salsa 27
Tiny Green Beans and Baby Red
    Potatoes in Salsa Vinaigrette 95
Torta de Calabacitas 106
Torte, Piñon Nut 237
Tortilla Soup 71
Trout, Jerry's World Famous Baked 197
Trout, Pan-Fried San Juan 198
Tuna Macaroni Salad 94
Turnovers, Mushroom 35
24-Hour Vegetable Salad 86
22-Minute Cake 209
Twice Baked Chile Potatoes 120
Twila's Eggless Fruit Ice Cream 248
Tyrone Steak 143

U

Ultimate Sandwich Bread, The 46

V

Valley-of-Fire Pecans 19
Vegetables
    Bart's Barbecue Green Beans 114
    Black Beans with Garlic and Chipotle
        Chiles 112
    Calabacitas 105
    Calico Corn 101
    Cattle King Potatoes 119
    Corn Cakes with Calabacitas and
        Queso Blanco Salsa 102
    Eggplant Mexicano 109
    Garlic Potatoes 120
    Ginger Yams 121
    Green Chile Corn Casserole 101

    Grilled Polenta with Red Chile Sauce
        and Black Beans 110
    Holiday Squash 108
    Hominy Cheese Casserole 100
    Hungarian Stuffed Bell Peppers 118
    Indian-Style Pinto Beans 113
    Roasted Scarlet Potatoes 119
    Sautéed Kale with Garlic and Vinegar
        116
    Southwestern Spinach 115
    Spicy and Saucy Stir-Fry 99
    Spinach Bake 115
    Stuffed Sweet Peppers 117
    Sweet Potato and Apple Casserole 121
    Torta de Calabacitas 106
    Tiny Green Beans and Baby Red
        Potatoes in Salsa Vinaigrette 95
    Twice Baked Chile Potatoes 120
    Vegetable Enchilada 100
    Zucchini Boats 108
    Zucchini Casserole 107
    Zucchini Casserole, Diabetic 107
    Zucchini Relish 122
    Zuñi Succotash 98
Venison
    Burgundy Venison Steak Tips 168
    Wok Venison 169
Viennese Crescents 223

W

Wedding Cakes, Mexican 226
Wilted Lettuce Salad 87
Wok Venison 169
Won Tons, Green Chile 28

Y

Yams, Ginger 121

Z

Zucchini
    Fettucine with Zucchini-Basil Sauce
        124
    Zucchini Boats 108
    Zucchini Casserole 107
    Zucchini Casserole, Diabetic 107
    Zucchini Relish 122
Zuñi Succotash 98

Special Discount Offers!

The Best of the Month Club

Experience the taste of our nation, one state at a time!

Individuals may purchase BEST OF THE BEST STATE COOKBOOKS on a monthly (or bi-monthly) basis by joining the **Best of the Month Club**. Best of the Month Club members enjoy a 20% discount off the list price of each book. Individuals who already own certain state cookbooks may specify which new states they wish to receive. No minimum purchase is required; individuals may cancel at any time. For more information on this purchasing option, call 1-800-343-1583.

Special Discount

The entire 41-volume BEST OF THE BEST STATE COOKBOOK SERIES can be purchased for $521.21, a 25% discount off the total individual price of $694.95.

Individual BEST cookbooks can be purchased for $16.95 per copy plus $4.00 shipping for any number of cookbooks ordered. See order form on next page.

Join today! 1-800-343-1583

Speak directly to one of our friendly customer service representatives, or visit our website at **www.quailridge.com** to order online.

Recipe Hall of Fame Collection

The extensive recipe database of Quail Ridge Press' acclaimed BEST OF THE BEST STATE COOKBOOK SERIES is the inspiration behind the RECIPE HALL OF FAME COLLECTION. These HALL OF FAME recipes have achieved extra distinction for consistently producing superb dishes. *The Recipe Hall of Fame Cookbook* features over 400 choice dishes for a variety of meals. The *Recipe Hall of Fame Dessert Cookbook* consists entirely of extraordinary desserts. The *Recipe Hall of Fame Quick & Easy Cookbook* contains over 500 recipes that require minimum effort but produce maximum enjoyment. *The Recipe Hall of Fame Cookbook II* brings you more of the family favorites you've come to expect with over 400 all-new, easy-to-follow recipes. Appetizers to desserts, quick dishes to masterpiece presentations, the RECIPE HALL OF FAME COLLECTION has it all.

All books: Paperbound • 7x10 • Illustrations • Index
The Recipe Hall of Fame Cookbook • 304 pages • $19.95
Recipe Hall of Fame Dessert Cookbook • 240 pages • $16.95
Recipe Hall of Fame Quick & Easy Cookbook • 304 pages • $19.95
The Recipe Hall of Fame Cookbook II • 304 pages • $19.95

NOTE: The four HALL OF FAME cookbooks can be ordered individually at the price noted above or can be purchased as a four-cookbook set for **$40.00**, almost a 50% discount off the total list price of $76.80. Over 1,600 incredible HALL OF FAME recipes for about three cents each—an amazing value!

Best of the Best State Cookbook Series

Best of the Best from
ALABAMA
288 pages, $16.95

Best of the Best from
ALASKA
288 pages, $16.95

Best of the Best from
ARIZONA
288 pages, $16.95

Best of the Best from
ARKANSAS
288 pages, $16.95

Best of the Best from
BIG SKY
Montana and Wyoming
288 pages, $16.95

Best of the Best from
CALIFORNIA
384 pages, $16.95

Best of the Best from
COLORADO
288 pages, $16.95

Best of the Best from
FLORIDA
288 pages, $16.95

Best of the Best from
GEORGIA
336 pages, $16.95

Best of the Best from the
GREAT PLAINS
North and South Dakota, Nebraska, and Kansas
288 pages, $16.95

Best of the Best from
HAWAI'I
288 pages, $16.95

Best of the Best from
IDAHO
288 pages, $16.95

Best of the Best from
ILLINOIS
288 pages, $16.95

Best of the Best from
INDIANA
288 pages, $16.95

Best of the Best from
IOWA
288 pages, $16.95

Best of the Best from
KENTUCKY
288 pages, $16.95

Best of the Best from
LOUISIANA
288 pages, $16.95

Best of the Best from
LOUISIANA II
288 pages, $16.95

Best of the Best from
MICHIGAN
288 pages, $16.95

Best of the Best from the
MID-ATLANTIC
Maryland, Delaware, New Jersey, and Washington, D.C.
288 pages, $16.95

Best of the Best from
MINNESOTA
288 pages, $16.95

Best of the Best from
MISSISSIPPI
288 pages, $16.95

Best of the Best from
MISSOURI
304 pages, $16.95

Best of the Best from
NEVADA
288 pages, $16.95

Best of the Best from
NEW ENGLAND
Rhode Island, Connecticut, Massachusetts, Vermont, New Hampshire, and Maine
368 pages, $16.95

Best of the Best from
NEW MEXICO
288 pages, $16.95

Best of the Best from
NEW YORK
288 pages, $16.95

Best of the Best from
NO. CAROLINA
288 pages, $16.95

Best of the Best from
OHIO
352 pages, $16.95

Best of the Best from
OKLAHOMA
288 pages, $16.95

Best of the Best from
OREGON
288 pages, $16.95

Best of the Best from
PENNSYLVANIA
320 pages, $16.95

Best of the Best from
SO. CAROLINA
288 pages, $16.95

Best of the Best from
TENNESSEE
288 pages, $16.95

Best of the Best from
TEXAS
352 pages, $16.95

Best of the Best from
TEXAS II
352 pages, $16.95

Best of the Best from
UTAH
288 pages, $16.95

Best of the Best from
VIRGINIA
320 pages, $16.95

Best of the Best from
WASHINGTON
288 pages, $16.95

Best of the Best from
WEST VIRGINIA
288 pages, $16.95

Best of the Best from
WISCONSIN
288 pages, $16.95

All cookbooks are 6x9 inches, ringbound, contain photographs, illustrations and index.

Special discount offers available! *(See previous page for details.)*

To order by credit card, call toll-free **1-800-343-1583** or visit our website at **www.quailridge.com.**
Use the form below to send check or money order.

Call 1-800-343-1583 or email **info@quailridge.com** *to request a free catalog of all of our publications.*

Order form

Use this form for sending check or money order to:
QUAIL RIDGE PRESS • P. O. Box 123 • Brandon, MS 39043

❏ Check enclosed

Charge to: ❏ Visa ❏ MC ❏ AmEx ❏ Disc

Card # _____

Expiration Date _____

Signature _____

Name _____

Address _____

City/State/Zip _____

Phone # _____

Email Address _____

Qty.	Title of Book (State) or Set	Total

Subtotal _____

7% Tax for MS residents _____

Postage ($4.00 any number of books) + 4.00

Total _____